AROUND ALONE

EMMA RICHARDS

AROUND ALONE

To Derek,

best wishes,

Emma x

MACMILLAN

First published 2004 by Macmillan
an imprint of Pan Macmillan Ltd
Pan Macmillan, 20 New Wharf Road, London N1 9RR
Basingstoke and Oxford
Associated companies throughout the world
www.panmacmillan.com

ISBN 1 4050 4586 8 HB
ISBN 1 4050 4804 2 TPB

1 3 5 7 9 8 6 4 2

A CIP catalogue record for this book is available from
the British Library.

Typeset by SetSystems Ltd, Saffron Walden, Essex
Printed and bound in Great Britain by
Mackays of Chatham plc, Chatham, Kent

For Mum and Dad

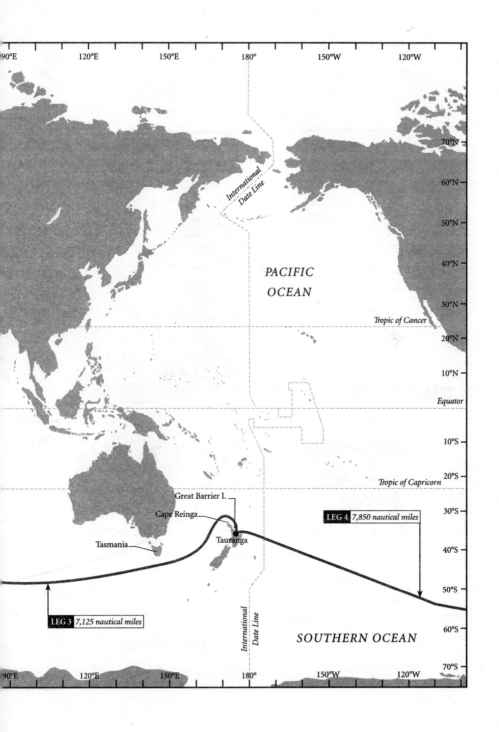

Introduction and Acknowledgements

I have been told by many people that writing a book would be one of the most difficult things I would ever undertake. I was told the same about sailing around the world single-handed, so I have taken on the challenge in the same way.

I don't tend to dwell on obstacles or the fact that I constantly take on too many projects. I still want to complete them to the best of my ability. Some people may call that total denial, others a coping strategy. I prefer the latter!

I take on challenges one step at a time, one mile at a time, one page at a time. I have goals and time frames. Thinking about writing a book, like thinking about sailing around the world, was a pretty daunting task. I had goals for both. On my voyage I never thought to myself: 'I am about to set off on a solo circumnavigation of 29,000 nautical miles.' Instead I told myself my first task was to get out of New York Harbour without hitting another boat, touching the bottom or hitting the bridge . . . one manoeuvre at a time, one hour at a time, one leg at a time before taking the next one. Writing this book, I also tried to keep the bigger picture in my head while focusing on the detail.

Just as the Around Alone race was a team effort, contrary to what the name implies, so writing this book, and achieving everything it recounts, has been a team effort. Nick Harris has helped structure my thoughts into something I hope is readable and of which I am certainly proud. I am also indebted to George Morley and Natasha Martin, my editors at Pan Macmillan, and to my literary agent Jonathan Harris who helped make it happen.

Everyone involved in the Around Alone – skippers, family, shore crew, organizers – have their own stories about the race. This is mine, and it has been tough to fit in everything that happened. It was such a big project, such a big year, that it is impossible to thank everyone individually who positively affected my race. So to everyone who sent an email of encouragement, everyone who called to say 'keep going', and all the people, many of them strangers, who cheered or waved from a clifftop or dock, thank you.

For me, this race has made me increasingly realize my priorities in life, my family and friends, and the differences that little things make: a smile, a hug. I have always sought challenges to see what I could do, how much I could achieve and those challenges are changing. I hope to sail around the world again, with a crew, but I also have some ideas and plans that may or may not come to fruition one day. But it's all about having a dream and daring to follow it.

Thank yous

Nick Harris. I am a sailor not a writer.
Thanks for helping me stay afloat in a world of words

Andrew Pindar, for all of your support and encouragement
since the day I met you and Caroline at the end of May 1999.
Thank you

My family

Thank you for all of your unquestioning support as I grow up,
not only in my early years but also through this race and since
it's finished!

Mum and Dad

Andy, Jules and Callum

Dave and Pippa

Philippa and Tom

Great-aunt Biddy, her son Simon, and Lynne

Cousin Joan

Mike, for being there

Jane and Marc

My shore team

Robin, Josh, Brian, Laurent, Mark, Ollie, Fraser

All my competitors in the race for making it so good –
Bernard, Thierry, Simone, Graham, Bruce, Patrick, Brad, Tim,
Derek, Koji, Pops, Alan

The Race organizers, especially Kels, Mary and Andrew

Sir Robin Knox-Johnston

Photographers, Marc Turner, Thierry Martinez, Billy Black, Roy Riley and Mark Pepper

The team at Pitch PR, Henry and Victoria, have worked through nearly three years of my projects with Pindar. Thank you.

My sponsors

Pindar, all 1300 employees

AlphaGraphics

HSBC

Henri-Lloyd

Harken

Radii

Stratos

Ocean Safety

Kelvin Hughes

Admiralty Charts

Raymarine

Also

Tracy Edwards for giving me the opportunity to go ocean racing at its best. Sorry we didn't get the big one

Scott Kennedy and Mike Voucas for you support

Helensburgh Sailing Club where it all began

Royal Southern Yacht Club

All the yacht clubs that have helped me throughout

PROLOGUE

What if I break a bone up here?
What if one of the blows to the head knocks me out?
At what point will another boat be diverted to start a search?
Is there another boat anywhere near?
Will they be able to find me?
What state will I be in?
How is anyone going to board if the weather's like this?

Numerous thoughts ran through my head as I struggled to stay calm. I was in the middle of the South Atlantic, 80 feet up a mast in high winds, aboard *Pindar*, the boat in which I was trying to race solo around the world. The questions were mostly practical and the answers likewise.

The sap of dread started to rise when I thought about my mum and dad. They'd been told I was going up the mast to make a repair. They knew they wouldn't hear anything for two hours, maybe three. But after five hours of hearing nothing, they'd really be starting to worry.

I was concerned about my physical well-being. But the one thing that truly terrified me was an image in my head of someone telling my parents I'd been killed. How on earth would they cope with that, not knowing exactly how I'd died, not knowing whether I'd been in pain or struggling or frightened at the end? Never knowing. It didn't bear thinking about.

It had been only a few short months before that I'd made a flying visit to Scotland to tell them I was going to sail around the world. Dad had picked me up from Glasgow airport. He'd asked if I was up for a wedding or party, the kind of occasions for which I'd normally make a flying visit.

'No,' I said. 'I've got something to tell you, about my next race.'

'Route du Rhum?' asked my dad, referring to a forthcoming race from France to Guadeloupe.

'No. A different one.'

'Not the Around Alone?'

Silence. The Around Alone, a 29,000-mile race around the world, starting and ending in Newport, Rhode Island via Devon, Cape Town, the Southern Ocean, New Zealand, Cape Horn and Brazil, is the longest solo race in world sport.

'Around Alone? You're telling your mum yourself.'

My mum often doesn't sleep when I'm at sea. She's the kind of mum who still instinctively goes to grab your hand when you cross the road, even though all four of us children left home at least ten years ago. She was in the kitchen when we got back from the airport. I came straight out with it.

She said it was a great idea, that she and Dad would travel round the world to visit me at the stopovers. She said it'd be great to see all those places, they'd be there to support me. She just kept talking.

Up that mast, in the image in my head, she wasn't talking at all. She was just standing there. And I was just holding on, wondering why.

Should I risk the seafood? That was the most pressing question I sought to answer the night before I set off to sail around the world. It was 11 September 2002, the first anniversary of the terrorist attacks on America, and I was in a restaurant in Newport, Rhode Island, having a last private meal with Mum and Dad before the start of the race.

The next morning I'd leave Newport and embark on a 160-mile ceremonial prologue, with seven guests, around Long Island to New York. And from there, alone, I would set out on the greatest challenge of my life.

I had so many doubts on my mind that night that it was simpler to suppress them than to try to talk them away. I could not comprehend what I was about to do. Being alone at sea for large parts of the next eight months held no allure whatsoever. I'm not the kind of person who takes any pleasure from being by myself. If you experience something wonderful, why not share it? If you hit trouble, why not have someone else there to help?

My entry for the race had been submitted only six weeks earlier. The decision to enter was ultimately made because I felt I could do the race, not because I was desperate to do it. Most people plan these things long in advance, often years. In the whirl of my own last-gasp preparations there had been no time to take it in and certainly no time to sit around fretting about it. The decision had been made and I got on with it. Those few hours in the restaurant were a welcome chance to sit in one place for a while.

There's something very special about Newport. It oozes history, from the museums that celebrate its days as a thriving colonial trading hub to the spectacular mansions built by the social elite, the Vanderbilts and their ilk, in the Jazz Age. For a century it was the venue for the America's Cup and it remains a spiritual home to the sailing community of the States and well beyond.

I've spent some great moments in the harbour. I first sailed into it as part of the all-female crew on Tracy Edwards's *Royal & SunAlliance* in 1997 before an attempt at a transatlantic record. In the summer of 2000 I arrived there as winner in my first solo ocean race. My last visit prior to the Around Alone, aboard Tracy's *Maiden II* in the spring of 2002, had also been celebratory. We'd just broken the speed record for a voyage from Antigua. And so to the Around Alone.

We ate at the Cooke House that night, down on Bannister's Wharf. It's a quintessentially Newport kind of place, a big old building made of white timber with shuttered windows and a Stars and Stripes over the door. It's always buzzing, regardless of whether the town is busy, and that evening was no exception. We found a quietish table in the corner. All I wanted was to spend a few uninterrupted hours with Mum and Dad, with no one asking how I felt, why I was doing this, what I ate on board, how I went to the loo. They already knew that stuff and anything they didn't know they decided not to ask.

We hardly mentioned the race at all and I kept my most

immediate fear to myself. I wasn't worried about storms or icebergs or collisions with unidentified objects in the dead of night. If I'd known what was going to happen in the coming months things might have been different. But my biggest worry then, trifling though it might sound, was getting out of New York Harbour in one piece. At all costs I just wanted to avoid crashing into another boat and prematurely scuppering my hopes – or worse, someone else's – before we reached the open sea. The harbour is busy at the best of times but on race day, as we crossed the start line off Battery Park, it would be heaving. The beginning of the race was the final act of the 'Sail For America' gathering, a parade of hundreds of sailboats on the Hudson River to commemorate the events of 9/11.

Looking back, that mundane fear of a bump served to keep out more negative thoughts about crossing the North Atlantic. The bad weather and treacherous seas off the Grand Banks are notorious. Maritime traffic is always a hazard, as are whales, industrial debris and any number of random and potentially disastrous breakages.

As for pressure . . .

Everyone close to me assured me that there were no expectations and that as long as I got back to land safely, even if I didn't get far out of New York Harbour, nothing else mattered. The media helped in that respect because coverage of my participation – and I was constantly amazed by the interest – was encouraging in demanding nothing of my performance. I wasn't unfairly compared to anyone else, just told to do my best. My role as the only woman and the youngest person in the race was highlighted repeatedly. By proxy, all my excuses went in early.

But that didn't stop me from wanting to compete as well as survive. And then there was the pressure of knowing that my sponsors, Pindar, after whom my boat was named, had supported me for three years and believed in me. There's nothing like someone believing in you to make you feel pressure.

On top of this I felt worryingly unprepared. There was no question that the boat was as safe as she could be. She was. The safety spec was the same for every boat in the fleet. But there were umpteen other practical details that might have made life on board easier that I'd had no time to address before the first leg. One of those was the installation of bigger winches to ease the physical demands of raising the sails. Another was a lengthier acclimatization to an unfamiliar boat. An extra month would have been good. Two years would have been better, maybe with a couple of shorter preparatory races thrown in.

But these were not the kind of things we talked about. Mum was subdued already, partly because of what might lie ahead for me and partly because she was fretting about Dad, who would be joining me on the prologue. I didn't question her lack of confidence that I would look after him!

Their main concern, as always, was that I came back safely, and that I wore my harness at all times to ensure that I didn't fall overboard when there was no one around to pick me up. And that I wouldn't phone them to say I was heading straight into some dreadful unavoidable storm and then never phone again.

Still, they didn't make too much of even these things. They knew it wouldn't change anything. Instead we talked about what I might do when the race was over, how I might spend my life if I had to get a 'proper job'. It was the kind of conversation I'd have with them occasionally. I'd never known the answers before and I didn't know them that evening.

Who can tell what's going to happen? If someone had told me five years previously, when I made my first tentative inquiries

about getting involved in ocean racing, that I'd be heading off
around the world by myself on a 60-foot boat by the time I was
twenty-seven, I'd have laughed in their face.

So we just ended up talking about normal stuff. My dad,
Bryan, was entering a hectic final year researching and teaching
at the University of Glasgow before retirement. My mum, Mar-
garet, who had shut the family B&B they run back at home on
the west coast of Scotland, was enjoying her break from looking
after guests.

Their trip had doubled as a typical holiday inasmuch as it
was spent supporting one of their sailing-obsessed children in her
latest venture. The previous year they'd been out to Italy with my
two brothers, spending quality time with their grandson while
their sons and daughter-in-law went racing in their respective
boats. Now, after a fortnight in Newport and New York, catching up with old friends and colleagues while I dashed around
getting ready for the Around Alone, it was almost time to go.
They'd be coming out to meet me at various stages along the way
but that was for later. Which brings us back to that most pressing
question. Seafood? I liked the thought of oysters but the last thing
I wanted was any risk of a rogue mollusc wreaking havoc with
my digestive system. I compromised with fish and it arrived
with an enormous pile of pasta. The carbs were going to come in
handy.

•

I was born in Belgium, not a country famous for its sailors,
but there was never much doubt that I'd take to the water.
My parents met through sailing at university. When they moved
to Brussels with Dad's work in 1966 they continued sailing at
a local club based at an inland lake. The arrival of four kids

– Andy in 1970, Dave in 1971, Philippa in 1973 and me, the baby, in 1974 – did little to dampen their enthusiasm.

Before we came along Dad sailed a Laser dinghy, an old design these days but still, as an Olympic class, one of the best in the world. A growing family required a more practical alternative. Dad built one.

He's been a whiz with anything mechanical or technical for as long as I can remember. In Brussels he was working at the Von Karman Institute for Fluid Dynamics, a postgraduate teaching and research institute where he was involved with high-speed aerodynamics research. If you could pronounce all that, let alone understand it, how hard could it be to construct a boat?

The dinghy he made was a Mirror. It was wooden, almost 11 feet long, and wider and deeper than the Laser, with air tanks under the decks. Even if the cockpit filled with water it didn't sink, which came in handy with four small children. Not that we were too concerned about safety at that age.

One day, when I was about four, Philippa and I were minding our own business, flying our kites, when our Belgian neighbours intervened and put an abrupt stop to it. 'Do you know where your children are?' they asked Mum. 'Yes,' she replied, slightly indignant. 'They're playing in their room.'

To us, it seemed perfectly normal to sit two storeys up on the guttering outside our window. Mum nearly had a heart attack before she persuaded us to climb back inside.

Apart from teaching me that you mustn't dangle your legs while flying a kite, Belgium didn't leave much of an impression. Apparently I was bilingual as a toddler although you wouldn't have known it by the time I came to learn French at school in Scotland aged eleven. I scraped through exams by the skin of my teeth and never really spoke the language again until I was twenty-five and started getting involved in the French ocean racing circuit.

I pick up words very quickly then string them together very badly. I still speak with no grammar although I make myself understood most of the time. My vocabulary is based around the boatyard though, so a dinner-party conversation about current affairs only really flows if current affairs are being dominated by boatyards.

We left Brussels when I was four and a half. Dad was offered a job as professor of aerospace engineering at Glasgow University and it was a good time to transfer us kids to a British school. We moved to Helensburgh on the Clyde estuary, 30 miles north-west of Glasgow. With the help of my godmother, Sue Vaughan, who already lived there, Mum and Dad found a suitable house that needed little doing to it. That was a bonus after they'd had to spend three years renovating our run-down place in Brussels. So was the fact that our new home was a stone's throw from the waterfront and just along the coast road from a sailing club.

They always say there's no place like home. I've lived in Hampshire and on the Isle of Wight, I spent a year studying in America and I've been lucky enough to travel all over the world through sailing. But the Gareloch, shaped like a witch's finger and nestling between the coast road and the Rosneath Peninsula, really is home to me.

I spent the best part of my childhood there. If we weren't sailing on the loch, we were walking up the hills above Helensburgh and looking down at it. On a clear, dry day with no haze you can see Loch Lomond to the east, and to the west – over the Gareloch and the Clyde – the Isles of Bute and Arran and a ladder of sea lochs.

Sailing was the main family activity and as I grew up I spent more and more of my time on the Gareloch. Helensburgh's full of families who sail and if we weren't out on the water we'd be hanging around at the sailing club.

We must have been a real handful for Mum – who when I was born had four of us aged under five – but I obviously wasn't conscious of that when we were young. My parents were just parents, there to praise us when we did something good, tell us off when we got into mischief (which was often but never usually serious) and encourage us to try all kinds of hobbies and activities.

Given Dad's line of work, it was probably always inevitable that some of it would rub off on us, and it did. I remember Philippa, aged eleven, building a car that was powered by an elastic band and would stop at the edge of the table without any outside help. Maybe it was something she'd learnt from Dave but her teachers at school were obviously impressed and she was given great encouragement to develop her talent. The result has been a successful career in engineering with British Aerospace and the shipbuilders Vosper Thornycroft.

Dave and Andy were always making things, usually aircraft and boats respectively. Dave once spent a whole day making a hot-air balloon out of tissue paper, complete with basket and fuelled by meths dipped in cotton wool. The whole thing disappeared in a flash of flame the moment he lit it. Such setbacks never fazed him and he had a successful model made within hours and then something else on the workbench the next day. Using Dad's jig saw, he started making wooden toys and puzzles for all the neighbours' kids. That made him some tidy profits one summer, at least until everyone we knew had already bought something. Andy and his friends would build remote-control boats that they'd sail, modify, crash and then rebuild.

I think it was inevitable that Philippa and I would grow up with tomboy streaks in us. We certainly wore a lot of the boys' hand-me-down clothes, which was fine by us, although it did make Mum's job harder if she needed to get us into dresses. It had to be a family wedding or some such special occasion to invoke such measures in those days.

Whether it was something to do with designing a gadget or purely for the fun of it, I remember we'd sometimes get to scribble on Dad's blackboard in his office. It wasn't until the inquisitive stage of my early teens that I had any notion of what he actually did. I was impressed though with the various books in his study that had his name on them. Only much later did I realize they were full of groundbreaking research.

I remember not spending too much time with Dad during the week when we were very small. We'd see him at dinner-time, then he would go and finish his work in his study. He'd often be up and out of the house before we got up for breakfast. Probably for that reason weekends were special and if we weren't sailing then we'd be out as a family, climbing hills. The mantra always seemed to be 'just to the top of this hill' but when we got there, we'd have a rest – and an apple or chocolate digestive and a drink of water – and be off again. We did some healthy-sized hikes for little people! Those walks typified the positive influence of my parents and the encouragement they gave in bringing us up. Even in small ways, they instilled a sense that anything was possible with a bit of effort, and that you get out of life what you put into it. They made us feel confident and that has undoubtedly underpinned everything I have done since.

I've often been told that I'm just like my dad and I certainly share more of his facial features than I do Mum's. I'm also a practical person, like him, but whereas I see him as a doer *and* a thinker, I could never claim his cerebral application. My attitude to things is much less likely to be 'We should ponder this for a while' than 'Let's do it, and now!'

Andy, Dave, Philippa and I all played the piano and at times had various other hobbies, one of which was tennis – I was useless and still am – but by our teens we'd pretty much given up most other things. Sailing took over, as it did for most of our friends.

I just loved being outside in the fresh air, getting in a boat and heading off for hours on end. That sense of freedom, of being in charge of your own little piece of the world, was exhilarating, not that I'd have described it like that then. It was just fun. We spent every weekend and most of our evenings sailing and we didn't stop in the winter. When I look back now I think it's crazy that we'd go out for pleasure in numbing cold and rain and wind but we did it. We knew nothing different and there was nothing better.

The first boats I sailed were a Mirror and an Optimist, which is the most popular boat for learners. Dad built both of them and we all sailed them. Andy and Dave were really competitive and always focused on getting the best results they could, whether they were racing each other or involved in some competition or other.

They've both had successful sailing careers since. Andy has been racing since he was nine and after winning umpteen titles across Scotland in various dinghy classes, he made it to the British sailing team and only narrowly missed selection for the 1996 Olympics in Atlanta. Dave was competing at senior level in his teens and won the UK national championships in 1988 in the 420 class, which is just a step down the ladder from the two-man 470 Olympic class.

For the past six years or so they've been sailing together in skiffs, and in the last few years in 18-foot skiffs, which are the fastest dinghies around. They're very light boats with a massive sail area and they hurtle along at about 30 knots of boat speed, which is huge. It's a pure adrenalin sport, hanging off the side in permanent danger of a spectacular flip. I'd definitely like to give it a go some day. Andy and Dave are among the best in the world, and that's not just the view of a biased little sister.

When we were kids I was intrigued by the buzz that the boys got from winning. I wanted to be part of that and by the time I was ten I was entering races with Andy in the Mirror, a class often crewed by younger sailors. I'd watch how intensely Andy worked and try calmly to take it all in.

Sometimes, maybe I was too calm. Once when I was out with Andy, around the time we started racing together, we capsized in bad weather just off Helensburgh. I got trapped under the boat but Andy managed to stay clear and scramble on to the upturned hull. It was a miserable day, windy and choppy, and Andy was going frantic wondering where I was in case I was trapped and drowning. He was swimming around looking for me, climbing on to the boat to get a better view. I'd found a nice pocket of air and was quite happy. Eventually I swam out and helped him to right the boat.

I went racing with Andy all over the place in the Scottish Traveller series, at club level to begin with. There was something on almost every weekend and night racing on Wednesdays. It took up every spare moment and I loved it.

When I was eleven we entered the European Championships, a week-long event that was held in Scotland that year, and finished in the top fifteen. The following summer, 1987, our campaign of events and regattas culminated in the World

Championships in Sligo. I remember hearing that we'd qualified but then being slightly disappointed that we'd only be going across the Irish Sea to compete. One of the recent championships had been in Sydney. When it dawned on me that Australia would have been out of the question financially, I realized what we *were* doing was pretty cool anyway.

It turned out to be a great event with some terrific sailing in the full Atlantic waves as they crashed towards the coast. It was so exciting just to be there, let alone make any impression. We came nineteenth overall, which I thought was quite good. 'We could have done a bit better,' I remember Andy saying. But we had to be proud of it. It was a senior fleet and Andy had only just turned seventeen and I was twelve.

Being youngsters in an older crowd always made me feel good about what we were doing and even better when we beat people older than us. That trip to Sligo reinforced my view that sailors tend to have a good sense of camaraderie whatever their backgrounds, with plenty of joking around. I'll always remember the official briefing at the beginning of the week when everyone got a chance to query the rules, ask about amendments and question the race committee about possible changes to the schedule if the wind changed or died. Right at the end there was a final call of: 'Any other questions?' This Irish guy stuck his hand up. 'Can you tell me . . .' he began, in all seriousness, '. . . why is it that orange jam is called marmalade?'

Andy and I stopped competing together soon after Sligo. I was growing too fast to be his lightweight partner and he moved up to bigger boats. I took over the helm in the Mirror and also went back to racing my Optimist.

When I was thirteen, the season after I stopped sailing with Andy, I persuaded my best friend Jane Ross to start. I was on the helm and there was no one at the club who could join me who was both the right size and didn't already have a crewmate lined up for the coming season. We already had the boat so Jane just needed a buoyancy aid and some old trainers and we were away. She didn't take much persuading although she didn't come out quite as often as the rest of us. (That's probably why she plays the violin so well today *and* thrashes me at tennis.) We sailed in the Mirror together for a couple of years, and then my results in the Optimist secured me a place in the Scottish sailing squad.

Being part of the squad involved sailing every weekend. In the winter there was squad training on the isle of Cumbrae off Largs once a month. In between there'd be events based at the Helensburgh sailing club, including the aptly named Frostbite series. These races were often cancelled due to gales but there was still plenty of good sailing – if you ignored having to break the ice off the boat covers and from the bilges every time you went out. The squad sailing also meant taking part in various championships around the UK and Europe. It was all-consuming but fun. And the more fun we had, the better we got.

I'd also become quite the little competitor, no doubt partly due to the influence of Andy and Dave. As my sister Philippa likes to remind me, even as a young teenager I'd picked up a catchphrase. I'd heard it being used by an older sailor in the 420 squad, I think, and it must have been quite comical to see me, not long out of pigtails, with it written on my boat. There was one time, she recalls, when we were out together racing around a local landmark known as The Sugar Ship. It's a huge sugar tanker that upturned on the Clyde in the 1960s and lies there to this day, protruding from the water. It was a bit choppy that particular day but I still wanted to get the best from the boat and was pushing for speed. Philippa didn't want us to capsize and she recalls me asking her why she wasn't sitting out better, making us go faster. I pointed to the boom, where I'd inscribed my new motto: 'No pain, no gain'. I quit the Scottish squads when I went to America for a year just before my seventeenth birthday. I left school, the local comprehensive, Hermitage Academy, in 1991, after my fifth year. I neither loved nor hated school. I just got on with it, doing what I had to do while looking forward to my activities out of school, mainly my sailing. I had no grand ambitions or concrete plans about what I wanted to do when I grew up. Most of all I wanted to enjoy what I was doing and live for the moment.

I was a far from exceptional student but I worked hard, kept my head down and got the results I needed for university. After my fifth year at school I already had all the qualifications I needed for university under the Scottish education system, but I didn't want to go straight there. Andy and Philippa had both gone directly from fifth year to university but unlike me had been at the older end of their academic years. My other brother, Dave, hadn't wanted to start university at sixteen either so had stayed on at school for a sixth year. Although it was useful to give him a head-start in his later studies, he wishes he had done some travelling or something else a bit more adventurous instead. I didn't want to fall into that trap *or* go straight to university, so I applied for an exchange programme in America to fill the spare year. I'd seen a poster advertising it and ended up doing 12th grade in a high school in Georgetown, Delaware.

I spent eleven months in Georgetown, a quiet farming town, though I'm still not sure whether the culture shock was greater for me, as a sixteen-year-old visitor, or for the town. There were quite a few other European teenage students and au pairs in the vicinity and most of us had experienced the odd drink before we arrived. We all got our fingers slapped for drinking beer or 'wine coolers' at some stage, even though they contained all of 2 per cent alcohol.

I lived with a family with two young kids who also had foster children coming and going. School was much the same as I imagine it is everywhere, the main difference being that extracurricular activities had a large dose of beach culture. Rehobeth Beach, only a few miles away, was quite the social hangout, although I did no sailing at all the whole time I was there.

I did learn to drive though, while I was still sixteen, which meant that when I got back to Scotland I was allowed to drive on my US licence for a year despite the fact I hadn't taken a British driving test. This was a source of much amusement – and no little terror – for friends in the car when I would pull out of a junction and be driving on the wrong side of the road. When I did take the test at home I failed because I'd picked up all kinds of bad habits. I passed the second time after a few lessons.

Fun though America was, I was glad to get back home to my friends, not to mention sailing, which had been such a big part of my life for so long and then absent for what seemed an age. I had no real appetite for rejoining the Scottish squads. With my studies at Glasgow University and all the other distractions that university life offered, I really didn't have the time to dedicate myself to a serious campaign in the 470s, where the tacit aim would have been the Olympics, which was the main option available. Earning a degree had to take priority.

I still ended up doing some sailing in the 470s during my second year, with a crew from Southampton. I'd study during the week, spend Wednesday afternoons doing university sailing, work in an Irish bar in the evenings and then borrow Mum's car every other weekend to go down south or to the training centre on the isle of Cumbrae. I realized pretty quickly that I'd taken on too much and my studies would suffer by the time I reached third year. I gave up the travelling and instead took on captaincy of the university team, regaining a social life I'd seemed to be losing in the process.

I continued working behind the bar, increasing my shifts to three a week to improve my standard of living. That meant I could spend my student loan on a mountain bike and skiing instead. By my final year, the bar work had stepped up a notch to become wine waitressing at the Glasgow Hilton. The tips improved, that's for sure.

The university sailing I did was a huge amount of fun and very competitive but I still had no real aim to develop my sailing into a career. If I'd wanted to do so at that stage, the Scottish squads would have been the best route.

If I said I had any firm alternative career plan, I'd be lying. The word 'plan' would be far too definitive. I had an interest in sports physiotherapy, so I studied Sports Medicine and graduated with a 2:1 Honours degree, which was better than I'd expected after a pretty full university life. The degree gave me the platform to do a Masters in physiotherapy and follow that as a career. But the Masters would have taken two years and I decided to take a year out before committing to it. Maybe, I thought, if I just take that break, and perhaps do something sailing-related in the meantime, the decision about the Masters would make itself. Sailing was about to become more than a hobby.

After I graduated in June 1996 I booked a two-month trip to the Cayman Islands for that September. The main aim was to visit some friends but I thought I'd also be able to make it a working holiday. The question was what to do with my time before I went. In July I headed for Hamble, a village on the south coast of England which is the heart of the sailing community down there. Many of the best sailors I'd encountered in competitions came from the area. With plenty of summer jobs apparently available in the marine industry, I thought I'd go down and see if I could find a couple of months' work. I ended up living in Southampton, 6 miles from Hamble.

The first place I looked for a job – I was looking for anything just to get me started and pay the rent – was down at the Hamble marina. I cycled there from Southampton.

As fate would have it, the first boat I saw was a massive 92-foot catamaran, formerly called *ENZA*, that I'd just read a book about. Two years earlier, Sir Peter Blake and Sir Robin Knox-Johnston had sailed her non-stop around the world in a record-breaking time of 74 days and 22 hours to capture the Jules Verne trophy, an award held at any one time by the crew that holds the monitored record for the fastest circumnavigation. *ENZA* was sitting there, looking huge and awesome, and there were people all over her, obviously preparing her for something.

I went over to one of the guys working on her. I asked if there was any chance of a bit of work, any odd jobs, and he asked if I was there because of the adverts. I had no idea what he was talking about. When he told me that Tracy Edwards was putting together an all-female crew to attempt to beat *ENZA*'s round-the-world record, and in the very same boat, the project sounded amazing. The Jules Verne trophy was at stake. Tracy's crew wouldn't be 'racing' in terms of coming up against another boat but they would be racing against the best-ever previous time for the journey round the world. I was hooked.

It was totally implausible, of course, because apart from not knowing anyone involved I had no real experience of yachts. Nearly all my sailing had been in dinghies, which are small boats without keels that you don't sail mid-ocean. Yachts are generally larger boats with keels, which are basically lumps of lead that hang from the bottom of the boat to help keep them upright. Most yachts can be ocean-going. I certainly had no experience of multi-hulls or of ocean racing. *ENZA* was a monster multi-hull and her *raison d'être* was ocean racing and record-breaking ocean voyages. 'Why don't you go and talk to Tracy anyway?' the guy said, and pointed me in the direction of her office.

For all her achievements, I knew little about Tracy except that she'd been the first skipper of an all-female crew in the Whitbread round-the-world race, aboard *Maiden*, in 1989–90. (The quadrennial Whitbread was brought under the auspices of Volvo in 1998, since when it has been known as the Volvo Ocean Race.) They'd finished a very creditable second in their class but had been the undoubted winners in terms of public acclaim. Something like 50,000 people turned out to greet them when they sailed back into Southampton. I'd seen Tracy on *This Is Your Life* and I'd read her book about the Whitbread but I didn't know what to expect from meeting her face to face. The only person I knew who'd met her was my best friend Jane, who at one stage was keen to become a journalist and had sat in on an interview with Tracy during work experience. All Jane had said was that Tracy was about 3 feet 10 inches, chain-smoked all the way through the interview, and gave the impression that she was one tough little lady.

I found her office and stood outside for a few moments working out exactly what I was going to say. I felt quite shy, which was a normal state of affairs, despite most people telling me that I come across as confident. I also felt nervous, never having met Tracy before. But then I reasoned that she'd have had a string of people looking for work and there was no real reason why my application would stick out, for better or worse.

I knocked on the door and was ushered in by Sue, the receptionist. I explained that I was looking for work and was shown into the next office, where Tracy was sitting behind her desk, elbow-deep in paperwork. I offered her my hand and heard myself saying something like, 'Hi, my name's Emma and I've heard you're looking for crew to sail around the world.' I didn't mention that I'd first heard it about three minutes ago. 'I've only sailed dinghies before and I've got very little experience on yachts but I'd love to be involved in any capacity and could start work as soon as anything comes up.'

Tracy was naturally a bit hesitant but asked me for a CV. Crewing wasn't mentioned but she said that if I wanted to do some odd jobs for the minimum wage, at least until she had a sponsorship deal tied up, then she'd see what she could do. I was glad of the opportunity, said yes straight away and promised myself that there was no way I was going to mess this up. I ended up cleaning the bilges and vacuuming the dust out of the boat, doing the kind of stuff that no one else wanted to do. But I couldn't have been happier. I had enough guaranteed work for a couple of months to pay the rent and I was involved in a project, albeit only on the fringes, that anyone who loved sailing would bend over backwards for.

In September I set off for the Cayman Islands as planned but kept in touch with Tracy by fax. My holiday turned out to be mainly just that because I had problems getting a working visa, something I didn't know I needed and hadn't organized. I spent most of the time thinking about that catamaran in Hamble marina, and what a dream it would be to sail round the world as part of its crew. The dream had no basis in fact because Tracy had never mentioned I was a candidate for consideration and I'd never asked about my chances. And then when I got back to Southampton, at the end of the November, the entire project was thrown into doubt. Tracy's prospective sponsor had pulled out and she was forced to lay off the majority of the people working for her, me included.

That's how I came to work for British Gas, in a job that was simultaneously the most tedious I've ever done and the greatest motivational kick up the backside I could ever have wished for.

I found it through a temping agency whose remit was to fill 400 vacancies for an expansion of British Gas's customer services department, based at a new call centre. What a nightmare! I'm an outdoors person and I get itchy feet if I have to sit still anywhere for more than a couple of hours, unless it's in a pub. And suddenly I was working in an office, constrained by a desk and a headset, taking up to twenty calls an hour, eight hours a day, most of them beginning: 'Good morning, British Gas, this is Emma speaking, how can I help you?' The only variety came after midday, when the calls began with 'Good afternoon, British Gas, this is Emma speaking, how can I help you?'

I dealt with pensioners calling in tears because they'd had erroneous bills for millions of pounds. I had people who were frustrated and angry because they'd spent their entire lunch-hour waiting for their call to be answered so that they could tell someone they'd been cut off by mistake, only to have me redirect them. I had thousands of routine calls about payments and dodgy cookers and meter readings and supply problems. And maybe, about once a fortnight, someone would ring up to pass on their thanks to British Gas for good service. Even then, there was always the suspicion that they were only calling because they were lonely and / or had nothing better to do with their time. Rewarding it was not.

I met people working at the call centre who, once upon a time, had started temping there, like me, to fill in a couple of months between doing other things. I got chatting one day to a girl called Sarah, who was a few years older than me. She was cheerful about her job in a resigned kind of way. She'd started as a temp after finishing college because she'd needed some cash while she looked for something longer-term. Two months had turned to six, and she told me by that time she'd 'fallen into it' and got used to having the income. She hadn't found the work particularly objectionable, certainly not as dull as I was finding it. So she'd kept an eye out for something else but as nothing came up, she'd made less effort to look. She said that before she got married, having a nine-to-five job meant she could concentrate on enjoying herself the rest of the time. Afterwards, when she'd started a family, she'd been able to fit her work round it.

'So how long have you been here?' I asked, curious to know where stop-gap employment could lead.

'It must be almost eight years.'

The day I heard that was the day I decided I just had to make the sailing work, even if it meant an age cleaning boats. It wasn't long afterwards, in February 1997, that I got a call from Sue in Tracy's office. 'Tracy's found a sponsor, do you want your job back?'

I left British Gas the same day.

•

Back in Hamble, I took up where I'd left off, working on the boat, by then provisionally named *Royal & SunAlliance* after the project's new sponsor. Once we finally launched her in early

May 1997, I began sailing on her. I never asked what my chances were of being offered a place on the crew, nor did Tracy give any hints. She needed to find the right combination of people with appropriate experience and what she saw as the right attitude. Candidates came and went. Even the numbers changed because it wasn't mandatory to have a fixed number of crew for a Jules Verne attempt. That kept everyone on their toes.

Over the course of that project, from summer 1996 to spring 1998, Tracy showed me that anything was possible with determination. It wasn't her achievements in themselves that had greatest resonance for me, ground-breaking as they'd been. Before *Maiden* she'd sailed in the 1985–6 Whitbread as the cook and only woman aboard *Atlantic Privateer*. After *Maiden* Tracy endured all manner of turmoil in her private life but bounced back to get *Royal & SunAlliance* off the ground at huge financial and emotional cost. What struck me was her determination to see things through, motivate others and resist pressures that threatened to crush her spirit.

I was completely unaware of many of those pressures at the time, like the fact that she'd borrowed £1 million in the run-up to the *Royal & SunAlliance* project and risked losing her home, her life savings and the savings of several close friends unless she found a backer. Also unbeknown to most of us on the crew, there were times when she felt the project was beyond her and that her control was slipping away. I certainly had no idea until later that she came within a whisker of quitting the whole thing, and quite late on, under the strain. To me she was precisely the tough little lady that Jane had briefly described and I respected the way she had strong ideas and stuck to them, regardless of whether others thought she was right.

I respect the drive that has got Tracy where she is today. She has put together some great projects and is a very dedicated lady. I like her socially too. She's got some great stories from her adventures.

If Tracy hadn't gone with her instincts, I'd never have made it on to the crew. I still can't believe that I was one of the eleven most experienced people in the world she could have found for the job. I know I wasn't. That was obvious to me from my total lack of ocean experience alone.

I was very eager to please. On the one hand, such an approach among a group of old-hand sailors may have come across as being *too* keen. On the other, when Tracy asked me to do something or adopt a new role, I made sure I gave it my all. When *Royal & SunAlliance*'s doctor-elect pulled out, Tracy asked if I'd take up the duties because of my quasi-medical background. I studied to expand my knowledge and spent time at the A&E department of the local hospital watching people being stitched up and having their broken limbs set in plaster. When Jo Gooding, *Royal & SunAlliance*'s proposed camerawoman, pulled out, I took on her mantle too and attended a filming course at the BBC. The objective was to make a documentary of our voyage, which we subsequently did.

Years later I was flattered when Tracy said I'd made myself indispensable through 'sheer hard work, enthusiasm and ability'. To be honest, I was just doing what I was asked or told and trying to make the best of it. I put that down to youthful enthusiasm. It's what I had to offer.

In the final crew of eleven, there were nine other strong women, each hand-picked by Tracy for their experience, zeal or both. I don't think any of us knew whether we'd have a real chance of breaking the record until we were two-thirds of the way around the world and it was still in our sights. The bottom line is that we knew Tracy believed it. That drove her and inspired me.

The first time I went sailing with her stood out for a different reason. I still didn't know her all that well but we'd all had a great first day on the water. The boat was quick, more like a powerboat, skimming over the water with its amazing acceleration, than a sailboat. You really had to see *Royal & SunAlliance* in the flesh to appreciate what an incredible machine she was.

She had two vast hulls, each one shaped like a thin, elongated ocean liner. They were joined by three crossbeams more than 40 feet wide, with netting strung between. The navigation station, aka 'the Pod', located centrally between the back two beams, was the control centre, housing all the computers, communications devices and chart table. It also had bunks for the skipper and the navigator. Inside the port hull there was the galley – a two-ring stove and a sink – as well as enough room for three people to squeeze in to sleep. The starboard hull housed another tiny sleeping area and the head (toilet). All the other space was for storage.

The depth of the hull was less than 7 feet, which set against the length and width made the whole structure seem very flat. (You could almost imagine a giant picking her up and skimming her out across the waves.) And then there was the mast, towering 102 feet. When the sails were raised and full of wind, it was almost as though she'd picked *herself* up and was doing the skimming on her own.

Even that first day's sailing gave us notice she was going to be quick, clocking an effortless 17 knots out on the Solent. Everyone was buzzing and Tracy was relieved that all her efforts were coming to fruition. I felt I was doing my best. No doubt, it had been a good day.

As we were motoring up the last stretch of the Hamble River to the dock I got chatting to Tracy about sailing and its effect on relationships. She started talking about how she was in the middle of a divorce. At twenty-two, I didn't have much experience in that area. Marriage, let alone divorce, had never been on my horizon and I knew very few people who were divorced. All I could think of to say was: 'Well, you won't make the same mistake twice, will you?'

Silence.

'Emma,' said Tracy, 'this is my second divorce.'

I suddenly found myself needing to be busy elsewhere, preparing docklines. My gaffe had no detrimental effect on my position in the crew but sailing has definitely taught me a few things about diplomacy since. Likewise I've seen the extent to which the ocean-racing profession plays havoc with relationships. It's not a lifestyle that's conducive to romance, if you want to spend long periods of uninterrupted time together. On a broader level, you can easily end up distanced from family and friends unless you make a real effort.

I've missed umpteen weddings, birthdays, reunions, special occasions and family get-togethers in the past seven years due to sailing. That's not a moan, it's just a price you pay. I'd have to feel pretty irreplaceable in my work for that to change. More importantly, I'd have to feel totally comfortable that I'd made my boat the fastest, safest vessel it could be to the extent that no more could be done and I could leave for a break just before a race or something. That's always going to be an unlikely scenario for most sailors, me included.

Back then, in 1997, as spring turned into summer, it was less of an issue. It wasn't my place to call the shots and I was just thrilled to be part of the campaign. How lucky was that? One minute I was walking in off the street looking for an odd job related to boats. A few months later Tracy Edwards was asking me how I'd feel about giving up my daily bike ride from Southampton, where I was still staying. 'Why?' I asked. 'Because the crew house is in Hamble,' said Tracy. And suddenly I was on my way to an attempt on the Jules Verne trophy, albeit as a small cog in an enormous machine.

Royal & SunAlliance, who were sponsoring Tracy to the tune of £3.2 million in the hope of raising international awareness about their recent merger, had their own small army making the campaign work for them.

Then there was Ed Danby, a great guy whom Tracy brought on board as her project manager. He was opinionated and he spoke VERY LOUDLY but I respected the job that he did, often in tough circumstances. A lot was expected of him. He'd been part of the crew when Sir Peter Blake and Robin Knox-Johnston broke the circumnavigation record, and knew the boat inside out. He didn't sail on our record attempt but was as close to it as possible in spirit.

Then there was the rest of the crew. Tracy needed someone other than herself with experience of the Southern Ocean. She asked Adrienne Cahalan, an Australian rated as the best female navigator in the world, if she'd be interested. Adrienne flew around the world to join up. She had a great sense of humour and was a good leader in terms of having confidence in her tactical decisions. At sea she kept our spirits up, laughing at the fact that she had to stay warm and dry inside to make decent decisions as the rest of us froze outside. Miki Von Koskull, a Finn, was hired as another watch leader. She's a likeable pro with a no-nonsense approach. Only Tracy, Adrienne and Miki had any Southern Ocean experience. They'd all sailed in the Whitbread.

Five of the others had varying experience as charter-boat skippers, and of racing, inshore and offshore, including Emma Westmacott and Helena Darvelid, who were both watch leaders. Hannah Harwood was a former UK women's match racing champion who then lived in Bahrain, where she taught sailing. She was physically strong and had an equally strong personality. You could always rely on her and you always knew where you stood with her, which I liked. Miranda Merron – extremely bright, very well-spoken and good at staying calm under pressure – had several years' experience in match racing and ocean racing. She was in charge of safety on board. Since *Royal & SunAlliance* we've raced together often and become firm friends. Frédérique Brule, aka Fred, was a French romantic in the broadest sense, arty and poetic and cool.

And then there was a trio of 'nippers' in Sam Davies, Sharon Ferris and me. We were all in our early twenties. I'd been twenty-one when I'd walked into Hamble marina that fateful day and I was the baby of the bunch. Sam was the rigger and it was her principal job to climb the mast to do the rig checks and any repairs. She always had an air of confidence about her and could give anyone a run for their money in the party stakes. Sharon, an Olympic dinghy sailor from New Zealand, was probably my best mate on the crew during the *Royal & SunAlliance* campaign. She spoke her mind, pushed hard, and you knew you could always rely on her.

As the crew was starting to take shape through the spring of 1997 (it wasn't actually finalized until late in the year) the goalposts moved in terms of the record we were chasing. In

March, Olivier de Kersauson, a Frenchman sailing a boat called *Sport Elec*, beat *ENZA*'s circumnavigation record, going around the world non-stop in 71 days, 14 hours and 22 minutes. But that only served to strengthen our resolve. After *Royal & Sun-Alliance* was formally launched in late May we headed across to New York to prepare for an attempt on the transatlantic speed record on a voyage that would also act as a chance for some practice under pressure.

We had to wait until 22 June for a suitable weather window but even then it wasn't plain sailing. We made good progress in the first few days but after we'd crossed over the Grand Banks off Newfoundland the temperature dropped below freezing. We hit iceberg territory though thankfully no icebergs. We passed over the *Titanic* without incident.

We effectively lost any chance of the record soon afterwards when we ran into a high-pressure system that took the wind from our sails. We abandoned our attempt. The year rolled on, the clock ticked down. We completed our sailing programme – including sailing around Britain and Ireland, which was fun – and moved ever closer to the big one.

Towards the end of 1997 we were placed on standby. At twenty-four hours' notice we'd need to be able to get packed and ready to go. If an appropriate weather system that would provide a slingshot effect for our first few days south started to develop, we'd have to take it.

It was a nervy wait and everything we arranged in our lives away from Hamble had to have a sufficient degree of flexibility to allow us to answer the call. My eldest brother, Andy, got married two weeks into our standby period, just before Christmas. I accepted the invitation to his wedding to Juliette on the shaky understanding that I might not be there. They made me a bridesmaid's dress just in case and fortunately I got to wear it.

Over Christmas we were 'stood down' for a few days so we could go wherever we wanted to spend the holiday period. I went home to Scotland, driving up and back with my brother Dave, who was living in Guildford. Between Christmas and New Year we were told that we definitely wouldn't get the weather we needed within the next five days. We had permission to go away for a break on the strict understanding that any dangerous activities were banned. It would be no use to anyone if one of us got injured. A couple of days later I bumped into Sharon in the Alps, where we'd both gone snowboarding! She'd just done her first day on the slopes and was a natural. I guess most of us didn't really consider skiing and snowboarding as dangerous. We were about to sail off around the world in a crazy boat and it was all relative. We certainly weren't rebelling in any way even though, once regrouped back in Hamble, everyone seemed to have a story about a skiing trip or other forbidden activity. None of us had come back with any broken bones. Luckily.

As the waiting dragged on we went on various fun trips, organized by Tracy and the sponsors. One was a team-building weekend down in Devon where we had to do all sorts of practical tests. We waltzed through them, as you'd expect if you'd seen the camaraderie between us. Another trip took us to Wales, where Tracy had a farm, and we had a great day riding in the hills. That proved more dangerous than any situation any of us had encountered on the slopes. Helena was given a horse that got quite jumpy and threw her off a couple of times but we all emerged unscathed. I'd done so little riding previously that I ended up on this little pony that kept on skipping to keep up with the horses with longer legs. I knew the feeling.

The call finally arrived on the evening of Sunday, 1 February, 1998. 'This is it, girls,' Tracy said when she phoned the crew house. 'I want you ready in the morning.' Then she hung up. There was a mad scramble to pack and say our goodbyes and before we knew it we were off.

Our start line was just off Ushant, the most westerly of the islands off France, about 14 miles from the coast of Finistère. We left Hamble on Monday afternoon and got to Ushant on Tuesday morning. We had a bit of a wait as the race officials took their places and the media helicopters, circling overhead, did their stuff. We made all our last-minute checks and at 10.53 on 3 February, we were off.

Our route, as per usual for record attempts, was due to take us out into the Bay of Biscay, down through the Atlantic, into the Southern Ocean, around Antarctica, up past Cape Horn and homewards, keeping all the Capes to the left.

It's impossible to describe a typical day on the trip because there was no such thing. Some days breezed past quite happily with the numbers staying high and the conditions in our favour. (The 'numbers' are the rate of knots and our distance covered each hour.) Others were fretful and slow, spent dealing with repairs or trying to keep things together during atrocious weather. The only constant was the daily ritual at 10.53 of finding out how far we'd progressed in the previous twenty-four hours. Most days we were happy to discover the record was still there for the taking.

The major dramas were the storms in the Southern Ocean, which has a well-deserved reputation for being the most inhospitable expanse of water on the planet. We took relentless beatings for days at a stretch in freezing conditions and with noise levels so extreme you couldn't hear yourself scream. The wind would rush from 30 knots to 40, then up again to 50 and above. This was combined with waves of 40 feet and more, each one carrying thousands of tonnes of water. From the helm you'd see nothing but a foaming mass of white, when you could see anything at all.

Sometimes it would've been more comfortable not to look. Cresting high waves and then slamming downwards into the wave in front can be a hairy experience. Personally I found it worse when I was inside, when I couldn't anticipate the next crash, or when to hold on, or when I was about to be propelled 15 feet into a wall. You can't think about it too often otherwise you'd never untie yourself from your bunk.

As for worrying or being afraid, I've never really worried or been afraid as part of a team in those situations, at least not due to the conditions in themselves, however bad they are. What is there worth worrying about, really? If you worry in life, you die. If you don't worry, you die anyway. Why worry when it's not going to change anything?

On a practical level, if the conditions are so bad that they should rationally be scaring the hell out of you, the chances are you'll have more than enough urgent tasks to do to keep your mind off them. That's certainly how it was for me on *Royal & SunAlliance* and numerous times since. If you're on deck and trying to steer, then that's what you do. It can be physically exhausting and requires every last bit of your energy to be focused. If something breaks, you need to fix it. (There is rarely a time when something doesn't need fixing.) If you start taking on water you need to bail it out. Once you do get back inside you need to get your outer wet clothes off and hung up and drag your damp, thermal-layered body into your damp sleeping bag.

You hope you will warm up quickly so you can sleep, ideally long enough so that when you wake your clothes are in a slightly drier state. You need to make sure the wet clothes aren't dripping on to your dry stuff. Or anyone else's dry stuff. You need to use the loo, which alone can take an age if you're wearing layer upon layer. You need to eat.

Aboard *Royal & SunAlliance* there were times when we did get fairly close to our limits. But you don't show it. You can't show it. What good would that do anyone? Panic spreads and no one wants to be the instigator. It was much more common in the stormy dark hours – literally and metaphorically – to make an attempt at gallows humour. Or should that be galley humour? As I recall, we spent more time saying things like 'Dangerous this sailing, dinner just jumped out of the pan at her . . .' than 'Oh my God, are we actually going to get out of this place in one piece?'

Of course it was the first time down in the Southern Ocean for eight of us so we didn't know what to expect anyway. When Tracy or Adrienne told us they'd seen worse, we believed them. We didn't know then they were lying.

Coping with what the ocean was throwing at us ended up being among the high points of my voyage. All my personal highs involved situations where I felt like a valuable part of the team and not just the youngest nipper. One of those came during the fifth week as we were battling against another mad storm and high seas. All the wind instruments went down. It's imperative in a fast boat like that to know where the true wind is coming from and we had no way of telling. I had to steer the boat for a long, long time without relief while someone stood behind me reading the numbers. I could barely see because of the power and volume of the water in my face. There was no moon, no stars, no light. I was just staring into the blackness trying to pick up the outlines of the waves. I was steering on instinct. Tracy later described it as 'like running along a cliff top and never once slowing down or pulling away because you're scared of heights or the wind'. She went as far as calling it 'a sixth sense' and even 'genius'. I don't know about that but it was bloody painful. When I could continue steering no longer I almost toppled off the wheel because my shoulders ached so badly. All I wanted to do was get dry and lie down but I felt good about my sailing and good that I was contributing something meaningful.

My camera work, at the time at least, was less of a pleasure. It was my responsibility – and I felt it – to make sure we had enough footage to make an hour-long documentary at the end. I had to film people during their lowest moments and quiz them about why they were feeling low, as if it weren't patently obvious most of the time. I had to be in the right place at the right time in a situation where right places and times didn't often happen.

It was a job that certainly didn't make us go any faster and didn't teach me anything about ocean racing. It was also a pain trying to film with various different audiences in mind. The BBC wanted clips and they didn't want any branding. The sponsors wanted as much branding as possible. It was a fine line and I often got it wrong. But it was part of the sponsorship deal and I had to do it – over and over again sometimes, when the wind ruined a take or the outside cameras had shaken loose and were recording empty skies.

It's hard now to say whether the good times outweighed the bad. That's not how I judged it. Some things left a lasting impression, like the harsh beauty of the Southern Ocean's moods.

Others were just silly, like being covered in rancid leftovers as part of a 'crossing the Equator' initiation ceremony for those of us doing it for the first time.

Yet that was all part of the fabric of the journey. There were some very tough times, but they made the good times even better. The whole experience was by far and away the most life-affirming thing that I'd ever done.

I always get asked if we got on. I can honestly say that every one of us was out there to break the record. Everyone was focused on one goal. Every day, every minute and every last manoeuvre counts. There is no time to waste and no time for not getting on. It's different from being in a school playground or an office, where you may have no choice who you play or work with. It's an incredible feeling to work in a team like the one we had aboard *Royal & SunAlliance* and I wish that everyone could experience that kind of unity of purpose. I have no doubt it would improve the world we live in.

The end, when it came, was brutal. Day 43, it was. We thought we'd survived a gargantuan storm that had been chasing us for days and had given us a massive hiding. We were almost out of it and the waves were easing. Then along came a freak one, 50 feet and rising, we had too much sail up for the conditions and when we surfed at high speed down a wave with no way out, the boat stopped dead. The mast snapped a few minutes later. Pandemonium was followed by calm practicality. Our attempt was over but we began a structured assembly of a jury rig (a makeshift mast and sail) that served us well as we headed to port in Chile. It took two weeks to get there. We said our goodbyes and went our separate ways. Our journey stayed at the forefront of my mind for a long time.

I'd still intended, before the start, to maybe go back to

university and do my Masters in physiotherapy. But after experiencing what I had and having emerged stronger in so many ways, there was no way I was going back to studying while I still had so much to learn about ocean racing. When I got home I knew I had to find some way back to it, even if it meant putting together a project of my own.

In the meantime I needed to find a new job to pay the bills, preferably one related to sailing. Because of the filming on *Royal & SunAlliance* I applied for a post at a south-coast media company, Airwaves Media Productions, which specialized in sailing. I got the job. AMP specializes in producing TV programmes and digital video production, local event radio, Internet radio and other audio productions. This impressive coverage includes the BT Global Challenge, the Volvo Ocean Race and the Around Alone as well as Eventing, Le Mans 24hr race, Cowes week, Wimbledon and Matchplay Golf. To begin with I was mainly doing onboard filming and post-production editing and then moved on to the odd producing job and even interviewing and presenting. I loved it. My new bosses, Dick Johnson and Steve Ancsell, quickly became good friends as well as employers.

They knew I wanted to pursue my new-found passion for ocean racing, and when I'd identified a target race – which was the double-handed Transat Jacques Vabre, from France to Colombia, in November 1999 – they put all AMP's resources at my disposal. I used their office to formulate and print proposals, write letters, make calls, develop contacts, you name it.

The key ingredient to any project is financial backing. Without that there's little chance of being able to afford to hire a boat or a shore crew or equipment, or pay for entry fees, insurance and living expenses. Dick and Steve both helped me look for sponsorship and it was through my work with AMP, albeit indirectly, that I met Andrew Pindar. Less than twenty-four hours after first meeting him in 1999 I asked him to write me a cheque for £3,000. He did, and in doing so became my sponsor. My whole way of life was about to change.

My participation in the Around Alone had a complicated genesis. At different times it seemed in turn to be a challenge, a mistake, an accident, an escape, a dream, a career move, an irritation, a breeze, a gale, a good move for my sponsor and a recipe for disaster. And I can't rule out the possibility that when the idea was first mooted, in the early spring of 2002, a couple of Caribbean rum 'n' cokes played their part in making the whole idea more intoxicating.

But without two specific events – meeting Andrew Pindar in 1999 and then winning my first solo ocean race a year later – I doubt I would have ever contemplated being on that start line.

I first met Andrew at a dinner at the Royal Southampton Yacht Club in early June 1999. The only reason I was there was because I'd been invited by Paul Covell, a director of Sun Chemical, a global ink company, who was a recreational sailor. A few weeks earlier he'd been on a volunteers' training trip for the BT Global Challenge and I'd been on board filming it as part of my job with AMP. I'd ended up showing Paul how to improve his tacking and we'd got chatting about my sailing 'career'.

A few days later he phoned and asked if I'd be interested in doing a day's crewing aboard a boat he was chartering for a corporate event. The dinner at the RSYC, the night before, was a precursor to that event. Andrew, head of the printing company Pindar, was one of the guests along with his wife Caroline. I was actually placed at a table alongside Peter Wilkinson, Pindar's marketing director.

The first shock of the night came when I picked up the menu. Apparently there were two 'special guests' in attendance. One was Sir Chay Blyth, a former Yachtsman of the Year and Man of the Year, who had been knighted for his services to sailing in 1997. The other, to my astonishment, was me.

I didn't know where to look. The information on the menu was correct. I had indeed been the youngest member of the crew on Tracy Edwards's *Royal & SunAlliance* during the 1998 attempt on the Jules Verne trophy. But first, to be blunt, we'd failed. And second, even if we hadn't, I didn't know how I was qualified to be called a special guest at anything. Sir Chay Blyth, yes. But Emma Richards?! The only upside to my embarrassment was that I had no need to introduce myself to anyone and I could happily chat about my hopes for the TJV and how it was looking increasingly unlikely that my attempt would ever get off the ground.

I first thought of that race as a realistic target at the end of 1998 after sailing across the Atlantic during a short stint working for Ellen MacArthur. Ellen had just won the Route du Rhum solo event from St Malo in northern France to Pointe-à-Pitre in Guadeloupe in a race that most people now consider was the turning point in her career. Sam Davies and I, who had sailed together on *Royal & SunAlliance*, had been working as Ellen's shore crew, and our last task was to deliver the boat from Guadeloupe back to the UK.

The boat, which Ellen sailed as *Kingfisher* in the Route du

Rhum, had previously been Pete Goss's *Aqua Quorum*, a 50-foot monohull. Obviously Sam and I were not in race conditions and there was no time pressure on us to push ourselves but it was demonstrably a great boat and I realized that a double-handed transatlantic race was not beyond my capabilities. Sam and I agreed we'd try to do the TJV in 1999 together, preferably on *Aqua Quorum*.

By June 1999 I still hadn't secured sponsorship and Sam had taken up another offer of guaranteed work elsewhere. Instead I asked Miranda Merron, another former *Royal & SunAlliance* crew member, if she'd be interested. During our Jules Verne attempt Miranda and I had talked about sailing together at some stage, albeit in dinghies. She said she'd be up for the TJV but that still left the small problem of cash. I reckoned we'd need to raise £150,000 to fund our campaign. We probably had about £50 spare between us.

Peter Wilkinson listened politely to my woes and I thought no more about it until the next day, when I happened to be crewing on the boat on which Andrew and his wife Caroline were guests. This was no accident: Caroline was the only other female on a day's sailing involving twenty-four people and she was the reason I was invited in the first place. Caroline, not Andrew, is the keen sailor. He openly admits he prefers power boats. We got chatting and he said that Peter had mentioned I was looking for funding and he might be able to put me in touch with potential sponsors.

Andrew struck me from the start as the kind of guy who said what he meant and meant what he said. He's affable and attentive but he knows where the bottom line is, as you'd expect from a successful businessman. I had absolutely nothing to lose by being straight with him and I told him what I needed.

He didn't flinch when I mentioned £150,000. That was the

absolute maximum that I reckoned the whole thing would cost including boat hire, insurance premiums, entry fees, new sails, safety equipment and other kit. When I first sat down to do the budget I'd adopted the motto of 'under-promise and over-deliver'. As I explained to Andrew, not all the backing needed to be in cash. If some of it arrived in kind as equipment, that was fine. And maybe it wouldn't end up costing anywhere near £150,000. I wasn't usually so confident but I even found myself pitching it to him as a way that a potential sponsor could actually make money.

'Supposing someone underwrites the whole thing,' I said, 'to a maximum of £150,000. The boat would sail under their name and in their colours but it might be possible for the sponsor to sublet the headline sponsorship and find five or six other companies who'd each pay £20,000–£30,000 to come aboard as co-sponsors.' I was going out on a limb here, having no idea whether it would be possible to find any co-sponsors or how much they might be willing to pay. But that's how I figured the ocean racing business worked, in theory at least. And it obviously sounded like a more attractive proposition if there was a theoretical profit in it rather than a simple £150,000 hole in a sponsor's bank account.

Andrew made positive noises about finding me a sponsor through some of his contacts and said to leave it with him. He called me the following day.

'Emma, it's Andrew Pindar. I've had no response from anyone.'

My heart sank. I had three days to raise at least a deposit on *Aqua Quorum* or else Pete Goss would be leasing it to someone else.

'I've had no response because Pindar would like to sponsor you.'

I didn't know what to say. While I was mumbling, 'That's brilliant, thanks,' he started to explain how he thought it would be in everyone's interests to have a six-month arrangement, starting immediately and lasting until after the race. Pindar would underwrite the sponsorship and pay me a living wage. In return, we'd work together to get the best value possible for Andrew and his company. It sounded to me like the deal of a lifetime. I was quietly trying to take it all in – only in my head was I screaming YEEESSSSSSS!!! – when I suddenly had a thought.

'Andrew, can you write Pete Goss a cheque? For £3,000? Today?'

The deposit for the boat was on Pete's desk the following morning.

The TJV ended up costing around £100,000, with Pindar paying about half and several co-sponsors making up the balance. We begged and borrowed through the summer to keep our costs down (on sails, equipment and safety gear) and took delivery of the boat in September. We had a memorable trip from Southampton to the start line in Le Havre, carrying Caroline Pindar and some of her friends, one of whom was very seasick. She couldn't have been more charming about it if she'd tried. And then, on Saturday 16 October 1999, Miranda and I set off.

We had no inkling that day how dramatic – or tragic – that year's edition of the Transat Jacques Vabre was going to be. I felt proud that we'd made it as far as this with a venture that I'd put together, albeit with huge amounts of help from lots of different people. There was also relief that we could finally get racing, and some apprehension that whatever the result we might not give Andrew a good run for his money.

The storm hit the fleet on the Wednesday. Hurricane Irene inflicted her most devastating damage on the boats ahead of us, the multi-hulls and the 60-foot monohulls. Paul Vatine, one of the most experienced skippers in the fleet, was killed when the trimaran he was sailing with Jean Maurel, a fellow Frenchman, capsized. Paul had been at the helm when his boat was flipped by wild seas and winds of 50 to 60 knots. His body was never found. Jean was rescued.

Four multi-hulls and three monohulls were put out of the race by the end of the first week. Ellen MacArthur and Yves Parlier aboard *Aquitaine Innovations-Kingfisher* were among others who suffered structural damage. The storm left them in real danger of losing their mast and they had to repair their rigging mid-race.

Aboard *Pindar* we had to cope with a broken forestay, which is one of the crucial braces that support the mast. As soon as we realized it had broken, we took the decision to turn around and sail downwind in the opposite direction to which we needed to go. Continuing upwind was exerting potentially disastrous pressure on the broken forestay. It could have brought the whole mast down.

The repair was a complicated procedure. It involved several draining trips up the mast for both Miranda and me and the effective dismantling, repairing and re-assembly of the forestay. Pivotal to our success was the almost miraculous discovery that a small but vital pin from the broken forestay had been thrown not into the sea but on to the deck. The chances of it landing there in the first place, and then us spotting it before it was washed away, must have been millions to one against. Maybe it *was* washed away, but Neptune, in a benevolent mood and taking pity on us, had spat it back.

We made the repair. It took almost twenty-four hours. Physically shattered but elated that we were able to continue, we actually went on to win our class. It was incredible. Andrew's response was: 'Great, what next?'

We agreed I'd extend my arrangement with Pindar for another two years. Andrew would pay me a salary and help in any way he could to facilitate projects to be agreed between us. I'd sail in races under Pindar's colours and be involved in corporate events as their in-house sailor. I'd also have the freedom to dabble in other projects, going out 'on loan' from Pindar if and when other jobs arose. We shook hands on it, as we had on our initial six-month partnership. Five years on, we have yet to sign a formal contract.

•

My first solo ocean race, the second key plank in my journey from AMP to the Around Alone, was in the summer following the TJV. I had never considered doing any single-handed sailing until Pete Goss encouraged me to think about it after that race.

Pete first came to public attention, certainly to my attention, when he took part in the Vendée Globe non-stop, solo round-the-world race in 1996–7. Aged thirty-four, he sold his house to fund his trip and survived on a tiny budget in one of the smallest boats against bigger and richer competitors. Although he didn't win, he set a record for the fastest British solo navigation.

His greatest achievement on that voyage came in ferocious conditions in the Southern Ocean. A fellow competitor, Raphael Dinelli, capsized in the middle of a hurricane and sent out a Mayday. Pete, 160 miles distant and heading farther away, reversed course and spent the best part of two days sailing upwind in heavy seas to rescue him. Raphael was frostbitten, suffering from hypothermia and in real danger of dying. Pete's intervention saved his life. He was awarded France's highest decoration, the Légion d'Honneur, and was later the best man at Raphael's wedding.

Pete is one of the most inspirational people I've ever met and I could listen to him talk for any length of time. He was very generous in providing me with the chance to sail *Aqua Quorum* and he was never less than captivating when trying to encourage me to take on new challenges. He speaks in a gentle but positive way and I've never seen him flustered. His confidence is almost hypnotic.

On a practical note, he is also great at parking. Boats, that is. He never used to have an engine on board *Aqua Quorum*, partly because of the cost and partly because you're not allowed to use one when you're ocean racing anyway, so why have one? Most boats have them in any case for safety, not to mention simple berthing, but not Pete. Thus he could sail that boat to the dock with precision and make it look leisurely.

When Pete first said he thought I should consider a solo voyage, it really meant something. There was even a target race, the transatlantic Europe 1 New Man Star (commonly abbreviated to Ostar, its former name) from Plymouth to Newport, Rhode Island, starting in June 2000. But in the immediate aftermath of the successful TJV, the preparation for that was left on the back burner while Miranda and I concentrated our efforts on a second double-hander in the spring of 2000.

The AG2R runs from Lorient in Brittany, via Madeira, to St Barths in the French West Indies. The boats, identical for every crew, are French-designed 30-foot Figaro-Beneteau monohulls. We spent eight weeks in preparation. During that time I went back to the UK for a week while Miranda was doing a weather-based course in French that I wouldn't have understood a word of. While back in the UK I did a qualifier for the Ostar. One new autopilot of two had been fitted to the boat.

Back in France, we crossed the start line on Sunday, 16 April. We had high hopes of holding our own amongst a fleet of forty-two boats and some of the most experienced sailors in the business. But our forestay snapped after two days and our race was over. We were lying in eleventh place when we were forced to retire.

No ocean racer enjoys having to head for land knowing all the preparation has been in vain. We were no different and we effed and blinded, Miranda in several languages. (She speaks five fluently.) But the very nature of our sport, which loops in so many broken circles around all our hopes and plans, is uncertainty. You can spend months or years preparing for a race and then see it ended within hours because of a freak wave or sudden squall. You never take for granted that you'll make it home, let alone win. Sometimes you just have to shrug off the bad days and look forward to the next good one.

My response to our AG2R misfortune was to redouble my efforts for the Ostar, a decision inspired by Pete and encouraged by Andrew. The race was due to start on 4 June and though it was desperately late in the day, I still had more time to get ready than if we'd completed the AG2R. I had a month, in fact. But it simply wasn't enough. I was completely unprepared and the boat – the fabulous *Aqua Quorum*, again, renamed *Pindar* for the duration, again – had not had the second new autopilot tested. Autopilots are vital in allowing you to get on with tasks and nap safely in the knowledge that you're headed in the right direction. Untested, there was a good chance they'd malfunction. I sailed anyway.

The great unknown for me was the solitude. The journey to

Newport would take somewhere upwards of two weeks and I had never before spent so much as twenty-four hours totally by myself, even on land. I had no idea how I'd react to not having face-to-face contact with another human being for an entire fortnight. I'm not the kind of person who seeks fundamental truths through being alone and I never will be. I've always felt happiest in the company of close friends, having a laugh and a drink or three.

On a practical level, I wasn't sure how I would handle the boat on my own after an accumulated lack of sleep. As part of a large crew you always have chances to rest, if not every day. Even with only two of you there's some room for manoeuvre. Alone, I didn't know what to expect.

I knew there were some skippers on the racing circuit who underwent individual monitoring of the effects of sleep deprivation in preparation. They'd wear watch-like devices that would record their work patterns via their heart rate and would calculate the optimal periods when they should be sleeping or napping. My strategy was no more complicated than hoping I'd get ten or twenty minutes of kip here and there and that if I suffered from debilitating tiredness there'd be a chance for an hour or two on the trot. The chance rarely arose.

The fleet was hit by a storm before the middle of the first week. When it later passed over land, the winds hit almost 100 mph and Scotland recorded one of its deepest low pressures ever. The last reading I noticed on my wind instruments before they were blown off the top of the mast was 60 knots (about 70 mph).

The loss of the instruments was bad but the way that the electronics were configured meant other systems were also corrupted. The control units in the cockpit, which had seals that couldn't cope with the pounding waves, had already been flooded. There *was* a simple fix – unplugging everything and plugging it back in again until it all worked – but this didn't become apparent until after a flash of panic and a few stressful phone calls.

Within the first few days I lost any means of electronic navigation. I'd been trying to run the two onboard computers via an inverter that could not produce sufficient power. One computer was running my nav program (navigational software) and the other my comms program (which controls all electronic communications). With a lack of voltage they tripped regularly. I kept rebooting them because I had no idea of the problem at the time. The navigation computer whirred and died. The other computer, which was very basic and required little power, carried on working. But it had no CD ROM so I couldn't load my nav program. Hence I had to resort to paper charts and a pencil for the rest of the trip. This is easy to do but far from ideal. It's time-consuming, you can't overlay weather charts, you can't show distances and angles and play around with the tactical decisions, and wet hands and wet sleeves do you no favours at all.

When the autopilots stopped working I felt a complete, if temporary, loss of control. These days I'd do some trouble-shooting tests as a matter of routine but then I just didn't know enough about electronics. Luckily I had a good sail combination up that made the boat easy to steer in a reasonably straight line, and then I got on the satellite phone to an electrician who knew the system well and talked me through the repair.

I was constantly frustrated by things that seemed out of my control. If anything had the potential to go wrong it did. I don't think there was a single occasion when I felt, 'Thank goodness that didn't happen ten minutes ago.' Disruptions happened when

I already had something else to deal with. Even 'good' days held their dangers.

One bright, sunny afternoon I was still fretting about the possibility of a collision with a fishing boat when I saw a much bigger ship heading in my direction. I'd been worrying about fishing boats because in big seas they can be hard to pick up on the radar. If you're both in troughs you can't see each other. Sometimes you think you've momentarily seen a fishing boat so you keep staring. You hope that from the top of the next wave crest it will either be clearly visible some distance away (and thus avoidable) or else won't be there at all. The worry is that you'll rise to a crest, straining for a view and then ... BOO! (And bang.)

Such thoughts were running through my head when I saw this ship. I called on the radio and asked if they could see me. I was a mile away in a bright yellow boat with shiny white sails set against a dark sea looking right into their bridge. I thought their radio operator must be located somewhere else because he asked if I was at a specific location and gave co-ordinates of somewhere 10 miles away.

'No,' I said, as calmly and deliberately as I could. 'Look out of your starboard window. I am the person waving at you.'

'Oh yes, I see you now, thanks and out.'

They simply hadn't seen me. That meant that my Active Echo, a device that sends out a signal to make me look big on shipping radar, had stopped working.

The most stressful single situation arose when I was about to cross the busy shipping channel just before you reach Nantucket Shoals, a treacherous area of submerged ridges and sandbanks spreading east and south of Nantucket Island. I was sailing in thick fog and on choppy seas and I was on deck trying to use my sense of hearing to help me spot ships. I had my radar on but it was slightly offset, which means it was giving readings that were slightly out. A ship that appeared to be to one side and off my path, for example, might actually have been on a collision course. Centring the radar still hadn't been ticked off my continuously growing jobs list. It was really one of those things that I should have done before I started the race but it hadn't been a priority. There hadn't been enough time for everything and it hadn't been done, simple as that.

When the fog had become so thick that I couldn't see beyond my bow, I went back below, left the boat steering by pilot and sat down to watch the radar and the progress of ships. I really needed to charge the batteries that power all the electronic systems, including the radar and the autopilot. But I wanted to leave the recharging as late as possible, giving me more time to negotiate the dangerous channel, using my senses of hearing and smell from deck if necessary. I'd be able to smell a ship passing to windward of me, at least.

Leaving the batteries until the last possible moment was always going to put me under pressure. In between watching the radar, listening and sniffing for ships, plotting my position regularly on paper and estimating how much time I had until I was clear of the shipping channel, the batteries ran to a dangerously low voltage.

As soon as I was out of the channel I tried to start the generator to charge them. The generator spluttered and stopped. I tried again. Same thing. I thought there must be an air bubble in the fuel line so bled the generator's engine. It started, spluttered and stopped again.

There was enough fuel sloshing around in the tank but I thought – or more accurately, wished – there might simply be more air bubbles than usual as we were in a bad chop and a top-up would sort it out. I tried to fill the tank from my last 5-gallon jerry can but the funnel wouldn't prop itself up and it was impossible to steady it *and* hold the heavy can with one hand *and* steady myself against the rocking motion of the boat all at the same time in order to put the diesel in the tank. It was messy and frustrating and I was scared that the batteries would die at any moment. If that happened there'd be no autopilots steering the boat and I would be out of control in a dangerous area. For all I knew, a ship could have been bearing down on me at that moment.

I grabbed some spare hose, stuck one end in the jerry can (which was balancing on the fuel tank I was trying to fill) and sucked on the other end. When the revolting diesel started pouring into my mouth, I stuck my thumb on the end of the hose and transferred it to the fuel tank. I secured it with some electrical tape to hold it in place, then tied the jerry securely to the top of the fuel tank so it wouldn't fall off while it was emptying. I ran outside to spit the diesel from my mouth.

Back inside, I tried to bleed the engine again with no luck. Frantic, I called Jim Doxey, a retired engineer from Bristol who had worked with Pete. He talked me through a solution that involved opening more of the engine valves, and while he was on the phone I started the engine. I told Jim he was the best and hung up.

There were tools and puddles of diesel everywhere but I had no time to clear up because I needed to plot my position. I did, only to discover I was almost on the sandbanks. I needed to tack immediately. I dashed straight back up on deck, tacked, pulled out a reef to increase my speed and went back down to clear up.

I was only 100 miles from the finish by that point but the

potential for disaster was constant. Shortly afterwards I got caught on a fishing buoy that had been laid with no clear marker. It took me about fifteen minutes to release myself and I didn't sleep again until the finish.

How I won that race I still don't know. At times I thought my brain was either going to explode or shut down. But the ocean can be a great leveller and everyone else had their own problems to deal with. In a fleet of seventy-one boats across all the different classes, monohull and multi-hull, thirty-two skippers were forced to retire or abandon their boats after capsizing. Those who came out on top had earned it, including Ellen MacArthur, who won her class in the 60-foot monohulls, and Francis Joyon, who won the 60-foot trimaran class. (Francis's subsequent achievements have included pulverizing the solo non-stop round-the-world record in seventy-two days on a voyage that ended in February 2004.)

In my class of 50-footers, the starters had thinned to three boats realistically hunting for the lead by the end of the first week. The others had been left behind. We went through three big storms and each one took its toll on someone. That left a trio of Alex Thomson (another Brit), Andrea Gancia (from Italy) and me, the sole female representative in the class, scrapping it out in the last couple of days. At various stages I was up to 17 miles in the lead and 50 miles behind, depending on the scale of my problems and theirs at any one time. I happened to make it out of the final frontal system first. It's very easy, using hindsight alone, to say it was a good race, but I ended up in so many spots of bother it didn't feel like it at the time or for a long time afterwards.

Every hurdle had left me frustrated or angry or both, mainly at myself, for having let things go wrong, even when there was really no blame to be apportioned. I constantly kept wondering why I'd put myself through it.

The loneliness was bizarre more than anything. I couldn't and didn't go a single day without talking to somebody, even if it was only a simple 'Hello and I'm fine' to the race committee. But I did miss speaking with people face to face, I did miss physical contact and I did yearn for someone to share the pressures of being so hassled almost every moment of every day. It was a strange kind of loneliness, evolved from being desperate to have someone to share the workload, the good moments and the nightmares.

The achievement took a while to sink in. I'd done a single-handed transatlantic race and not only finished safely but won. I'd stood on the dock and made my Steve Redgrave-esque statement to my family and friends along the lines of 'If you ever see me going near a solo ocean race again you have my permission to shoot me.'

And then, as weeks turned to months after the race, I started tossing various scenarios around my head. What if I'd had my nav program available? What if I'd prepared better and had systems that had been tested? What if my knowledge of engines and electronics had been better? What if I hadn't lost ground due to lack of information about the Gulf Stream? What if I just knew then what I know now? I might even have increased my winning margin.

And so my stone-cold certainty that I would never again do a solo race (ever, ever, ever) became ever so slightly less certain.

•

Pete Goss had an idea. Under normal circumstances that fact alone would have meant me taking it on board and giving it some consideration. But what he was suggesting was so far out of the ball park that my immediate and final decision was: 'Not a chance, mate.'

'You know what your Ostar result means, don't you, Emma?' was how he'd begun that particular conversation, sometime in late June 2000. 'You're instantly qualified for the Vendée Globe.'

The 2000–1 edition of the quadrennial Vendée, non-stop and solo around the world, was due to start in four months' time, on 5 November. Pete set out his case. He said I'd just proved that I could cope with a solo race and done so by fire-fighting my way through it. He said he knew it hadn't been easy but if anything, that showed I was *more* capable of doing a longer race because it meant I didn't let setbacks get me down. What doesn't kill you makes you stronger and all that. He also said that *Aqua Quorum* would be ready and waiting if only I said the word. Take the chance *now* seemed to be the message. *Carpe diem.* You never know what the future is going to bring and these opportunities don't come up all that often. I listened.

'I don't want to do it,' I said. At that moment, still only days after the end of the Ostar, it swayed me less than zilch that I already had access to a boat, a sponsor and the undoubted support of everyone around me. A lot of sailors would have bent over backwards – on broken glass, while giving away their right arm – for that kind of backing. But I really had not enjoyed the Ostar and I'd never been keen to go solo sailing anyway, I just fell into it. At times I'd positively hated it. It had given me no pleasure that by starting without the right preparation I'd put myself in stressful, dangerous, frustrating situations hour after hour, day after day. I'd taken very little satisfaction even from winning. Of course it was a buzz, of course it was good to have proved to myself I could cope. But I wasn't about to fall into the trap of convincing myself it'd all been hunky dory once it was over. It had been horrible. It was still raw.

Even if I'd wanted to do the Vendée – and I didn't – I would have had insufficient time to prepare. Most sailors give themselves several years to get ready, physically and mentally, for a solo circumnavigation. They go into it prepared. At that point I would have gone to the Vendée still thinking that electronics was a branch of the dark arts. As for all the drawbacks of sailing solo, the mere suggestion of spending 120 days or more at sea on my own was too crazy to think about.

'No. Absolutely not. Not a chance. Now, who fancies a drink?'

Pete had a queue of takers who wanted *Aqua Quorum* for the Vendée and he leased it to a French guy, Patrice Carpentier, who sailed it as *VM Matériaux* and ending up winning his class (for 50-footers) by a distance. It was a fantastic result and he almost made it look easy although I knew that isn't how it was.

Another Frenchman, Michel Desjoyeaux, finished as the over-all winner by taking the 60-foot class, while Ellen MacArthur took second place behind him. It was an amazing race that catapulted her to international recognition. Her achievement was remarkable for her personally, for British sailing and for women's sailing.

After that Vendée finished – in February 2001 – I did, very briefly, wonder how I might have coped had I entered after all. It was an impossible question to answer. I quickly left such 'what might have beens' in their proper place – the past – and no further notion of sailing solo again crossed my mind during the rest of that year.

It wasn't until early 2002 that I allowed even the theoretical possibility of single-handed racing to worm its way into my head. I was in the Southern Ocean as part of a crew competing in the Volvo Ocean Race, as was my friend and former *Royal & SunAlliance* crew-mate, Miranda Merron. She was toying with the idea of submitting a provisional entry for the 2004 Vendée, which she subsequently did. We had a few general chats about the pros and cons of solo racing but even then I had no real intention of doing it again, let alone over a big distance.

My focus in the wake of the Ostar had switched back to other projects. Among other things I took part in the Round Britain race, the Oops Cup, the Archipelago Raid, a second Transat Jacques Vabre and umpteen non-racing engagements and assignments for Pindar. It was a valuable time when I expanded my experience and knowledge, on and off the water.

The Round Britain Race was in August 2000, not long after the Ostar, and I entered double-handed with Miranda. We wanted as much practice together as we could get, so she flew out to Rhode Island to meet me post-Ostar to deliver the boat back across the Atlantic together. I was knackered, but we didn't have a lot of time so left Newport all of eight days after I'd arrived.

Our intention was to try to set a record for the fastest Atlantic crossing by an all-female crew. There wasn't one at the time so if we'd wanted it, bar sinking, it would've been ours. But after a fast run for the vast majority of the trip, the wind died completely within a few hundred miles of Britain. We could have kept on sailing, inching with frustration towards home but knowing the record would be ours. The alternative was to motor the last stretch, abandon our attempt and tell the various monitoring officials that they could put away their stopwatches. We opted for the latter. We weren't too keen on setting a very slow record that would've looked more like a cruise than the mostly speedy run we'd had.

Back in the UK, Pindar had organized various homecoming receptions and lunches in Scarborough, where their headquarters are based. But the last part of our trip was so slow that we docked in the Scilly Isles instead of back in Southampton as intended, left the boat there and were flown in a small plane to Scarborough. It was a beautiful sunny day, the views were fantastic, and the flight gave us almost a couple of hours just to sit back and enjoy the ride.

We landed a few minutes before a charity lunch we were due to attend. We weren't told the identities of the guest speakers until we'd sat down. 'You should prepare something,' whispered Peter Wilkinson, Pindar's marketing director, giving us several minutes' notice. I briefly contemplated delivering an instructive talk about the benefits of being well prepared for challenges and how forward planning was essential. Unfortunately I'd not had enough time to prepare one. That made a change.

From Scarborough I went to France for a couple of days' break and then came back to start the Round Britain race. I was still exhausted and looking forward to sleeping for a week. Instead we set off, the weather turned nasty and there was little opportunity for a few solid hours' rest, let alone days.

I wished that just for once we'd have it easy but it wasn't to be. This was especially frustrating for Miranda, who'd already done two events with me that year – the AG2R and the transatlantic record attempt – neither of which had worked out. It was important that we put in a good performance, and she coped brilliantly with me being tired and both of us wishing for smoother conditions that rarely came along and never lasted.

The racing proved dramatic. Not long after the start, a 4,000-ton freighter off the coast of Dorset hit one of the smaller double-handed boats. The collision ripped out their mast and put a hole in their stern but thankfully there were no serious injuries. Traffic is one of the numerous hazards of coastal sailing and the Round Britain is almost wholly that for nearly 2,000 miles. *Aqua Quorum*, sailing under Pindar's name and colours, helped us to handle it. After some big storms, some brief calm, a bit of frustration and some good spinnaker sailing, we went on to win the double-handed class, setting a Round Britain record for an all-female crew in the process.

The winter of 2000 into 2001 was spent doing all the things that come as part and parcel of ocean racing when you're not actually at sea. I spent time doing corporate work with Pindar, meeting with accountants, fixing budgets and catching up with the various people involved in our campaigns. I started planning for summer 2001, which was going to be busy, and made the rounds of the various boat shows. I had meetings and lunches with assorted directors from different sections of the Pindar business, discussing marketing, branding and the countless details that underpin the corporate financing of my profession. As often as I could I went sailing. Surely that was the whole point, wasn't it? It was for me.

The first event of that summer was the Oops Cup, with the Oops standing for Open Ocean Performance Sixties. It was run by Atlant, a company in Stockholm that manages events and syndicates for ocean racing. It involved three 60-foot multi-hulls in eight races that took in four Scandinavian capitals with corporate sailing days in between. My two 'bosses' were Anna Drougge, a Swede with Volvo Ocean Race experience who was the skipper of the boat and fun to sail with, and Magnus Olsson, a veteran of several Whitbread races who came in as our racing skipper. Also on board was Miki Von Koskull, with whom I'd worked on *Royal & SunAlliance* and who had a wealth of knowledge. As a sailor you never stop learning, so the Oops Cup was a good chance to work with some seasoned pros. It was also a lot of fun.

Henrik, a fireman by trade and a giant of a bloke, was another member of the crew. He was the powerhouse on the boat, grinding in the sails during all the manoeuvres. He worked himself so hard that at times he seemed in danger of rupturing blood vessels, if not actually exploding. We also had two senior crew-mates, old friends of Magnus, old in more ways than one. They were as welcoming and committed as they were entertaining. Yuppe, our navigator, was colour-blind and the focal point of much good-natured banter. Hasse, who was blind in one eye, trimmed the mainsheet and was always exhorting, 'More power!' or 'I want to see blood!' They evidently enjoyed racing with Magnus, as we all did, and I moved to my next assignment with a renewed sense of sailing as a pleasure which can be relished by all.

The Archipelago Raid was next. Like the Oops, it was organized by Atlant, but it was staged solely in the Stockholm archipelago, a beautiful part of the world comprising 24,000 islands, islets and skerries. It's a crazy race, double-handed in 18-foot catamarans, where the basic idea is to hurtle virtually non-stop around the archipelago for four days via twenty checkpoints. The only snag is that the checkpoints are located in some weird and wonderful places – on beaches, in boats, on pontoons, in lighthouses, next to buoys. You're only told where they are four or five at a time, when you stop at one of the race headquarters. You have a maximum of an hour for each stop at HQ in between groups of checkpoints to plot your next course, eat, make repairs, empty the hulls of leaked water and do anything else required to keep going. The emphasis is on expert navigation, quick sailing and the ability to cope with as little sleep as possible – ideally none – for four days.

I raced with Ronan Cointo, a Breton who'd done most of his sailing on the French Figaro-Beneteau circuit. We weren't particularly well prepared and didn't know the boats too well but we came fourth of seven and had a lot of fun in the process. It's certainly a race I'd like to try again. Sweden is a great host country and the archipelago is a stunning place to sail. Being out on the water as the summer clouds filter the sunset into a hundred shades of trickling orange and yellow is quite breathtaking.

In November I entered my second Transat Jacques Vabre, which in 2001 ran from Le Havre in France to Bahia de Salvador in Brazil. I sailed with Miki Von Koskull in one of the three 60-foot multi-hulls that had been involved in the Oops Cup, although it wasn't the one we'd been on then. This one was more than a decade old and had an illustrious history. In 1990, as *Pierre 1er*, she had been sailed to victory by the French yachtswoman Florence Arthaud in the Route du Rhum. The American adventurer Steve Fossett subsequently bought her and sailed her as *Lakota*, breaking a number of speed records.

Unfortunately, against a fleet of new ORMA 60s in the TJV she really wasn't up to speed but it was still a good opportunity for us and we managed some decent sailing. We completed the race ninth of fourteen, albeit with the boat not in the best of shape. I was pretty content to hand her back at the end. We'd had a good enough time but a racing machine she was not.

Competing in the TJV meant I'd initially had to decline an offer to crew aboard *Amer Sports Too* in the 2001–2 Volvo Ocean Race. The race started in September and the TJV was a priority. But as things transpired, *Amer Sports Too* had a crew change after the first three legs and both Miranda Merron and I were asked to take part from there onwards. Miranda had also just done the TJV so we both headed to Auckland to catch our boat. My plan was to sail just one leg, maybe two, because Tracy Edwards had a new project in the pipeline with a maxi-catamaran, *Maiden II*. I'd told her I'd be there as soon as she got the campaign off the ground and the Volvo was an opportunity not to miss in the meantime.

Grant Dalton, one of New Zealand's most successful yachts-men, was in overall charge of *Amer Sports Too* although we had an all-female crew skippered by Lisa McDonald, an American. I ended up sailing the fourth leg, from Auckland to Rio de Janeiro, which left at the end of January, and the fifth, from Rio to Miami, which finished in March.

We had some fantastic sailing. Compared to the short-handed events I'd been doing it was great to be able to push a boat to its absolute limits. I spent quite a bit of time at the helm and I loved being back in the Southern Ocean with so many people. Even some hairy days with icebergs didn't detract from that. At one stage we were dodging potentially lethal little 'growler' bergs at night, during storms, as we picked our way through expansive fields of the really massive guys. (Growlers are small icebergs that break away from big ones.)

It was while we were down in the Southern Ocean that Miranda and I got talking about single-handed races. Miranda was looking for money and sponsors to enter the 2004 Vendée Globe. As I recall, we were trying to build a theoretical case about why it might be good to do a solo circumnavigation. I think most of our conclusions were based around it offering a totally different kind of racing. The emphasis, we decided, was not purely on squeezing every last knot of speed out of a boat but more on strategy, mental strength and the application of a whole variety of skills.

We reckoned you'd make your decisions very differently from a fully crewed yacht, for a start. Safety would go up the agenda and speed slightly down it. You'd have no one else on board to rely on in sticky situations. We also wondered whether you'd be inclined to push slightly less hard not only for safety's sake *per se* but because you'd always want to keep a small physical reserve within yourself in case of a 'major situation'.

And then, I think, we concluded that that was all very well, but what was the point of doing it if you were going to ease off the throttle too much? We happily batted such questions back and forth, with the rest of the crew not even remotely seeing the attraction of solo racing. Miranda had an eye on the Vendée thirty months thence. I didn't have a serious thought in my head about that race or the Around Alone.

As my Volvo sojourn came to its end in Miami, my preoccupation was with *Maiden II* and how I'd managed to upset both my current skipper, Lisa, and my next one, Tracy. I wasn't in Lisa's good books because she was hoping that I'd be able to stay on until the end of the race. I'd done two long legs of more than 11,000 miles altogether but the race still had four more legs totalling about 5,000 miles to go.

I wasn't in Tracy's best books either because I left *Amer Sports Too* so late that I only had a long weekend between arriving in Miami and needing to be in La Ciotat in the south of France to depart on *Maiden II*. We were heading first to Spain and then off on various record attempts, the first being across the Atlantic to the Caribbean. I made it by the skin of my teeth but I was pretty shattered.

The record attempt, from Cadiz to San Salvador, was going to follow the Route of Discovery, so called after the course on which Christopher Columbus set off to discover the New World in 1492. The target record was 10 days, 14 hours and 53 minutes, set by Grant Dalton aboard *Club Med*, which Tracy subsequently bought and renamed *Maiden II*. She was a sleek 110-foot maxi-cat and evidently capable of doing the speed. But as Tracy said before we embarked, 'This is a difficult record, as you have to have near perfect wind conditions. We're taking the view that the crossing is for training, but if we get the wind conditions we need then we'll go for it.'

We went for it. There was an experienced mixed crew of sixteen, including six of us who'd sailed on *Royal & SunAlliance*. Aside from me there was Adrienne Cahalan, Helena Darvelid, Miki, Sam Davies and Sharon Ferris. Tracy was otherwise engaged and Brian Thompson filled in as skipper.

The attempt, which saw us cross the start line in the second week of April, turned out to be a good time to catch up on some sleep. We had a watch system that gave us each four hours on duty, four off and four on standby (most of which was off) in every twelve-hour period. Every day thus meant eight hours on watch, in two intense stints of four. But then there were eight hours off (mostly spent sleeping) and eight hours in which to cook, eat or read one of the two books on board, knowing it might be 'all hands on deck' at any moment.

When the boat was set up and sailing well, three people could handle it. Having four or five on each watch was plenty and having the same again on standby was also adequate for sail changes and manoeuvres. The record was within our grasp until the final stage of the crossing. The trade winds died as we neared the Bahamas with less than a couple of hundred miles to go. It happens, and it's frustrating, but there's nothing you can do about it, so we called it a day not far from the finish. We changed course and headed for Antigua, our next destination.

We were there for Antigua Week, a kind of Cowes Week of the Caribbean, and for the following week too. We did some corporate sailing with guests. We swam. We trained. And, purely on the principle of 'When in Rome, do as the Romans do', we also had our fair share of rum.

It was during the time in Antigua that Andrew Pindar came out to visit, have a sail on *Maiden II* and hold a catch-up meeting about future projects. He'd also brought along a friend, Robin Gray. Their fathers had known each other for a long time and they'd been mates since they were kids. As soon as Andrew arrived in Antigua he rushed to the boat to see me. Robin wasn't with him.

Andrew suggested that it might be a good time to hire a dedicated Pindar sailing manager, someone whose job it would be to help me facilitate projects. Until then I'd been my own project manager, coming up with ideas, taking them to Andrew, getting the go-ahead and then being in charge. By April 2002 I'd gained all kinds of experience, under Pindar's wing and elsewhere, as in the Volvo and with Tracy on *Maiden II*. But it really was time to start getting my teeth back into another big project of my own, something that would take me up to a new level. Andrew floated the idea that Robin could be the man to become Pindar's racing manager.

'Sounds like a plan to me,' I said. And with that Andrew took a small box from his pocket and showed me Robin's new business cards, printed and ready to use. Such are the advantages of being in the printing business, I guess!

One evening while they were there, we all sat down over a

rum 'n' coke or three to start discussing our racing options. The first race mentioned was the Route du Rhum, which seemed only appropriate as we were knocking back the stuff at the time. That year's edition of the race, running from St Malo to Pointe-à-Pitre, was due to start in November, just over six months from then.

I knew I didn't enjoy racing solo but at least I'd be better prepared than in the Ostar and would have more than two years' greater experience under my belt by the time I got to the start. My certainty about not sailing single-handed again had also started to thaw slightly, probably helped by my debates with Miranda. It was feasible. It was only across the Atlantic.

'Right then, what are the practicalities?' I said.

The evening wore on and we talked about how we might go about chartering the right boat and how much that charter would cost. And I'd need a few months' training in it. And what about sails?

We'd need a new suite of sails, which might cost tens of thousands. Insurance for the duration might be as much again. Throw in all the other expenses, including a shore crew and logistical support and technical help, and we'd be looking at a lot more than we'd ever spent on anything previously. That's how it would have to be if we wanted to enter with a fighting chance of winning. And why would we want to do anything else?

It was a warm evening and I got up to visit the bar and have a stroll on the balcony to take in some air. Within a few hours we'd pretty much knocked down most of the hurdles that I'd thought would prevent me sailing solo again. Maybe it wasn't such a total no-no. I went back to the table not knowing the conversation was about to take another mighty tack.

'So,' said Andrew. 'The Route du Rhum is feasible. Emma, you're happy we explore it further?'

I nodded.

'The only drawback I see is that for the money we might spend we could get *more* value out of something else.'

I nodded. Robin nodded.

'You know,' said Andrew, 'there *are* races that might not cost all that much more, certainly not pro rata, but would give us all a better chance to get more from it.'

We all nodded. Heady stuff, rum. Before I knew it we were talking about the possibility of doing the Around Alone, the longest solo race in any sport in the world at 29,000 miles.

'It *is* broken into five legs,' someone said.

Five legs. That's what I was thinking. Perhaps it wouldn't be a long, daunting, lonely, impossible race at all. It might just be five long, daunting, lonely, almost plausible *legs* of an impossible race instead. It all added up to the same total, of course. But for me to have any chance whatsoever of contemplating the Around Alone, I needed to be thinking in the latter fashion. That's what I did.

And so we started going through how the logistics and costs of an eight-month round-the-world race compared to those of a two-week Route du Rhum. There were big differences, undoubtedly, but not as big as you'd expect. Charter fees, insurance and sails would all cost more, but equated to proportionately much less per month over the duration of a campaign, that might exponentially increase publicity opportunities for Pindar. The boat might cost around twice as much but that would be for a hire that would last up to ten times longer. Insurance would similarly be more economical over time, as would sails.

The major extra costs would be in funding a shore crew to attend the start and finish in Rhode Island and the four interim stopovers in England, South Africa, New Zealand and Brazil.

It would be no small venture and everyone would need wages, travel costs, accommodation and expenses. Still, judged on a monthly cost, it seemed the Around Alone might make more sense than the Route du Rhum.

The marketing potential for Pindar was obvious. It would be a huge race compared to anything we'd done before. As a British-based company that had expanded to America and within Europe, its name would be taken around the world. I'd also be getting the chance to see new places, like Cape Town, which I'd never visited before.

The 'pros' kept on stacking up. The only major 'con' was the fact that I was no enthusiast of sailing alone. That went into the mix with all the other factors, including the benefits I'd reap from spending a lot of time with one boat instead of having it for a short period and handing it back. Andrew and Robin would spend a day or two weighing it all up. When I went to bed that night my head was swimming. And it wasn't just the rum.

By the time they headed back to England, we'd made a resolution. It was a provisional 'yes' to the Around Alone. It had been a practical decision. It had not come from a burning desire to sail around the world alone. It had ultimately been 'Why not?' as opposed to 'Why?'. Life's biggest decisions aren't always illuminated by fireworks.

With those pivotal few days out of the way, I turned my attention back to *Maiden II*'s next speed record attempt, between Antigua and Newport. Brian Thompson was again our skipper for it and we pushed the boat to her absolute limits. We claimed the record in an incredible time of 94 hours and 31 minutes, hitting 40 knots – the fastest the boat had ever gone – just before we crossed the line. It was a great feeling and a great achievement for a deserving team who had plenty more adventures ahead of them. I had other business to attend to. I said my goodbyes and headed home.

Back in England at the end of May, our provisional 'yes' to the Around Alone began to look more provisional by the day. We did some sailing on the boat that we had in mind to charter. She was an Open 60 belonging to a British sailor, Josh Hall, who'd sailed her as *Gartmore* in the previous Around Alone in 1998–9. Josh was forced to retire from that race after losing the top of his mast but he did complete the 2000–1 Vendée, finishing ninth. The sailing we did in late May 2002 didn't give me much confidence.

The boat still needed a lot of work. She'd been dismasted for a third time not long before. She hadn't been sailed for a few months and my gut reaction was that she had basically run out of luck. Sailors thrive on a belief in luck and I didn't feel lucky about this. Andrew and Robin were content to agree. They'd been having their own doubts. It was going to be an expensive project – six big figures, they reckoned – and there was no guarantee of a return.

'Yes' turned to 'maybe not'. We each had our own reasons for the indecision. Andrew was worried about the responsibility. If something happened to me out there, regardless of how willingly I'd gone, it had the potential to look awful for Pindar. Who, after all, would want their company's name associated with the death of a twenty-seven-year-old woman who'd met her end sailing a boat with their name plastered all over the side and the sails?

As for me, I had doubts about the boat, doubts about the lack of time and doubts about solo sailing at all, which persisted.

Some days I'd wake up thinking: 'Solo around the world – are you crazy, Emma?' Sense prevailed. 'Maybe not' swung towards 'No'. Until mid-June, that is.

It took one good week's sailing for the subject to revive itself. Admittedly it was a very good week's sailing. It was down in the Solent and we had company guests on board. They loved it and the enthusiasm was infectious. The weather was perfect. The boat was fine. My mood, maybe buoyed by having had the prospect of the Around Alone lifted off my shoulders, was upbeat.

'Why *don't* you do this race then?' someone asked, addressing Andrew and me and the rest of Team Pindar collectively.

'Why don't we?' said Andrew.

'Why don't we?' I echoed.

I don't honestly know whether Andrew or I at that moment meant '*Why* don't we?' or 'Why *don't* we?', or whether it was just a plain 'Why don't we . . .' that tailed off unanswered.

Nothing had changed from a few weeks earlier and the 'Almost no'. Question marks still hung over the boat, the funding, the dangers, the time constraints and my enthusiasm. It *was* a beautiful day, though.

Ludicrously, implausibly, we agreed there and then that 'Yeah, maybe we can do it after all.'

We were about to embark on a process where there would be no time to think, let alone change our minds again.

'Are you sure, Emma?' said Andrew.

The sun was out. The water looked lovely. What the heck.

'Yes.'

The next day I booked a flight to Scotland. I had something to tell Mum and Dad.

•

I went into denial within hours of agreeing to do the race and even my visit to my parents made little difference. I'd hoped that by telling them about the Around Alone I'd go some way to convincing myself it was the right thing to do. Mum and Dad couldn't have been more supportive but as I flew back south I was still full of doubt. Around the world alone? When my only previous solo race, just two weeks long, had been hellish enough as it was? What on earth was I doing?

Mentally I tried to switch to autopilot but even that was playing up.

'The decision has been made and it's not going to change now,' my autopilot was telling me. 'It's just another project and here's the list of things we need to do.'

'Too much!' I protested to myself.

'Shut up and get on with it,' said autopilot. 'We've got six whole weeks.'

'It's not enough!' I protested. 'I'll never be ready.'

'You *have* to be,' said autopilot. 'You've got six weeks before the qualifier across the Atlantic and then a whole week afterwards to iron out any problems before you turn around and start the race. You'll only have 29,000 miles to go by then.'

'29,000 miles! Fricking heck, what AM I doing?' I thought.

'Oh, do stop moaning,' said autopilot. 'Don't think of it as a round-the-world race. It's just five separate back-to-back parts of one.'

'But what about the solitude?' I thought. 'I hated it last time.'

'You'll have me for company,' said autopilot.

'Precisely!' I thought. 'I'm talking to myself already and I'm not even at sea yet.'

Autopilot overruled me at that stage and I got on with my preparations.

I knew that I would probably be able to handle whatever the race threw up in terms of pure sailing challenges. Bad weather and nasty conditions are part of my profession and while they're sometimes unnerving they've never been a disincentive. Coping with the physical demands of solo racing, especially during sail changes, was certainly going to be tough, but then my approach would be to get through one task at a time and see how I got on.

Even the thought of having to be simultaneously my own engineer, electrician, strategist, computer geek, sail repairer, communications expert, cook, rigger, security guard and doctor was not in itself as daunting as it once had been. But when all those things were combined and then solitude, the defining ingredient of the race, was added, I hit a mental brick wall. Logically I knew I could do the race, and even fight for a place on the podium. Emotionally I was intimidated.

'LATE!' was the primary thought in my head during the weeks between the final 'Yes' and having to leave on my qualifier. I'd lost time through indecision. I'd been the last person to enter the race by a margin of some months. I felt like I was playing catch-up even before I got to the start line, let alone over it. And I was increasingly nervous that we would run out of time and I'd end up departing as a total mess.

Matters weren't helped by the fact that when the 'Yes' decision was finally made, I was in the middle of a one-month deal with a TV production company. I was assisting on an episode of the Channel 4 programme, *Faking It*. I'd been asked to be a 'mentor' on the programme. It wasn't paid work but had the potential to be a good laugh and it was sold as a good PR opportunity for Pindar.

The basic premise of *Faking It* is that a subject is transplanted into a totally alien profession (e.g. a vicar becomes a second-hand car salesman) to see whether they can 'fake it' in their new role. At the end of a month in their assumed lifestyle the subject is tested to see whether they can fool a panel of expert judges. I'd been asked to mentor Lucy, a twenty-eight-year-old stewardess who worked on cross-Channel freight ferries. She'd had no yachting experience but her objective was to fake it as an experienced skipper of a 72-foot racing yacht. Tracy Edwards and Chay Blyth were her other mentors.

When the producers initially asked me to be involved they said it would only require a couple of days per week for filming. Lucy came to live with me for the month and I spent every spare moment teaching her the basics of sailing, tutoring her on dinghies and helping her get to grips with sailing terminology. When the production team wanted us up at 5.30 a.m. to be ready to do 'wake-up' scenes an hour later, we were up. When they wanted to film late at night – to finish cutaways they hadn't done earlier, for example – we stayed up. It was all going fine.

But when the decision about the Around Alone was finalized, I had to travel to America for three days at short notice. I left late on a Monday and was back at dawn on the Friday, ready for filming. In between I'd been across the Atlantic and back, had meetings with the race organizers in Rhode Island and New York, checked out facilities at various locations and confirmed all the details of what I'd need to do before the race started.

Although I'd okayed the trip with the *Faking It* production team before I left, they were frosty when I got back. They then told Lucy to make it known via her video diary that she was convinced that if she failed her test it would be my fault for leaving her to her own devices! Conflict makes better television, I'm sure, but this was manufactured nonsense. I completed the month despite suspecting the producers would stitch me up and make me look uncommitted when the programme went out. They did. The narration painted my trip to America as a nuisance to Lucy without explaining that I was going to be leaving in a few weeks to sail solo round the world. Sad but true.

Thankfully, from Lucy's point of view, she did really well in her test. She skippered a crew to victory in a five-yacht regatta even though she didn't dupe all the judges. But by the end of the filming I felt that the production team had duped me. I was more stressed than ever and time was really running out.

We ended up chartering Josh Hall's boat despite our reservations. Quite frankly, we had no time to be picky. All the newer Open 60 options had already been snapped up either by other Around Alone participants or sailors entering that year's Route du Rhum. I wasn't at all confident that Josh's boat was right for me. In fact I was sure she would be too powerful for me to handle to her maximum capabilities. But it was the only option available.

The costs began to mount. The charter alone cost the equivalent of a terraced house in Hamble. The entry fee and the deposit on the mandatory ARGOS safety beacon cost the equivalent of having that house decorated, top to bottom. Insurance for the boat cost the same as a couple of executive cars, and I mean top of the range. A suite of sails cost the price of a 35-foot leisure yacht. And then there'd be all the costs of the shore crew, plus the cost of shipping a container of spares around the world, plus the cost of any repairs.

In an ideal world, I should have felt in control of every last detail of my race campaign. As it was, I didn't even really feel in control of the vessel that I'd be sailing in. We'd never hired a boat before that came with her owner and shore crew as part of the auxiliary package, as Josh's did. Previous owners had always been at the end of a phone if we'd needed them but they'd generally left us to it and I'd done things my own way.

For the Around Alone, there was no real option of that happening. There wasn't time to arrange my own team so that left us with Josh and his team instead. On the one hand that should've been a huge advantage. Josh knew his boat inside out and he's a great guy and fun to have a beer with. But when he was on board during my limited build-up time (and later, during stopovers) I found it tough to explain that the way I wanted things done was not necessarily the way he'd done them during the Vendée Globe. I wasn't assertive enough in telling him to back off and let me take control. I wasn't familiar enough with the boat to be especially assertive anyway. It was easier just to let Josh get on with it and then try to make it feel more like my boat each time I set off.

I wasn't really assertive enough because I guess I didn't really want to offend Josh. He has done so much solo racing and has been doing it for so many years that he can race solo in his sleep. I just raced differently. I had to aboard *Pindar*, Josh's boat, because I didn't have half his physical strength, which was the amount that the boat ideally needed to sail to her full potential.

It didn't help matters that there seemed to be friction between Josh and me. Whether he actually thought so or not, I felt he believed my sponsorship had fallen into my lap and I didn't work for it. He always seemed to have issues with not having quite enough money for his next race and I was never sure what he was thinking.

I felt I was constantly being pulled in opposite directions. There were things that needed doing to give me the optimum chance of success, like sorting out the boat and practising in her, which I had too little time for. And then there were requests

I knew I should be granting – from TV and radio, newspapers, magazines, PR people, sponsors, people holding meals in my honour, sailing clubs, schools, sea rangers, you name it – but I felt swamped. I did everything I could but felt persistently guilty that it still wasn't enough. It was stupid, really. There were so many people who wanted to help by giving me publicity or dinner or advice or a morale boost and yet it felt like I was being crushed. I'm a sailor. I just wanted to sail.

By the time it came to leave for my qualifying voyage, at the start of August, I was just desperate to get on with it. It was almost a means of escaping all the hassles. It seems ridiculous now, but I actually felt that heading off on my own, something I knew I didn't enjoy, had become preferable to staying put!

The last public engagement I had to attend before I left was the opening ceremony of Cowes Week 2002, on Saturday, 3 August. The organizers of this prestigious annual regatta began it with an early start gun in my honour! The plan was to cross the line and then sail to Brixham in Devon, with my shore crew on board, with the object of having one last pre-qualifier practice day with help at hand if I needed it. I'd then leave Brixham on the Sunday morning on my non-stop qualifier to America.

The departure from Cowes buoyed my spirits. It was amazing to take the start gun on such an occasion, and as we headed out of the Solent we had a rendezvous with *Maiden II*. She made *Pindar* look tiny as we sailed past The Needles. But almost as soon as I'd pointed her west towards Brixham, the wind died. We'd have gone nowhere fast if we'd tried to sail. Instead, we had to enlist the help of *Pindar*'s support boat, the *Hatherleigh*, a converted trawler that my sponsors use as a base – and bunkhouse and entertaining venue and floating pub – wherever we happen to be. Due to a lack of breeze, the *Hatherleigh* ended up towing us all the way to Brixham. My final day's practice had disappeared.

We arrived in Brixham late on the Saturday and I slept aboard the *Hatherleigh*. I awoke early the next morning, departure day, and the autopilots on *Pindar* still weren't working properly. It was a major concern. You need to be able to steer the boat even when you're busy doing other things. The guys tried to fix them. They still weren't right after lunch but I just had to go. I went.

The rules of the Around Alone dictate that competitors need to complete a 2,000-mile ocean passage prior to the start. This has to include some celestial navigation using the sun, moon, stars or planets with a sextant, tables and a clock. It's good old-fashioned navigating, which, despite being a chore if you're up to your neck in other problems, can also be quite satisfying.

My intended route from Brixham to Newport was 1,000 miles longer than the qualifier needed to be but seemed the best option because I had to get *Pindar* to Newport anyway. I was banking on a smooth trip of a little over two weeks, maybe as long as three, during which I'd get a chance to build a relationship with *Pindar* and learn how everything functioned. So much for best-laid plans. I ended up being at sea for four weeks, sailing almost 5,000 miles and stopping in Bermuda *en route*.

After feeling so stressed in the build-up, the first few hours were a massive relief. I'd had quite enough pre-race chat, unsolicited 'help' and general faffing around. I was just looking forward to being at sea without having to smile for any cameras or answer any questions. I actually had a first chance to sail the boat single-handed and prove to myself I could cope, physically as well as mentally.

The relief didn't last long as it started to dawn on me just how unready I was. I felt vulnerable due to things not working properly and I felt angry because it seemed things shouldn't have had to be like that. I was frustrated and distracted because I was worried about the autopilots. The boat might suddenly tack itself while I was in an awkward place, like on the fore deck trying to pull a sail down, or up the mast trying to fix something. Momentarily I thought about turning round and going back to Brixham. I didn't because I knew that when I got there everyone would already have gone. What would be the point of going back to Brixham knowing that the expert electronics knowledge wouldn't be there? I never actually considered pulling out. That would only have been an option if I'd been literally sinking. But daily I asked myself why I was doing this when it was proving so tough.

I pressed on, annoyed, mostly at myself. I had 3,000 miles ahead of me (I thought then) and I wasn't going to be able to get any more spares or stop again until I'd done them. I don't think I've ever felt so unprepared in my life and it was ultimately my fault. I should have been more forceful earlier about imposing a preparation structure that worked for me. I shouldn't have allowed other things to encroach on my time. I should've said no to a lot more people. But I hadn't and that was that. It was just me and *Pindar* now, and we had to get on with it.

One day into the qualifier, on 5 August, I heard that one of my fellow Around Alone competitors, Graham Dalton (brother of Grant), had suffered a dismasting during his own qualifier. Ultimately it didn't stop him taking part in the race but then, in early August, it was yet another reminder of how fragile such campaigns can be, even if they're well funded and have time on their side. I vowed to myself that getting to Newport in one piece was my sole aim. *Pindar* had already been dismasted three times during her life as *Gartmore* and I didn't want a fourth dismasting, one that might end my race before it started.

By 6 August, two days in, I was already missing the immediacy of contact with other people. On one occasion my phone rang and I couldn't get to it in time. And then there was no message! If I ever miss a telephone call on land and I have no way of telling who it is, I always ask the next person who rings whether they tried earlier. I think that's normal enough. But I was so gutted on that occasion that I actually made an entry in my diary to record the fact that someone had been trying to reach me but I'd missed it. At sea receiving a call can be the highlight of a day, a chance to talk to someone. That missed call was a missed opportunity for solace.

On 7 August I had to go up the mast, which is always potentially dangerous when you're on your own. It can also be arduous, even though I run and visit the gym as often as my schedule will allow in order to do daily cardiovascular training and keep sensibly fit. Even in good conditions with the boat stable there's a danger of a freak accident affecting either you or the boat while you're up there. If that happens, with no one else on hand to help, you're in trouble. On this occasion I had to go up to make a check on the masthead halyard block. (A halyard is a rope used to hoist a sail up the mast and hold it there. Blocks are pulleys through which halyards feed. The masthead halyard block is the halyard block at the head, or top, of the mast.)

The halyard system on *Pindar* was a two-to-one halyard, so the main halyard started at the masthead, ran all the way down to the deck, through a pulley, back up to the top of the mast, through the masthead block and then down again to a winch. This 'doubled halyard' allowed me to raise the sails more easily although it did take longer due to having to handle twice as much rope.

The reason I had to check the masthead block was that I'd

made a miscalculation when raising the spinnaker, which is the biggest of the headsails. (There are a variety of headsails for different conditions and they're utilized one or two at a time in conjunction with the mainsail.) I'd raised the spinnaker too high, accidentally forcing its halyard block to mesh with the masthead halyard block, damaging both blocks in the process. I brought the sail down before the chewed blocks could chafe through the halyard and sever it. But I couldn't be sure it wasn't *almost* chafed at the masthead block, and the only way I could find out was by going up and looking.

I had only two ways of getting to the top of the mast. One was via the masthead halyard, the other was up the main halyard. The latter option would have meant taking down the mainsail and sailing with just a small jib (a type of headsail), which would in turn have meant a more unstable boat motion and therefore a more difficult climb. The other option was to bite the bullet and climb using the masthead halyard, which was potentially chafed. I bit the bullet. Thankfully the halyard was in good shape and conditions were clement and I managed to replace the blocks without too much trouble.

There were a couple of lighter moments during the qualifier. One was on the first Saturday at sea, 10 August, when I called Miranda Merron for a chat. She was in the pub in Hamble, where I would've been if I hadn't been in the Atlantic. We discussed how I was getting on and I told her to have a drink for me.

'At the rate you're going,' she said, 'I think there might be time for more than one, don't you?'

Another heartening moment came when my progress had been slowed to a virtual standstill by lack of winds in the second week. It was a bright, sunny day and I was down in the cabin when I heard a tap-tapping sound against the hull. I ran up on deck and made it just in time to see a turtle floating towards the back of the boat. *Pindar* had obviously nudged its shell, sending it spinning along the length of the hull. I smiled at the cartoon-ish sight of this beautiful creature, spinning round and round, unharmed and apparently unfazed as it floated away.

By then *Pindar* and I hadn't been so much going round in circles as in a giant loop down into the Atlantic and then back up again. I'd made a decision at the start to sail downwind, with the wind, rather than upwind, against it. The downwind route was always going to be longer than if I'd gone straight across 'the top' of the Atlantic. But I took the longer route for a specific reason. The first leg of the race was going to be downwind and I wanted practice using the bigger, lighter downwind sails that I'd had no previous experience of using on an Open 60 on my own.

The risk in taking the downwind route was that I might end up in light winds for the second half of the trip. That's exactly what happened. First the Azores' windless high-pressure system expanded and spread south, following my direction. Wanting to get the most from each day's sailing, I tried to dodge it by heading even further south. Later, when I needed to head back north, I got stuck in light airs anyway.

My battle with the weather should have been an invaluable learning experience in terms of tracking the systems, trying to interpret their movement and making my tactical decisions based on my conclusions. It proved not to be because I lost the use of my Sat B system (which allows full access to a range of weather information) in the first week. It crashed and didn't recover for the duration of the qualifier. I was thus denied a chance to practise making all those decisions that are vital in race con-ditions, when you're not allowed outside assistance. Instead I had to rely on just such assistance, which was permitted during the qualifier. It came from a guy called Lee Bruce, a weather data expert based in Wolfeboro, New Hampshire. Using constantly updated information about systems, winds, currents, temperatures, waves and anything else that might affect the boat – compiled from multiple sources, including *Pindar*'s instruments – Lee was able to advise me on the best way to go. I asked him to keep me in as much wind as possible and he did. But by doing so, I ended up sailing around 5,000 miles instead of 3,000. By the time I started heading back north, on 17 August, I was getting caught in the Bermuda high-pressure system. I outlined my concerns in an email.

> *17 Aug 02*   3014.55N 06200.00W   Only 800 miles to Newport, still a few days and awkward systems to encounter but I'm still up for the challenge. I have had to resist the huge temptation of finishing my qualifier in Bermuda, and picking up my shore crew to sail the last bit in company (and ask my million questions about the boat!!)! By doing that I would certainly eliminate the chance I have of arriving in Newport by 1st of September after which I will have time penalties to take into leg 1 of the race. After another night of thunder squalls, hopefully today is a good time to catch up on some sleep and prepare myself for the last day of shipping and coastal hazards!

It was crucial that I made it to Newport by 1 September because that was the cut-off time for competitors to arrive. If I arrived afterwards, the race organizers would hand me a time penalty for the first leg of the race, something I was desperate to avoid. The race would be tough as it was. But I was also conscious that the last 800 miles might be tricky and time-consuming. From my Ostar experience in 2000 I was expecting problems until the moment I reached the dock. As I envisioned in the email, these might have included:

> . . . fishing buoys, fog in the shipping lanes, bleeding the diesel engine (generator) as the fuel runs out, therefore sweating about the pilot dying as the battery runs too low, and turning off the radar that is using too much power that you may need for the next half hour of fixing the generator problem, and stressing that the fog horns you can hear are only 2 boat lengths away. Then to finish off, when you think you have survived the worst of it, the breeze that has guaranteed you will be in before the pub shuts, dies (or in this case, probably minutes after the time penalty is set!) But at least I am expecting it this time, and I promise I will try to accept it in good humour! See you all soon, Emx

It was while I was in that anticipatory state of mind, heading towards Bermuda, that I encountered a lot of thunderclouds and more Doldrums-like weather. Again, I wasn't going anywhere fast and I was at risk of not making it to Rhode Island. I'd already done far in excess of the 2,000 miles I needed for the qualifier. I reckoned my best course was keep my stress levels down by ending it in Bermuda. I did. With the restrictions of being solo no longer in force, I filled up with diesel, picked up some of the shore crew and then sailed and motored to Newport. In the end, I made it with five hours to spare before the cut-off time for competitors to be in port ahead of the Around Alone.

It was a relief knowing I'd be able to start the race without having any penalty time to take into the first leg. But it was also daunting to acknowledge quite how much had gone wrong even on the qualifier. Luckily, none of the problems had proved dangerous. For the time being.

3

The countdown clock started ticking the moment I stepped ashore in Newport. We had ten days in which to fix all the problems on the boat, go up to Wolfeboro and do some intensive study about weather, finalize my preparations for the prologue, and make sure I had everything set for the first leg of the race.

My overriding concern was making *Pindar* a fit place to live, work and above all be competitive in during the coming months. As well as trying to make the boat as strong and safe as possible, I needed all the basics right to provide a platform on which I could hopefully prosper.

In any average twenty-four-hour period at sea I expected to sleep for four or five accumulated hours, broken into naps of between twenty and sixty minutes. These would mostly be taken on the long angled seat at the chart table in the cabin. Less frequently, during storms when there was a danger of being thrown around, I'd climb into one of the bunks. There were two, one on each side of the cabin. I'd pick whichever one was on the windward, high side.

Given good conditions and no urgent distractions, I'd try to have three meals a day plus two snacks. Typically I reckoned on having some cereal as soon as the sun came up, a muesli bar mid morning, half a pan of hot pasta at lunchtime, half a pan of cold leftover pasta for dinner and maybe a power bar during the night. Variety would come in the form of noodles or couscous for lunch and dinner. If I had advance warning that conditions would become too atrocious to cook, then I'd prepare a big pot of pasta beforehand and snack on it for several meals. Most of the sauces I had on board were tomato- or pesto-based and tasted fine cold. I'm not a fussy eater anyway.

Food supplies would be replenished carefully on a leg-by-leg basis so that I wasn't carrying anything that wasn't absolutely necessary. The 'larder inventory' for the first leg comprised four large bags of five-minute pasta, eight meal-sized portions of flavoured couscous, eight packs of noodles, some sauces and tubes of pesto, two bags of muesli, freeze-dried milk, packet soup, tea bags, muesli bars and power bars. I also took some effervescent vitamin C tablets, which were as much for flavouring the water as taking on board vitamin C. Later I'd take a treat for each leg, including some of my mum's banana bread and some Jaffa cakes after the UK stopover, and dried fruit, nuts and a bag of biltong (dried meat) after the Cape Town stopover.

When you're racing, the basic tasks that make the boat go faster fill the days. You need to keep the sails at the correct angle and in the right shape to eke maximum efficiency out of them, which means constant adjustments for each slight change in the wind speed and direction. When the wind increases or decreases out of the range of the sails you're using, you need to change them.

You need to check weather updates via the internet regularly, adjusting your route depending on what the weather files show. You need to contact the race organizers and your shore crew with regular updates, and check how the rest of the fleet has fared in the previous eight-hour period. Their progress can back up what your weather files have been telling you. Sometimes, if another boat has individually slowed, that might be a sign it has sustained damage.

In bad weather, when the autopilots can't steer with sufficient accuracy, you need to steer by hand. In good weather, you undertake repairs, checks and routine maintenance. There is no such thing as leisure time, although brief phone calls to friends can provide entertainment, as can sending and receiving emails while downloading weather files. Hand-steering in good weather – when you know the pilot could be doing as good a job – is an occasional indulgence.

As for real luxuries, and for me that includes long, hot baths – no chance. Bathing during a race is rudimentary at best. Buckets of seawater or rainwater in warm weather are luxuries. Baby wipes, talc, deodorant and sunscreen were the extent of my toiletry supplies for the Around Alone. Cleaning my teeth was less an exercise in daily hygiene than a good way of waking up properly after taking a nap.

In Newport, making the boat as comfortable as possible, even within meagre boundaries, came second to getting *Pindar* into racing shape. At the end of my qualifier I presented the shore crew with a long list of jobs to do. At the top of the list was the need to do something about the winches that are used to help raise, lower and trim the sails. As they were, they weren't big enough and didn't offer me sufficient extra help to – my physical strength, set against the otherwise all-male competition, was comparatively limited. We fitted a new set of winches that would hopefully redress that imbalance. As it transpired, we didn't put the finishing touch to this task until the first stopover, when a pedestal (a 'grinder' with two handles) was added to maximize the new winches' efficiency.

One thing that had needed immediate attention in Newport was the mast. We'd found a small hole in it so we needed to take it out of the boat, fix it and then replace it. The autopilots also needed fine-tuning, the electronics needed some tinkering and there were all manner of tests and checks to be done. As usual, I didn't feel we'd be prepared in time, and this was compounded by seeing that several of my competitors were ready and waiting to go a week before the prologue began. My shore crew were working at full space to try to make sure everything was done.

There were others who seemed as unprepared as I was, and some were so under-funded that they were having a hard time getting their entries ratified even at that late stage. Some of the skippers, for example, were having trouble affording the additional safety equipment that was required by the rules and one skipper looked like he might not be able to afford any insurance. Everyone got there in the end, however, by whatever means necessary. One of my competitors, Tim Kent, took what I thought was the most novel approach. He borrowed $50,000 from his ex-wife!

After leaving my list with the shore crew, I went up to Wolfeboro in New Hampshire, about 150 miles north of New-port, and spent three days learning more about weather from Lee Bruce. He'd taught me the basics on a previous occasion and so this time we focused on how I could speed up the process of finding and interpreting information. This involved learning which information sources were most accurate, which sites provided what details, and so on.

Those few days away gave me a welcome break from the

intensity of the build-up. I spent six hours each day studying and the rest of the time trying to relax and catch up on sleep. I had naps on the sofa in Lee's office after lunch while Lee and his wife Sherry continued working. When I woke up I'd get back to my studies.

Chronic exhaustion was starting to kick in and I needed to keep it at bay before the first leg. For a couple of years I'd hardly stopped for a break between the end of one event and the start of preparations for the next. For the previous month I'd been at sea alone learning to sail a new boat. I was feeling pressures on land too. Wolfeboro felt like a sanctuary.

I returned to Newport to find that 'Team Pindar' had been hard at work in my absence. My participation in the Around Alone would not have been possible without a varied supporting cast. Andrew Pindar, the figurehead of the team, always found space in his hectic business schedule to be in attendance for at least a few days whenever I was on land. He was always a big help, making it his personal responsibility to host a party of some kind in each location, as had become a Pindar tradition over the previous three years. He supported everyone in our team and made sure we had access to everything we needed, and it wasn't unusual to find him helping other skippers as well. Certainly the Pindar parties were open-house affairs for my fellow racers and their crews.

Robin Gray had eased into his new role as shore manager, which must have been quite a leap for a guy who'd spent his career until then in farming. He was great at organizing all the logistics and making sure, for example, that our container of equipment and spares (not to mention our shore crew) were always in the right place at the right time. Robin is a great networker and whenever we needed something, he always seemed to know exactly where to get it at the right price.

The shore crew, without whom the vital work at stopovers would have been impossible, saw a few personnel changes along the way but they were ably headed by Josh Hall, *Pindar*'s owner. His intricate knowledge of the boat, his background in solo sailing and his experience of making projects work on low budgets all contributed to the campaign.

Brian Harris, a hard-working, ever-smiling American, was the most experienced of the crew. He'd once owned his own boatyard. He managed my job list and concentrated on systems, engine maintenance and umpteen other things. He was totally focused on his work and got on with the job even when the schedule was so punishing there seemed no chance we'd get it all done.

Mark Wylie was our marine electrician. He'd worked on all of Josh's boats for around seventeen years. He was a nice guy and an expert in his field. He was also as messy as anyone I've ever met and prone to leaving his tools lying around. He was mostly excused though, because he did an excellent job.

The team also included a French guy, Laurent Mayer, who was a good boat builder and did repairs and maintenance, and Ollie Dewar, an old friend of Josh, who was a jack of all trades (in the nicest sense of the word) and ended up working for Pindar on our website side. Later I also brought Fraser Brown, a New Zealander, on to the team. He's a rigger by trade and has made a name for himself in multi-hull sailing. I'd sailed with him on *Maiden II* and he was the only member of the shore crew I personally added to the team.

It would have been impossible for me to have entered the

Around Alone without the help of so many others, not least my shore crew during stopovers. Their support was also invaluable for morale at sea, even though every aspect of the racing, from tactics to weather interpretation to the actual sailing of the boat, is self-managed and very much solo.

Apart from the shore crew being ready on the end of the phone to answer any questions about engines or electronics, the race rules did not permit external help with weather routing. That means they didn't allow someone else to advise me where to go. Such assistance is allowed in some races but not the Around Alone. That is a big part of my job at sea, deciding which route to take and how to get from A to B quicker than my opponents.

When I'm racing like that, it really is a self-management job as much as a sailing job. You have to manage each day at sea very carefully to ensure you are always heading in the best possible direction and angle to the wind, to keep yourself rested and fed and to maintain the boat.

When I reach land, the shore crew take over, almost like a baton race. That gives me time to rest up more and organize other parts of the whole sponsorship programme so that Pindar and the media have a chance to catch up with me and work with me. The boats with less sponsorship (i.e. most of the Class II boats) had less shore assistance and needed to spend more time working on the boats. But then they'd spend less time working with sponsors and the media. I like every aspect of the sponsorship and was glad of a break from the boat: sometimes it gets a little intense when all you need is to sleep and you can't just disappear and lie down.

Morale in Team Pindar was mostly good. If anything, I was the one who'd be responsible for upsetting the apple cart when my management went awry at various stages. Media commitments seemed to be never-ending but with our workaholic PR team – consisting principally of Henry Chappell and Victoria Fuller, from Henry's company, Pitch PR – there was never going to be any respite. I was often trying to do too much, often away from the boat, and the combination of physical tiredness, playing too many roles and the intensity of the challenge did nothing to calm me down. The guys on the shore crew would let me know if they thought I hadn't spent enough time with them, explaining my precise requirements. I was feeling the pressure but never really dwelt on it and didn't talk about it. That would have made it real. There were times when I wished I could walk away, leave them to it and not come back. But I just kept working through my jobs and obligations and enjoyed the precious time I did get to be alone and relax.

Sometimes I felt caught between wanting to get away and clear my head and needing to stay and make sure everything was being done as I needed it to be. I would get frustrated when I was being advised that such-and-such had 'worked very well for the Vendée Globe'. I was racing a different race in a different way, the only way I knew how. But I was rarely forceful in expressing my views. Josh and I had contrasting ideas and we knew it, so it was often prudent just to accept that and get on with things quietly. When things did become tense, at times when I felt *Pindar* wasn't really my boat in any case, I would just disappear for a day, making sure I was still in phone contact. Ultimately I was happy as long as my job list was covered, and if Brian had done the maintenance and servicing, which he always did without fail, I was happy.

For all the tensions, they were no more than you'd expect from a group of people working under pressure at close quarters in any environment. At the time, though, and in the days immediately prior to the start, it reached the stage where my brain was getting more than a little muddled. I'd be in the middle of an interview and not be able to remember if I'd already said something to that interviewer and was repeating myself or if I'd already said it but to a completely different interviewer. The journalists all wanted exclusive – separate – interviews but I would end up saying the same things to most of them and rarely got asked any new questions. All the interviews seemed to roll into one giant one that started first thing in the morning and ended last thing at night. Every conversation I had, be it with a journalist, my shore crew, my fellow competitors, my parents or even groups of school kids who came on visits to Newport harbour, started to roll into one. Confused? I was.

I was nervous and also excited – how could such an adventure fail to excite? But those days ticking away to the off were such a blur that there was no time for much of it to register in any meaningful way. I just had to keep focusing on the boat. It was going to be my life in the coming months and it needed all the attention I could muster.

I knew it was far from ideal. It *is* possible to find boats that are close to ideal, an obvious example being Ellen MacArthur's *Kingfisher*, aboard which Ellen came second in the Vendée Globe. She was specifically built for Ellen, around her, effectively by her, with everything tailored to her individual requirements. Due to simple lack of time, my choice for the Around Alone had been limited. We had only one choice and it was Josh's boat. She and I were going to have to get along.

Pindar had no lack of potential. She was a sleek, Open 60 racing yacht, like a giant surfboard – wide, flat and relatively light – and capable of incredible speeds of up to 36 knots. She was also typical of that type of boat, built with function, not frills, in mind.

The cockpit, where you stand on deck in a recess, led down to the cabin which was covered by the curving coachroof which extended forward of the hatch. The only other external fittings were the 82-foot mast and boom on deck, the 14-foot keel underneath, and two rudders at the back. The shape of the boat meant that if there'd been only one rudder in the middle the top would have come out of the water whenever the boat was heeled over, which was frequently.

The below-decks living area, the cabin, might best have been described as compact but not especially bijou. To enter you took a couple of steps down from deck level. Some safety equipment was stored under the steps, including an Emergency Position Indicating Radio Beacon. An EPIRB allows a boat or sailor to be found when they're in distress or imminent danger but all other means of contacting land directly have been lost.

The cabin was the only place inside *Pindar* where I could stand upright with no fear of bumping my head. When standing, the top quarter of my body was above deck (but inside the coachroof), with the lower three-quarters below decks and equating to the height of the ceiling inside.

After stepping down into the boat, looking forward there was a long seat running from left to right and then the chart table, surrounded by a bank of screens and the instrument panel. This area was the nav station, the nerve-centre of the boat, with all the key pieces of equipment in one place for easy use.

One laptop computer held all the navigation and communications programs. The other had everything backed up. The Satellite B system (Sat B) was connected to this and served two functions. First, it allowed high-speed access to the internet via satellite. Second, it could also be used as a back-up phone, although it functioned on a lot of amps and was a lot more expensive than other methods.

There was an Iridium phone, which allowed me to send and receive emails at the same speed as a regular phone line. It wasn't especially fast but only used as much power as a standard 12-volt phone charger. It was obviously also a telephone. Being less expensive to use than the Sat B, it was the phone I used most often. Another satellite system, Sat C, was left permanently open but could only be used for text communications. It was typically used to write short messages to the race committee. It was popular with all the competitors because it was a relatively inexpensive way of sending messages to one another.

The radar screen, which displayed the readings from an antenna in a dome a short way up the mast, provided information about shipping and other hazards. The radar would normally allow you to spot ships or anything else solid within 25 miles. It also had various programmable alarms and guards that would provide alerts under certain conditions. If, for example, I set it to tell me whether an object had breached a pre-determined radius around Pindar, a loud buzz would sound as a warning. This gave me time to check whether the object was just heavy cloud or something potentially more dangerous like a squall or a tanker or an iceberg.

The GPS, or Global Positioning System, pinpointed the boat's position and simultaneously fed the information into the navigational program on the computer. A compass was linked to the autopilot control, which told the rudder to steer in a certain direction. The autopilot control could be programmed either to follow a compass course or to steer at a certain angle from the wind. *Pindar* had two autopilots, as do most single-handed boats, because if one pilot goes down when you're on your own, you need a second pilot to steer while you're fixing it. Of course there are times when both pilots are running with errors, as I'd already discovered, and that's when things become really tough. Character-building, I think they call it!

Other vital kit in the nerve centre included the barometer, which gives you an indication of when you're likely to enter or leave frontal systems, and the wind instruments, linked to the anemometer at the top of the mast. The computer would work out the true direction and speed of the wind from the apparent readings, which were influenced by the speed and direction of the boat. Once you plotted a course, the computer would constantly update you on the distance remaining to the next way point. Most of this key data was also available on an instrument panel outside so that if I was on deck I didn't have to keep going down below to look at the computer.

Above the chart table there was a panel of switches that included the breaker circuits for all the different systems. From the seat it was possible to switch the power on or off to each different instrument or system as necessary, or control the bilge pumps that pumped water out of the bottom of the boat. At a glance I could also check the voltmeter to see whether the four on-board batteries that powered everything needed charging. If they did, I'd do that using the diesel engine.

At the right-hand end of the chart seat was the small galley (a one-ring alcohol-burning stove mounted on a gimbal, which mostly but not always kept the pan upright when Pindar heeled during cooking). Just aft and port side of the seat was a small sink.

The bunks, which were basic frames with canvas stretched across them, were slung parallel to the port and starboard hulls respectively. When the boat was heeled over, I'd always sleep on the windward (and thus higher) side, using my weight as much as a counterbalance as possible. It would have been impossible to stay in the bunks on some occasions so I used a rope and pulley system to keep them approximately horizontal.

Underneath the chart seat there was an engine, connected to the sail drive (propeller) under the boat. The engine was sealed during the race, with the seals checked before every departure and again on arrival in each port to ensure that the boat had not been powered by the engine.

There was little need – or room – for non-essential personal possessions, although I did have a few small knick-knacks and mascots at different stages of the journey. My favourite, a gift from my best friend Jane, was a miniature disco ball that hung from the chart table light and made cool patterns around the cabin, especially if it was sunny.

I also had a mini disc player that I could connect to deck speakers and I took a good supply of music. My sister Philippa had also recorded some compilations of songs and messages from people back home that did wonders for morale on my down days.

Aside from clothes, food, tools, spares and a water-maker – a little desalination unit to provide a daily supply of fresh water – that was pretty much the extent of contents of the cabin. I did initially have a toilet (a real saltwater pump model, albeit rudimentary) in one corner but this was taken out later to make the boat lighter.

Immediately aft of the cockpit were four of the ballast tanks, which were part of a six-tank system that allowed the boat to sail more efficiently. Sea water could be pumped in and out of the various tanks as necessary to increase stability or else add 'punch' via the forward tanks when ploughing through waves.

The rearmost compartment on the boat, aft of the four tanks, housed a variety of parts of the autopilots (which included the computer processor), the rudder drive and wiring. Forward of the cabin, aside from the other two ballast tanks, there was just storage space for the sails not in use or being kept in readiness on deck, and for spare rope, sheets, and climbing gear in case of a need to scale the mast. My sail inventory for the race, which included a suite capable of coping with myriad conditions, comprised a mainsail, a solent (an upwind jib, a jib being a triangular headsail), a staysail, a storm jib, a gennaker, a masthead spinnaker and a Code 5. Later in the race we also added a reacher.

As the shore crew spent the final days before the prologue working through as much of the job list as they could manage, I needed to make detailed checks of every inch of the boat, all the equipment and all the supplies. The time flew by and I still felt I had not spent enough time on the boat by myself.

The atmosphere in Newport shipyard was buzzing, with swarms of people from umpteen different countries milling around the pontoons as the shore crews did their fine-tuning. There's a little café in the shipyard called Belle's and it became a hub for everyone involved in the Around Alone. The race committee had established an office upstairs, where there was also a makeshift media centre. As the clock ticked down, so the hustle and bustle increased. There was an air of nervous anticipation.

11 September, the first anniversary of the terrorist attacks, was a strange kind of day in America for obvious reasons. The whole country seemed, quite naturally, to be focused on the enormity of that tragedy and its repercussions in the intervening year. In Newport shipyard people went about their work as normal. There was no lack of respect, indeed it would probably have been impossible to find anywhere in the States that day where there

wasn't a sombre tone, but our little world also felt slightly apart. The race community was not primarily made up of Americans for a start. And with the race prologue due to start the next day, everyone had their own preoccupations about the adventures and troubles that lay ahead.

My own clearest recollection of that 11 September was a visit by a group of around thirty schoolchildren who arrived for a tour of *Pindar* as part of an education initiative, the HSBC Global Education Challenge, which promotes extracurricular learning. Kids always ask the most innocent questions and they're invariably the hardest to answer.

'Will you be scared?' one asked.

'I hope not,' I said, not really sure what to say.

We set off on the 160-mile overnight prologue to New York the next day at 4 p.m. Although it was termed a 'prologue race', there was no onus on anyone to push their boat to the limit. It was more a chance for the skippers to have sponsors and guests on board for a short offshore run before the serious business of going solo commenced.

I'd had my last private pre-race dinner alone with Mum and Dad on the evening of 11 September and then Dad was one of seven guests aboard *Pindar* for the prologue. The others were Andrew Pindar, Josh Hall, Mark Wylie, Dick Johnson of AMP (who'd sorted all the onboard cameras for the race), Mike Voucas (the vice-president of Yellow Book, one of Pindar's biggest clients) and Bob Phelps (who owned an AlphaGraphics store in the States, of which Pindar own the franchise).

I was keen to take Dad because I wanted him to be a part of the experience. I'd insisted Andrew came because he hardly ever got to sail with us despite his big part in the whole thing. Mark came mainly because I still had issues with the electronics, even at that late stage, and the extra help in working things out was always welcome. Dick brought his camera to get some sailing footage for promotional reasons and the others were keen sailors and there to enjoy their day out.

Josh steered *Pindar* over the start line and continued at the helm for the first couple of hours. Mark and I concentrated on working on some glitches in the navigation program. We even had to use paper charts to plot our course through the channel west of Block Island, located east of Long Island, but managed to get things working eventually. It was stressful more because I knew I'd be embarking on a transatlantic trip within days than because we were close to the island and its shallows.

Although the atmosphere on the boat was relaxed and sociable, and everyone got a chance to steer, I didn't find it especially enjoyable. With Josh there I felt very much like a guest and not a skipper. This had its advantages, such as freeing me up to spend time with Mark, but it also felt very much like me handing the boat back over to someone else at a time when perhaps I should have felt more in control.

I don't know if that was how it was all meant to be but that's how it was. As long as our guests were enjoying themselves and I was getting some knowledge from the experience, it was fine. But I was more than glad when we rolled up the Hudson River into Manhattan and over the finish line. We were last in the fleet, which was irrelevant. At least we were there.

Dad said to me afterwards how awesome he'd found the whole experience. He'd never sailed an Open 60 before and he'd been taken aback by the scale of the boat and the level of difficulty he assumed one small person would have in controlling it through all weathers. It was evident that even in a small chop you needed to be holding on with one hand at all times, making other tasks that much more difficult. 'But I'm sure you'll be fine,' he said, probably more in hope than expectation.

And that was that. We'd reached the weekend of the race. The prologue had borne no relation whatsoever in my head to the challenge ahead. I was technically on my way. I had the right ideas in my head yet just didn't feel ready at all. I was ready and unready in equal measure. But then, wasn't that always the case?

4

When I awoke in my New York hotel room, early in the morning of 15 September, I had no inclination to move an inch. The curtains were closed but I could see hints of daylight at the edges.

I lay there for a while, pulling the duvet up to my chin and nestling my head into the pillows. There weren't going to be any more lie-ins for a while and I was in no rush to leave behind a cosy, stationary bed. How long could I delay the inevitable though? I needed to get up and pack my bags. I'd arranged to meet Mum and Dad for breakfast. I climbed out of bed and got on with it. I was very mechanical and methodical about it.

I can't remember what I ate that morning, but I'm sure it wasn't much. It was a quiet breakfast. No one really had much to say. I'd pretty much blanked out the enormity of what lay ahead. I was concentrating on one thing at a time. Packing. Eating. Giving my spare gear to my parents to take home. Checking out of the hotel. Picking up a fax from the hotel reception that gave the latest weather information in the Atlantic.

There was no rushing and no mad panic. It was time to go. We walked the eight blocks down to the boat. I didn't feel nervous any more. I didn't feel emotional or sad. My thoughts were already on the coming days and how I was going to get the best from the weather. The fax had indicated there was a lot of wind expected. I was pondering the start, about how I'd negotiate safely through the harbour, tack out of the Hudson River and get past the Ambrose Light into the open sea. Beyond that – who knew? I didn't think about it.

Down at the boats everything was a bit hectic. Last-minute preparations were under way. Families and supporters were starting to say their goodbyes and depart for the other side of Manhattan to board spectator boats. I said my own goodbyes to Mum and Dad and stepped aboard *Pindar*. I looked around at my fellow competitors, every one on the verge of their own adventures.

•

The idea for the Around Alone was first mooted in a marina pub in Newport, Rhode Island in 1979. It was there that a sailor called David White first talked of organizing a solo round-the-world yacht race. Although people had previously made single-handed voyages around the world, including Francis Chichester in 1966–7 and Robin Knox-Johnston in 1968–9, in the first non-stop solo navigation, there had never been a race contested on a regular basis.

David White's idea took three years to come to fruition but when it did, in 1982, the Around Alone, then known as the BOC Challenge, was born. It has been contested every four years since, with the 2002–3 race being the sixth edition. The only other regular solo round-the-world race, the Vendée Globe, has been running since 1989, also on a quadrennial basis. But at 29,000 miles the Around Alone is the longest solo race not only in sailing but also in the whole of world sport.

Before becoming a competitor, I knew bits and pieces about

the race, mostly its dramatic highs and lows, gleaned from yachting magazines or via stories passed on between sailors. The bare facts of what lay ahead – five legs across five oceans via four stopovers, each on a different continent – merely outlined the scale of the journey ahead. It was the anecdotal stuff – tales of endeavour and adversity and occasional glory – that made me stop and think (or just stop thinking).

Only eight of the seventeen starters in the 1982–3 inaugural race finished. A French guy, Philippe Jeantot, won every leg and took the Class I honours among the bigger boats. Yukoh Tada, a Zen Buddhist taxi driver from Tokyo, won Class II. Two other entrants were saved by fellow competitors when their boats sank, while a third wrecked his boat on rocks near Sydney. David White, who had had the original idea for the race, was forced to retire when his boat started to disintegrate during the first leg.

Philippe Jeantot also won the second race, in 1986–7, on that occasion against a larger, more professional fleet. Many of the entrants had spent years targeting the race and preparing boats especially for it. The race had its first fatality when Jacques de Roux disappeared, presumably washed overboard. His body was never recovered although his boat was found, unmanned, 250 miles from the finishing line of the second leg. The third race, in 1990–91 saw the death of another skipper, although not at sea. Yukoh Tada, a class winner eight years previously, committed suicide during one of the stopovers, apparently through disappointment in his performance.

In the fourth race, in 1994–5, Isabelle Autissier, a pioneering Frenchwoman who'd raised women's sailing to new levels, set an amazing pace in the first leg. She finished six days ahead of her nearest rival. In the second leg she was capsized and dismasted but managed to make it to the remote Kerguelen Islands in the

Southern Ocean to make emergency repairs. With a makeshift mast she attempted to catch up but was rolled over again by a rogue Southern Ocean wave and spent three days in a life raft before being rescued by the Australian navy. The same race claimed the life of the oldest competitor, Harry Mitchell, who disappeared near Cape Horn during the third leg. Neither his boat nor his body was ever found. The fifth race, in 1998–9, was won by an Italian, Giovanni Soldini, but not before he had dramatically rescued the tenacious Autissier, who had returned unbowed by her previous experiences but had again capsized in the Southern Ocean.

These are the kind of snapshots that reverberated whenever I thought too long or too hard about what I was going to attempt. In the five previous Around Alone races, eighty-seven sailors from fifteen different countries had set off and thirty-one of them had not made it to the finish line. Aside from the losses of life, the race had seen a variety of collisions, abandoned boats and capsizes. But then, given that the total distance sailed by the skippers had been more than two million miles, the safety record was good. My aim was to get *Pindar* through 29,000 miles and to finish as high up the field as possible.

Unlike the Vendée Globe, the Around Alone features stopovers. The races each have unique challenges, with the Vendée taking a shorter, non-stop route. Sustaining any one serious piece of damage during the Vendée usually means you're out of it, whereas in the Around Alone you at least have the theoretical chance of limping to the end of the leg and making repairs, albeit under time pressure.

The Around Alone's stopovers add their own intensity. Skippers know they'll get chances to make repairs and tend to push their boats to the limit, risking the kind of hammering a Vendée skipper might be inclined to avoid. The stop-start of the Around Alone also adds other pressures that you don't find in a non-stop race. Each time you make a stopover, the stored-up fatigue washes over you. A new race begins, onshore, to get the boat ready for the next leg. And then just when the fatigue from the last leg is showing signs of easing or your sleep patterns are beginning to normalize, you have to force a confused body and mind back into race mode to depart again.

On a practical level, the Vendée's non-stop circumnavigation by definition keeps you out in the ocean at all times, largely away from coastal hazards and heavy traffic. The stopovers of the Around Alone introduce a new dimension to the first few days and last few days of each leg, when you need to negotiate coastal waters, shipping channels and high volumes of other craft. You tend not to sleep much, if at all, in those periods, yet they are the precise sections of the race where your body is in need of most sleep. Towards the end of legs the accumulated sleep deficit is high. At the beginning, your body is still wanting more rest after a period on land.

In the months before the Around Alone, when I was trying to decide whether it was feasible or not, I had kept telling myself to think of it as five parts of one big race instead of one long trip. The reality of those parts was that each could last up to thirty-three days and there were five of them, each with a potentially hassle-strewn start, finish and stopover. My imagined manageable chunks would become bigger and less palatable by the mile.

As Sir Robin Knox-Johnston said, 'All around the world races are tough, some are tougher than others, however there is none more demanding on the individual than Around Alone.' I'm not going to argue with that. On 15 September 2002 I could barely envisage further than the Hudson River, let alone the entirety of the route that would take us back to Newport, just to the north, via the Antipodes.

The first leg, from New York to Torbay in Devon, was also going to be the shortest. At 3,000 miles it was deemed to be something of a downwind sprint, taking anywhere between eight and eighteen days.

The second leg, from Torbay to Cape Town, was going to be 7,000 miles, taking in a variety of climates. I was anticipating a few days of heavy upwind sailing to cross the notorious Bay of Biscay. The weather would probably be horrible until I reached the trade winds, and then the North Atlantic trades would take me to the Doldrums, which are a lottery. They can either ease you through (which is highly unlikely) or leave you stranded. There's no knowing which until you get there. Next would come the South Atlantic trades, skirting around the St Helena High before coming into Cape Town, which is awesome visually but an awful place to arrive as a sailor. If you misjudge your run-in, you risk being becalmed or else hit by huge winds. Table Mountain is beautiful but does terrible things to the wind. There are also whales everywhere and loads of shipping.

The third leg, from Cape Town to Tauranga in New Zealand, would be another long leg, just over 7,000 miles. It would take us through the Southern Ocean, the only place on the planet where waves can do full circuits of the globe in the sure knowledge they're never going to encounter land and be brought down to size. It can be a freezing, dangerous, violent place and you need to be careful in judging where on the 'Southern Ocean highway' you plot your course. You need to stay south of the high-pressure systems but north of the low-pressure systems that spin around the bottom of the earth, stirring up fearsome gales and the kind of waves you'd balk at in the cinema. Next we'd need to come back up into the Tasman Sea and make our way to Cape Reinga, the northernmost point of New Zealand. After turning that corner we'd come back down the east coast.

The fourth leg, from Tauranga to Salvador in Brazil, was going to be the longest, at almost 8,000 miles, and the toughest by reputation. It was going to take me back down into the Southern Ocean towards what is simultaneously the most fearsome and welcoming corner in ocean racing – Cape Horn. Before you reach the Cape you can never be sure what kind of monstrous ocean will greet you nor what kind of approach you'll have. It's often foggy and rarely calm. Then again, if and when you round Cape Horn safely, the start of the journey back north can be a tremendous relief, at least until the weather mutates to become hot, windless and frustrating.

The last 4,000 miles of the Around Alone, if we made it as far as Brazil, were going to be another sprint, although there was always the danger that the Doldrums would make the last leg more of a hurdles race, through treacle. If the Atlantic was moody, it might become more of a malevolent steeplechase.

Each competitor in the race was free to choose his or her own route between the start of each leg and the finish. Planning that route was an intrinsic part of the tactical challenge. There would be no such thing as a straight line that everyone would follow. Rather, imagine that each ocean was a massive off-road terrain that needed to be traversed however each skipper chose. Picking your way through weather systems to make gains by sailing the fastest routes would be the key. To do this would require using all our skills as navigators and meteorologists and tacticians.

As I stood in New York on *Pindar's* deck that September morning, waiting to depart, twelve other skippers were gathered alongside. Seven of us would be contesting the Open 60 class

(Class I), with six smaller boats, 40-footers and 50-footers, contesting Class II. In some respects I stood out as the only woman, the youngest person and the only Briton. But as I'd come to appreciate more than I could ever have imagined that day, each skipper would come to stand out at some stage in the journey. The fleet had diversity not only in terms of big-race experience but in nationalities, backgrounds, ages, motivations, backing and personalities. The Around Alone 'family', as I now collectively think of that assembled group, was as follows.

In Class I, racing against *Pindar* and me, there were Thierry Dubois, a Frenchman sailing a boat named *Solidaires*, Bernard Stamm, who was Swiss, aboard *Bobst Group-Armor Lux*, Graham Dalton, a New Zealander, aboard *Hexagon*, Simone Bianchetti, an Italian, aboard *Tiscali*, Bruce Schwab, an American, aboard *Ocean Planet*, and Patrick de Radigues, a Belgian, aboard *Garnier*.

In Class II there were Brad Van Liew, an American, aboard *Tommy Hilfiger Freedom America*, Derek Hatfield, a Canadian, aboard *Spirit of Canada*, John Dennis, a Canadian, aboard *Bayer Ascensia*, Tim Kent, an American, aboard *Everest Horizontal*, Kojiro Shiraishi, a Japanese, aboard *Spirit of Yukoh*, and Alan Paris, a Bermudan, aboard *BTC Velocity*.

Thierry Dubois was a fiery but charming character, driven by his convictions and a strong faith in his boat, *Solidaires*, the French word for solidarity. His project was very much based around that theme. He had used ocean racing as a platform to promote humanitarian causes, not least Amnesty International, and he was never less than passionate on the subject.

Prior to the Around Alone, Thierry had entered two Vendée Globes. In his first, the 1996–7 event where Pete Goss rescued Raphael Dinelli, Thierry's boat capsized in the Southern Ocean.

Rather than stay trapped in the upturned hull, he swam free and climbed on top of it. He managed to activate his EPIRB and within hours he saw an Australian plane fly overhead, which was very unusual. It was on a spotting mission to locate the where-abouts of another sailor, Tony Bullimore, who had also capsized, although Thierry didn't know that at the time.

Tony's boat was successfully located but there were no signs of life so the plane went back and dropped two life rafts for Thierry. He had to leave his upturned boat to try to grab them – they were held together with a length of rope – but he couldn't manage in the terrible weather and they blew away. Another two were dropped and he eventually scrambled to relative safety. He was in a life raft in appalling conditions for three days before an Australian navy vessel reached him. The same boat went on to find Tony Bullimore's upturned yacht and Tony was rescued having spent four hellish days inside thinking he might die. Thierry's stories from that Vendée Globe were quite amazing. In the next Vendée, in 2000–1, he had been forced to make a technical stop in New Zealand, meaning he was officially disqualified. He resumed racing none the less and went on to complete his circumnavigation.

I admired not only Thierry's sailing abilities but his single-mindedness and commitment. He had an unfailing desire to get the best from himself time and again, undaunted by the kind of previous nightmare experiences that would deter most people, me included. If he had something to say, he said it, even though it might have been controversial. Ultimately he cared deeply about any form of perceived injustice and wasn't afraid to act on it.

Bernard Stamm had also raced in the 2000–1 Vendée Globe although an autopilot failure had forced him to retire. He had built the boat he sailed in that race himself while searching for money, parts and equipment – including lead for his keel – from a variety of friends, supporters and suppliers. His enforced retirement from the Vendée had inspired his decision to enter the Around Alone, where he had only one aim: to win. He was a man on a mission and arrived at the start line with superb credentials, including a transatlantic record and a twenty-four-hour distance record on the same boat, both achieved in the wake of the Vendée and in the run-up to the Around Alone.

When Stamm was at sea, he was so utterly focused that he would make other driven professionals look like dawdlers. He pushed his boat to extremes and consequently suffered breakages. But he never eased up and he expected the same work ethic from his two-man shore team, who would have their work cut out at every stopover. I didn't have the extraordinary levels of confidence that Stamm had to put so much pressure on his boat. Nor did I think that I'd deal with setbacks with as little discernible effect on my confidence as Stamm's had had on his. I would be amazed by his ability to push the boundaries.

Away from the water Bernard, who has a lovely family, was good company, modest and popular. His pregnant partner and little girl came out to visit at each port, with his second daughter born during the Brazil stopover.

Graham Dalton, brother of the famous Kiwi sailor, Grant, arrived at the start line with a lot to live up to due to the family name. He'd had his boat built especially for the race and he had a huge backer in the form of HSBC. His campaign had the biggest sponsorship deal in the race. Graham, a teacher, wanted to use the race as a platform for the HSBC Global Education Campaign, something I was also going to be involved with.

Graham's boat, *Hexagon*, was one of the fastest designs at the time although he had encountered problems with it, including a dismasting during his qualifier. His new mast arrived in Newport just before the start of the race, something that can't have soothed his nerves. He also started the race with a time penalty because of his late arrival in Newport. But he was a big guy with a big, outspoken personality and he didn't hold back with his optimism. Only first place was good enough for him. Coming second was nowhere. That was the mantra. Graham had a steely, often brash aura that sent out a message that no one could touch him. His language was as colourful as a rainbow though rarely as pretty. Once you got used to him, though, you hardly noticed the swearing.

Simone Bianchetti had an altogether different way with words. He was a published poet and a romantic in every sense. He came from Cervia on Italy's Adriatic coast and was born to be at sea. He'd been in the Italian navy before becoming a professional skipper and one of his country's best-known yachtsmen, first in Mediterranean regattas and then in ocean racing. He'd taken part in a previous Around Alone (then the BOC Challenge) in 1994 but had had to abandon the race. His CV also included transatlantic racing and the 2001–2 Vendée Globe, in which he finished in twelfth place after a 121-day non-stop voyage. It was during that journey that he had become known for his poetry, which was subsequently published in both Italian and French.

Simone was a man of extreme emotions, in love with the ocean, where he felt at home, and with life, which he lived by the moment. He actually got married during the first stopover of the race.

He was the life and soul of any party and made his presence felt on social occasions. He was one of those people for whom the phrase 'larger than life' had a particular resonance and that is not something that comes solely with hindsight. He was a guy with big appetites – for adventure, for self-knowledge, for the kind of isolation and solitude that would drive me crazy – and if at times he was seen as an absolute madman, it was a term invariably used with affection.

Simone was often described as a troubled soul, and certainly I found some of his writing, which tended towards the deep and philosophical, beyond my comprehension. He seemed fulfilled one moment, apparently tormented the next. I liked him but I can't admit I identified with such swings of emotion. On land, at times, he seemed like a fish out of water. Perhaps it was only the ocean that provided an environment in which he could truly be himself.

No one was to know, at the start of the Around Alone, that it would be Simone's final voyage. He died in June 2003, the month after the race finished, aged thirty-five. The cause of death was attributed to respiratory and circulatory arrest. After a life on the ocean, and every thing he had been through, it might have been more fitting if he had disappeared at sea. I sometimes think it was a shame he didn't, just like some old seadog. The sea had looked after him throughout his life, after all.

Brad Van Liew was, in many ways, the complete opposite of Simone in terms of personality. He was one of the steadiest, most level-headed guys you could wish to meet. He came from California and had worked as a commercial pilot, doing some stunt flying as a hobby in between taking his clients – including Robbie Williams at one stage – wherever they needed to go. He'd been sailing in ocean races since he was twelve and had taken part in the previous Around Alone, finishing third in Class II that time in an older boat. In the 2002–3 race he was back on a mission to win. He had a good boat and good back-up, and he always joked that he was a student of the Around Alone and knew more about it than anyone. He was a warm, approachable guy, very friendly, endlessly supportive and never short of a word of encouragement. He was very much a stabilizing influence on our race 'family' and I know he desperately missed his own young family when he was away at sea.

Derek Hatfield was a former Mountie who'd built his boat from scratch. It was a 40-footer, the smallest boat in the fleet, but he'd done a beautiful job in building her from meagre resources. Although Derek was an experienced offshore sailor he'd still focused for the best part of four years on getting ready for this one adventure. Derek was quiet and had a real determination about him and I would get to know him better during the race. During the first stopover, for example, he was still raising money for his campaign, seeking $50 donations here and there. In return for their money, every single donor had their name painted on the side of his boat. During that first stopover Andrew Pindar and I both paid up and saw our names added. I was proud to be one of his supporters.

John Dennis was another Canadian, also racing in Class II. He was the oldest member of the fleet, at almost sixty, and he was also the first person with diabetes ever to enter a solo round-the-world race. John launched his campaign with a dual aim: to achieve a lifelong ambition to sail around the world and to raise awareness about diabetes. A drug company in the forefront of diabetes research supported him in this as his campaign sponsor. John soon acquired the nickname 'Pops', not only for his seniority and big white beard, but for the kindness he showed to all of us. John had an incredible belief in himself and he had my utmost respect not only for the way he treated others but for taking on the challenge with such a constraining condition in the first place.

Koji Shiraishi was an amazing character who'd sailed all the way from Japan – across the Pacific and through the Panama Canal – just to get to the start line. The journey had taken months and he only had a couple of weeks in Newport before the race started. By the time the fleet reached New Zealand, he would already have effectively sailed around the world in one trip. At the beginning, I found it tough to converse with Koji because of the language barrier, but his English would improve. He had great stamina and kept everyone entertained with regular video footage and photographs of his journey. His boat, a 40-footer called *Spirit of Yukoh*, had been named in honour of Yukoh Tada, his mentor, in whose memory Koji sailed.

Bruce Schwab was an American guy who had built a very radical, almost skinny boat with an unusual rig. He struck me as a creative dreamer but he was also quite scientific. When we were ashore his guitar never seemed to be far from his side. I didn't ever see him go busking but he was always exploring ways to fund his campaign, raising cash via donations or selling T-shirts. When I'd been in Antigua in April 2002, Bruce had been there as charter skipper of his race boat earning money for his project. At times he seemed to be living day-to-day financially. I'm not sure I could've coped with the stress of that on top of the stresses of the race. But Bruce seemed happy enough. He had work done on his boat even though he couldn't afford it, and then had faith that somehow things would work out. I don't think I'd ever have the nerve to operate like that, partly I think because money had seemed quite tight as I grew up and I'd been taught never to run up debts that I couldn't be sure of paying off. Even getting to the start was an accomplishment for Bruce and he seemed to view the rest as a bonus.

I would only meet Patrick de Radigues a couple of times.

I saw him briefly on the day of the start and in the pre-race briefings, and then again during the first stopover. He had a background in motorsport – cars and bikes – and had done two Vendée Globes prior to the Around Alone, although he had problems in both. I'm not certain that Patrick ever intended to do more than one leg of our race, and then only as practice for the Route du Rhum. But maybe if he'd said that before the start he wouldn't have been allowed to enter. As it transpired, he retired after the first leg and we never saw him again.

Alan Paris had been a hotelier for eighteen years and was a great guy whose wife and son came out to each stopover. He was always in high spirits, didn't seemed fazed by anything and would never be unduly concerned that his stopover breaks were shorter than everyone else's because he took longer to reach each port. After a lengthy spell at sea I'm desperate to wind down, socialize and rest. Alan seemed so organized with his boat, so comfortable with what he was doing, that he didn't let stresses like that get to him. He was in tune with his boat and nothing seemed to be a problem. He always had a smile on his face and the mood was always lighter for having him around.

Tim Kent was a scholarly American from Milwaukee, very articulate, very good at getting his point across. His speech at the final press conference really stood out for me. He talked about what the race meant to him, how it had always been his dream to sail around the world. He said he'd wanted to prove to his two daughters that if you really wanted to do something, it was possible. But in the end, he'd discovered, the support they'd given him had actually been the thing that kept him motivated.

The thirteenth and final entrant was me, a twenty-seven-year-old woman who had done one previous single-handed race and had shown plenty of signs of reluctance about doing another.

Come that day in September though, there was no turning back. My participation had become significant for many more people than me. It was important for Pindar, important for my family, quite possibly important for women's sailing. I didn't think of it then in such terms. Being the only woman in the race was neither a good nor a bad thing for me. It was ultimately irrelevant.

Short-handed ocean racing is one of the few sports where men and women compete as equals, even with the differences in weight and strength. The only time I ever really thought about being a woman in a male-dominated sport was when the umpteenth journalist in a day asked me about it. I really do see myself as just another competitor, only it takes me longer to go for a pee than the guys. Tracy Edwards and Ellen MacArthur had both raised the reputation of British sailing *per se*, not just women's sailing. If I was setting out to achieve anything, it was as a sailor, not as a female sailor.

Every skipper had their strengths and weaknesses, mental, physical and emotional. I was no different. But I did know it mattered to lots of people how I fared. And I had every intention of showing that there was no reason why I shouldn't compete, shouldn't be tactically as good, shouldn't be technically as competent, shouldn't fight for a place on the podium.

I took a deep breath as I cast off.

1. *(right)* My big brother Andy's first boat, before I was even around.

2. *(below)* A young Richards family on holiday, with my godmother Sue's two sons, Tom and Seb.

3. *(right)* Philippa and I helping Dad with our house in Brussels.

4. *(left)* Typical Richards family hill walk.

5. *(left)* Philippa, Dave and Andy helping Dad build the Mirror.

6. *(below)* Dave and I sailing the Optimist that Dad built.

7. *(left)* Mum, Philippa and I sailing in the Hebrides on our friends', the Sandersons', yacht.

8. *(below)* Andy taking us to a regatta in Mum's old car.

9. (*right*) The RYA Scottish Optimist squad, the only other single-handed boat I sailed!

10. (*below*) 420 youth training was the next step before the 470 senior squad, which I did only for one year.

11. (*below*) My brothers, Andy and Dave, and trimmer Andy Fairley on their current 18ft skiff, *Radii*. (Marc Turner)

12. *(left) Royal SunAlliance* days after we lost the rig in mid-Southern Ocean, taken from a Nimrod by one of my father's colleagues. (Ray Troll)

13. *(below)* Miranda and I crossing the finish line of the Transat Jacques Vabre in November 1999. (Dave Richards)

14. Miranda and I sailing on *Pindar Net* in the AG2R in April 2000. (Thierry Martinez)

15. At the finish of the Ostar in June 2000 with Andrew Pindar and Mike Golding. (Thierry Martinez)

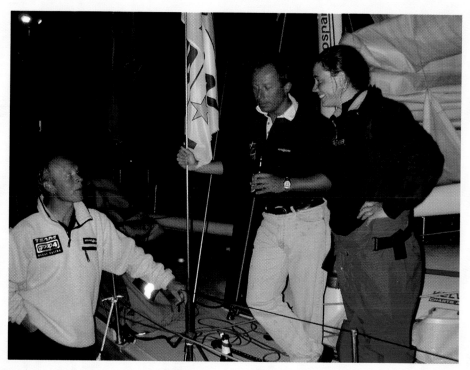

16. *(above)* **Miki and I training for the TJV in 2001 in the ORMA 60 trimaran** *Pindar Systems.*
(Thierry Martinez)

17. *(left)* *Amer Sports Too*, **sailing in Rio de Janiero during the Volvo Ocean race 2002.** (Carlo Borlenghi, Sea & See)

18. *(left)* **The start line of the Around Alone, September 2002, NY Harbour.**
(Ray Riley, Marine Pics)

19. *(below)* **Dawn, just as I finished the first leg, into Torbay. What a great feeling!** (Marc Turner)

20. *(above)* The start of the second leg out of Torbay, the *Hatherleigh* behind me, and my parents waving from the bow. (Marc Turner)

21. *(left)* At a scary height!

22. *(below)* The finish of the second leg, dawn, Table Mountain – a beautiful backdrop. (Ray Riley, Marine Pics)

5

New York Harbour can be busy at the best of times but the scene that day was something else. Crowds had gathered along the shore, waving and shouting. A flotilla of well-wishers and support boats was straining to get better views. The air was filled with the sound of horns and cheering.

The fleet circled in preparation for the start. The last few shore crew who had remained on the boats bade their farewells and disembarked. I really was on my own now. I hadn't sailed *Pindar* solo since arriving in Newport and a lot of changes had been made in the interim. Right, I thought, let's just try to get through the next few hours with as few errors as possible.

I caught sight of the spectator boat carrying Team Pindar and Mum and Dad. It was packed with family and friends and people who'd worked on the campaign. There were Pindar clients and employees, people I'd got to know in the previous three years. Andrew Pindar was there, and Andrew's parents, Tom and Margery. As usual, Andrew had said a few private words to me shortly before I boarded.

'Just get yourself back safely,' he'd said. 'Because at the end of the day, results are irrelevant. All that I care about, and all that your mum and dad care about, is that you come home in one piece.'

It was a perfect send-off. I knew Andrew meant what he said. Seeing everyone waving and cheering brought a lump to my throat. I waved back. It was an emotional moment but it couldn't last long. There was work to do. I wanted to secure a good position on the start line and began to manoeuvre in the right direction, gathering speed.

The start of a race is always important, not necessarily because it gives you a long-term advantage but because it sets the tone. Crossing the line first gives you a boost. You are given a precise time in the day and you know that you want to be sailing at full speed towards that line at the right time, ideally on the line as the gun goes. You are given a warning signal ten minutes before the off, and a preparatory signal five minutes before the gun, and then it is up to you how good a start you get, how you set up your sails and how well you time your run.

With a crew, starts are easier because you have different people in charge of different sails, someone calling what the other boats are up to (so you know what's happening) and the bowman calling distance to the line while standing right up on the bow. In solo racing it is more difficult because you are doing it all by yourself.

At the start of the first leg from New York Harbour, I was going a bit too fast towards the line just before the gun, which meant a risk of crossing too early, or worse, hitting something. I slowed down. I had a long journey ahead, there wasn't any need to rush this bit. I didn't want a collision or major incident before I got going.

I wasn't the only nervous skipper. Conditions were forecast to be windy and squally, which was unsettling for everyone, especially in the first few hours. In such a confined area as a busy harbour, with large numbers of spectator boats, there was always the chance of something going wrong. It would only take a couple of day-trippers on a launch, too eager to get too close to the fleet, to create a snarl-up or disrupt the whole starting procedure. That's what we'd been reminded of in the final skippers' briefing that morning anyway. I eased up a bit more, too much probably. I ended up near the back of the fleet as we crossed the line. No matter. We were off.

There was quite a bit of jostling for position as we headed out along the Hudson River. Graham Dalton on *Hexagon* had a great start but then I ended up crossing in front of him while tacking. Things got tricky very quickly. There were sandbanks and boats everywhere. We were expecting more wind than we initially had and I didn't have enough sail area up. Then the wind died altogether and I needed all of it up.

It took a good couple of hours to reach the open sea. So much for the forecast that had suggested we'd be rattling down the narrow channel and catapulted out into the Atlantic. We were closer to drifting than doing that. But at least when we did get to the open sea the wind picked up and I had the chance to put up bigger sails. I changed to my spinnaker, which took a lot of effort and twenty minutes to raise. I'd had it up for about twenty-five minutes when the wind increased again, above the 12–14 knot range in which the spinnaker worked best. I had to pull it down quickly and get the gennaker up. I was still only about 20 miles out of New York but already I felt tired. I knew there would be no rest at all the first night because there was so much traffic to negotiate.

There were a lot of ships with their anchors down, just sitting there with their lights on. There were also lots of fishing buoys, with little reflectors so radar could pick them up when they became hard to spot manually. Not that my radar was on all the time. There was so much shipping that it was easier and safer to be on deck looking out for it than to keep going down into the cabin to look on radar. My first night at sea was spent doing just that while wishing I didn't feel so exhausted. There was no chance of any sleep at all. I still hadn't had any when the first crisis arrived on the Monday afternoon.

The morning had been fine. I'd been making decent progress, clocking speeds up to 22 knots with an average of 18. I could also see a boat from the fleet ahead of me. I guessed that maybe it was Patrick de Radigues on *Garnier* but I wasn't close enough to be sure. It didn't matter. This was good downwind sailing, with the gennaker up and a full main, and things were about to become more interesting. We were crossing Nantucket Shoals.

The wind crept up past 30 knots. Some sailors keep the gennaker up in breezes that fast but I knew my safe limit was closer to 25 knots. I'd exceeded that already, and for too long, because I'd wanted to push on. But I knew I really needed to get the gennaker down. I comforted myself with the thought that there was so much wind I wouldn't slow too drastically when I'd done so. The problem arose with the furler system, which is a mechanism that allows you to deploy and store sails more easily. The key component is the furling wheel, which sits at the bottom of the stay – the rope to which the sail is attached – with a furling line to roll up or unroll the sail. When you use a furler system, the sail is not actually raised or lowered as such; rather, it is unrolled and rolled. If you imagine a sail rolled in on itself like a long, thin sausage, that is how it is stored when it is not in use.

I needed to take down the gennaker so I started to pull the furling line. The furler started twisting the sail but the force of the wind was exerting too much pressure and the furling line snapped. That meant I had to find another way to bring down the sail. Not only that, but I'd have to decide how and where to store the sail. Under normal circumstances it would be rolled neatly and dropped to the deck in the sausage shape, which fits easily down the hatch on the foredeck.

I toyed with the option of trying to rethread the furling line. That wasn't going to be easy, or especially safe, but I tried it anyway. To do so I climbed to the end of the pole sticking out of the front of the boat to reach the furler. There was nothing below me but churning water. *Pindar* was travelling at an average of 20 knots. When she careered down waves, she was going even faster. I spent ten minutes trying to rethread the line but I wasn't making any real progress. While dangling precariously over the front of the boat, it dawned on me that maybe this wasn't such a good idea. If I hit a big wave and it washed me off this pole, hence overboard, even with three harness lines attaching me to the deck, it might not just be my race that was over. I decided it would be a crazy way to make my exit. I was only one day into the race. I edged back on to the deck and thought again.

The sail needed to come down, no question. There was only one option left. I'd need to try to drop the gennaker down on to the deck by releasing the halyard. This would have been a simple procedure with a crew. If I'd had four people on hand I could have spaced them out along the bottom edge of the sail, eased the halyard and instructed them to pull it in. As long as the wind wasn't too fierce, four people would probably have been able to control the mass of sail and fold it before it blew over the side. But I didn't have four people on hand. Whatever I was going to do it would have to be feasible on my own.

I decided the best course of action was to steer the boat –

with the autopilot – further downwind. This would mean that the mainsail would act as a partial 'shadow' on the gennaker, reducing the amount of wind on the latter as I tried to bring it down. And then I'd ease the halyard a couple of feet, secure the bottom of the sail to the deck by its corners, ease the halyard a bit more, secure the next bit of sail, and so on until it was down. The problem was that to ease the halyard I needed to be at the mast and to secure the sail I needed to be towards the front. The procedure involved multiple little sprints and the 30 knots of wind did me no favours whatsoever. Every time I loosened the halyard, the sail started flapping frantically and dipping into the water. It was about as much as I could manage to lash each bit down in a fairly rudimentary fashion and then dash back to slacken the halyard again. It took a good hour and a half, during which time my mind was firmly focused on the job in hand and nothing else.

Unfortunately by sailing so that the mainsail shadowed the gennaker, I was sailing in the wrong direction. The intensity of the squalls had not really registered. Visibility was rapidly decreasing towards zero. On top of that, we were now indisputably over Nantucket Shoals. The intensity of the waves was telling me that. Shallower waters always tend to create bigger waves, like surf breaking on a beach.

I had one other problem. I'd been so preoccupied with getting the gennaker down that I hadn't been able to go below and check my precise location. I had no idea whether I'd already strayed into the shipping lane or whether I was about to run aground on the sandbanks. The low visibility made my imagination run wild and nightmare visions briefly ran through my head of me struggling to get the gennaker under control but losing control of the boat, leading to a collision with a ship. I was a little stressed, to say the least, and the absence of sleep – I hadn't had even a ten-minute nap, wasn't helping.

My concept of time had already become a bit skewed. The longer I was on deck trying to sort out the sails, the more I became convinced I was either about to run aground or be hit by a ship I hadn't seen. The mainsail was obscuring my view of what was behind us.

Eventually I got the sail down, readjusted my course so I was going in the right direction and began to pick up some speed. I still had to store the gennaker though. I went back on deck and looked at it – it was now a crumpled mess. There was no way I could roll it back into a neat sausage while it was on deck. This can only be done when it is hoisted to the top of the mast. It would need to be stuffed in the sail compartment for now and the only way to get it in there was by untying one bit at a time and pushing it through the hatch on the fore deck.

The wind was still too strong for me to untie more than a bit at a time without a risk of the sail flapping itself free and destroying itself. The problem was that the hatch was only 70 centimetres in diameter. That meant a lot of pushing. The sail consisted of 145 square metres of fabric. Matters were made more difficult because every time a wave hit us, gallons of water poured straight into the boat through the hatch, which would normally have been shut in such conditions.

Eventually, exhausted, I got the sail down below – along with plenty of seawater that didn't belong there – and I then went below decks to bilge out the worst of the water. I'd have to wait until the wind died to think about sorting out the sail and finishing the clear-up. That wasn't going to happen any time soon because almost immediately the conditions deteriorated again.

Despite not having the gennaker up, I still had plenty of sail area and we were moving quickly. Visibility was poor, though. There was a mass of very low cloud, like the densest fog you can imagine. And the squalls were unbelievable. One came through at 40 knots, with rain like I had never seen before. I could hardly breathe for water. The worst of the stuff was coming from behind me, sweeping over in airborne waves. As the 40-knot squall began to pass, I turned to look behind me to see what was coming my way next. What I saw almost killed me.

A massive supertanker, hundreds of metres long and weighing hundreds of thousands of tons, was towering ominously behind me. It had just passed behind me about half a mile away. On a sunny day I'd almost have been in its shadow. On a marginally different course, *Pindar* and I would have been wiped out like matchstick toys under a bulldozer. This thing was immense anyway but was piled several storeys high with huge containers, one on top of the other. I just stared as it carried on its way.

On a clear day I would have seen it easily before it had finished coming over the horizon. Either that or I would have picked it up on the radar, which would discern its line from 25 miles away. But with my other preoccupations, and the weather, and the fact that the low cloud and squalls had rendered the radar screen a mass of blobs and dense speckles, there'd been no chance. I was only peeking at the radar screen intermittently from the deck anyway. And you certainly can't hear shipping unless a boat blows its horn. Even if it had, the chances are that the noise of the wind would have drowned it out. On a crewed boat, someone might have stood a chance of spotting such hazards. Needless to say, I wasn't on a crewed boat. The incident did nothing to lessen the stress levels.

Later, during the first stopover, I got talking to Thierry Dubois about the whole gennaker nightmare scenario. He told me he knew precisely when my troubles had started. At the time when I'd been pushing to catch up with what I assumed was *Garnier*, I had in fact been on the heels of *Solidaires*. I don't think I'd have kept the gennaker up for as long if there hadn't been another boat in sight, and I jested to Thierry that he had been unwittingly responsible for encouraging me to make problems for myself!

'I saw you just behind me and I thought you were crazy to leave your gennaker up,' he said. 'I'd taken mine down a long time before that. I tried to call you on the radio and tell you but I guess you weren't listening or were out on deck trying to control it.' He joked about my craziness and said he didn't know how I'd managed to get through. In the dry, comfortable environment of that conversation it all seemed quite funny. At the time I couldn't have felt less like laughing. I'd only been out of New York for a day and I'd nearly come a cropper twice.

The upside was that the adrenalin rush in those opening days kept me going. Though frustrated by the gennaker and terrified by the tanker, I hadn't actually wished I was elsewhere at any stage. I was exhilarated, if anything, although in desperate need of some sleep. At least I wasn't seasick, which is thankfully an affliction I rarely suffer from. On the couple of occasions when I have been sick, other factors have tipped the balance, such as a typhoid inoculation the day before sailing offshore. I am also lucky in that I don't continue feeling the ocean after I get back to land. Some people get land legs which make them feel like they're swaying for a long time after they're back on land.

Sleep eventually came in the early hours of the Tuesday morning, in four twenty-minute naps that felt luxurious. In between two of those I also cooked some pasta, my first hot food since leaving New York. Some of it even ended up in my mouth, despite the bumpy conditions. The bonuses didn't last for long, though, and I was soon immersed in a new problem – computer failure.

The onboard computer was quite old. Every time I slammed over a big wave or the boat jarred for any reason, it would switch off and then reboot itself. The navigation program I was using was particularly slow in restarting each time and the communications program also had to run through a set-up procedure. It was table-thumpingly frustrating. Imagine your PC whirring into life at a snail's pace and not being ready to use for five or ten minutes after switching it on. Then imagine opening a program, waiting for another whirr, finally getting access to what you're after and then the whole thing crashing again. It was happening time after time and eventually I left it switched off. I just had to hope I wouldn't miss too much vital information that might either save me miles or warn me of especially bad weather.

At times when the seas were calmer and there was little chance of a slamming crash, I switched the computer on to find out exactly where I was and collect the eight-hourly position reports for the fleet. Most of the time in the first week I wished I hadn't bothered. I was last in Class I by some distance. Realizing how many miles I'd lost was thoroughly disheartening.

To be so far behind so soon in such a long race wasn't what I needed. Worse, it was my own fault. I should have taken the gennaker down sooner. I shouldn't have waited until the wind had created problems for me. Aiming to go faster, I'd made a bad call and ended up losing out. I hoped I'd learnt my lesson. I resolved I wasn't going to be so bothered about the other boats just yet, certainly not to the extent of chasing them without caution, as I'd done with Thierry. I had to concentrate on my own race.

Although there were no more major dramas over the next couple of days, the solitude began to kick in on the first Wednesday, 18 September. I was tired and frustrated, I still hadn't fixed the furler, and my nap routine hadn't taken shape as planned. The sky was still dotted with dark squall clouds that needed monitoring and the polling positions were providing no good news.

19 Sep 05:09 Another frustrating day, starting wth a 4hr becalmed patch a.m., meant I had a chance to get the crumpled heap of a gennaker out of the fore hatch and back up, but by the time I had that filling nicely the wind shifted to come out of the North, and very quickly got up to 30kts (the gennaker is safe down below). I have been under 3 reefs and staysail most of the evening and night, and each time I go to pull out a reef, the wind gusts to 30+again then slowly settles back nearer 25. My course is suffering as the wind has shifted to 25–30deg so I can't hold my ideal course therefore getting further behind the leaders . . . the computer keeps crashing under big waves each time we land again. took me an hour earlier just to have enough time between crashes to pick up the polling (I still didn't get to read it!).

Andrew Pindar called me later on the Thursday to see how I was getting on.

'Not great,' I said. 'I'm tired, I'm cold, I'm frustrated that I'm last in Class I. The computer keeps crashing, I've made a right mess of the sails and I almost got mowed down by a supertanker. But apart from that, everything's fine.'

'Emma,' he said, patience personified, 'forget about the position reports. Forget about trying to break your neck catching up. You've only just started what is going to be a very long race and there's no need to put extra pressure on yourself. As long as you remain in the race, you're competitive just by being there. And the bottom line is that if you can't go on or don't want to go on, at any stage, then you don't have to. Stop. No one will think any the worse if you did.'

Again, I knew he meant it. His unconditional support only made me more determined to deliver.

When we'd finished our brief conversation, I opened one of the three CDs that my sister Philippa had recorded for me for the journey. Somewhere south of Newfoundland I started jigging around to the strains of 'Ain't No Sunshine When She's Gone' and other songs. There weren't no sunshine where I was, either, but the CD sent my spirits soaring.

The music was interspersed with messages from family, friends, members of the *Maiden II* crew, Tracy and various members of the Pindar clan in its widest sense. It was quite an odd sensation sitting alone in a cabin filled with familiar voices. It made my week.

The polling report on the Friday did its best to spoil it again. I seemed to have reached a compromise with the temperamental computer but the payback was that it only presented me with bad news. By the Friday evening I was just over the eastern edge of the Grand Banks of Newfoundland, having covered 1,000 miles in five days. I was still lying seventh of seven in the Class I fleet.

Bernard Stamm was in first place, almost half-way to Brixham, 400 miles ahead of me. Thierry was 123 miles behind him, followed by Patrick, Simone and Bruce. That left Graham on *Hexagon* as my closest rival and even he was 60 miles closer to the finish, somewhere to the north-east of me.

As we headed across the Atlantic, the northerly wind turned icy cold. That meant two extra layers of clothing, two hats and pairs of gloves. But at least there was some decent breeze and I spent six hours hand-steering overnight with a full main in perfect surfing conditions under clear, moonlit skies. I could see the vast ocean ahead of me, mountainous waves, sometimes birds skimming the waves next to me, their wings fluttering millimetres from the surface. These are perfect conditions because you can surf down the waves as well as sail down them, as if you were surfing at a beach; you're using the shape and power of the waves. In a boat you can use the power of the wind to keep you going and then use the extra power of the waves to propel you even further and faster.

Early on the Saturday I decided to put up something more conservative and get some sleep. But as I was taking down the gennaker we were hit by a 34-knot gust. It whipped the gennaker straight over the front of the boat and I had to spend two hours getting it back on deck. Hadn't I already had to do this? I felt exhausted by the time I'd finished and went for a nap. I couldn't afford to sleep for long because I was in danger of being sucked into a big high-pressure system devoid of breeze and I needed to eke whatever mileage I could before that happened. While I was steering in the dying wind of the afternoon, I had a visit from a couple of small birds, who took the liberty of having a look around my cabin.

> *21 Sep* . . . I thought they would be scared out immediately by the smell of my socks . . . but these birds were down there ages so now I keep checking things, my jacket, mug, headtorch etc for any little surprises they may have left. Thats it, no more birds down below, new rule on the fine ship Pindar! OK one bird, I better stay and finish this!

With a week of the race gone, I spent much of Sunday fantasizing about home.

22 Sep   I hope you guys gave us a thought out here this morning, while I was thinking about most of you – mug of hot tea (or coffee) with fresh milk in it, fat Sunday paper in hand, read the headlines, the sports pages and maybe a quick flick through any good telly on, then have a glass of fresh cold OJ, hot toast or maybe as its Sunday, a full cooked brekkie! then read more of the paper. A walk into town, kicking the leaves (have they fallen yet? lost count of seasons!) . . . Sunday lunch with your mates in the local pub, and if you are sensible, go straight home from late lunch and relax for the rest of the afternoon with a little Grandstand and prepare for your week ahead! What a thought!

My week ahead was going to be spent playing catch-up, hoping for an unlikely turn of events that might propel me through the field. News that Bruce had broken his boom on *Ocean Planet* was double-edged. Instinctively I felt for him and hoped it wouldn't damage his chances of continuing. Once I knew he was safe, well and continuing, it had to be viewed as a chance to get past him and into sixth place at least.

By the Monday afternoon, the Class I fleet had effectively split into three races within the class. Stamm was out in front but Thierry had closed the gap to less than 60 miles. In the second group, about 300 miles further back, were Graham, Patrick and Simone, all within 30 miles of each other and apparently vying for the third spot on the first-leg podium. Some 140 miles further back again were Bruce, who was slowing, and me, on the verge of overtaking him, albeit to the north and out of his sight.

By the Tuesday morning I'd gone past and was almost 50 miles ahead of *Ocean Planet*. But I wasn't making up much ground on *Garnier*, *Tiscali* and *Hexagon*, who were all still some 100 miles ahead of me.

I began a short debate with myself about whether to raise the gennaker to transform a good day's surfing into something altogether faster. It can really make you fly in constant breeze but I was all too aware of the drawbacks if the wind were suddenly to rise above its range. A 38-knot squall came through and put an end to my procrastination. I erred on the side of caution and the gennaker stayed down. I then had a bout of 'wheel envy' when thinking about Graham aboard *Hexagon*. When I was hand-steering on *Pindar* I had to make do with a tiller. Graham had a proper steering wheel, the kind I'd used on *Royal & SunAlliance* and during the Volvo Ocean Race, when I'd spent a lot of time at the helm. It's much easier and more comfortable to handle a wheel than a tiller for long periods of time. If I'd had one on *Pindar*, it would also have been easier to imagine I was in fact on a crewed boat with twelve mates.

My morale was in need of another boost. Conditions were deteriorating and I barely had time to do anything but steer. My email update on the Wednesday was restricted to a paragraph.

25 Sep I hope everyone is getting this horrible stuff, huge waves, too much wind and its constant 40kts, not just gusts! The boat is screeching and complaining with every pounding, can't wait for it to stop, hope there is not too much damage (to the whole fleet not just Pindar!) Em x

By Thursday morning there'd been a few changes in the rates of progress. Stamm was less than 100 miles from the finish with Thierry another 100 miles behind him. *Garnier* and *Tiscali* were 350 miles farther back. About 50 miles behind them was Graham on *Hexagon*. And *he* was within *my* horizon! If I made another push, I thought fifth place was attainable. The push would need to be strategic though because I was still having problems with the sails.

I took a tactical decision to dive south, hoping that it would leave me well placed for entering the English Channel as the wind shifted round to the south-east. It was a gamble because although the numbers told me I was travelling at a decent rate, the tack south meant that I was effectively standing still in terms of distance to finish. I just hoped the strategy would pay dividends later. I should have been on the edge of my chart table seat at that stage. We were into the endgame of the first leg and everything was likely to hang on the jostling in the next twenty-four hours. I was tired though, and took what I intended to be a short nap. It lasted four hours! At the precise time when I should have been fretting and unable to keep still, I managed my longest unbroken stretch of sleep in the leg. It left me feeling almost brand new.

By Friday morning, Stamm had won the leg, setting a new monohull record for a single-handed Atlantic crossing in the process. Thierry had finished in second place and the race was on for third. My priority was to get ahead of Graham into fifth.

27 Sep I am sitting writing this wearing a balaclava and hat combination for indoor evening wear, outdoors I have an extra waterproof one on top. Everything is wet, inside and outside, and anything that was velcroed (and I mean well-velcroed) has long since come away from the walls, pockets with manuals, spare hatch covers etc. The slamming is less now than the past few days which is a relief but its not over yet, about 440 miles to the finish where I will be able to breathe a sigh of relief, and the boat too, then let the shore team (the best in the world, I might add) look more closely at my long and extensive work list! . . .

By the morning of 28 September, my fourteenth day at sea, I'd overtaken *Hexagon* and was within 50 miles of *Garnier* and

Tiscali. They both had around 150 miles to the finish and I started to believe I might be able to close them down.

> *28 Sep*   We are definitely nearing civilization again – I have just sailed through a fleet of fishing boats, a few cargo ships in the distance (where they belong), some Biscay dolphins played around the boat for a little while, and I have just come down below having had a couple of hours of beautiful steering under the bright 3/4 moon . . . didn't think that's what you wanted to hear. The smell of competition is fierce, I may have made a bunch of boat handling (more specifically – sail handling) errors at the beginning of the race but I've not spent 10 days climbing back into the fleet to finish a couple of miles behind these guys! I'm finally feeling good about the decision I made to tack South . . .

Although I had a headache, brought on by a combination of grinding my teeth and the repetitive pierce of the radar reacting to traffic, I put some loud music through the speakers to keep me wide awake.

By Saturday night I was past *Tiscali* and by Sunday morning, coming past the Lizard in the early hours, I was closing on *Garnier*. To round off a perfect twenty-four hours I then took a call on the radio from Michael Ellison of the World Sailing Speed Record Council. He informed me that I was now a record holder for becoming the fastest woman to complete a solo west-to-east transatlantic crossing in a monohull.

I crossed the finish line at 7.07 a.m. in fourth place. This was effectively upgraded to third due to Patrick de Radrigues's withdrawal. The scrutineers were first to climb aboard to make their mandatory checks on the engine seal. Mum, Dad, Philippa and the shore crew piled on afterwards and I lost myself somewhere in the midst of the group hug.

I had a magnum of champagne open and drained within minutes. Within an hour I was sitting in a press conference, nursing a drink. Maybe this wasn't going to be so bad after all.

Only four legs and 26,000 miles to go.

6

I **never imagined** my racing career would be the catalyst for a late-night, transvestite-led frenzy in a Devon town. Nor that it would lead to my dad's cousin Joan becoming a temporary chef to the former pilot of a major pop star. Nor, for that matter, that it would lead to me appearing on Breakfast TV, *Radio Five Live* and *Woman's Hour* on the same day that a newspaper cancelled an interview because I had too many arms. These things all happened during the first stopover of the Around Alone, as did a variety of stressful incidents that almost drove me nuts. Not that I foresaw any of that as I crossed the finish line in Torbay, where the Brixham Yacht Club had established a wonderfully hospitable race village.

The bay was a great place to finish the leg. It was especially so that morning, with 25 knots of wind ushering me home in the wake of a beautiful dawn. The Brixham lifeboat that had waved me off two months previously was there to accompany me back in. Mum and Dad had been up most of the night waiting for my arrival and friends had travelled from all over the place to come and see me.

The local community was hugely supportive of the race and a lot of people from the bay area had given up time to get involved and look after the skippers and their shore crews and supporters. My dad's cousin Joan was buzzing around all over the place, looking after all sorts of people. One day she heard that Brad Van Liew was partial to pizza but had discovered that there wasn't a pizza restaurant in Brixham. She baked one especially and delivered it to his boat. Quite what Brad, a laid-back Californian, thought when Joan arrived on the pontoon carrying a box of homemade margarita, I'm not sure. There was no stopping Joan once she'd started. She was great. My great-aunt Biddy also chipped in, baking cakes as usual for the crew of the *Hatherleigh*: Peter the skipper, Charlie the engineer and Darren the manager were always aboard and part of the extended family.

We also had support from local businesses including the Rising Sun, a fishermen's pub nearby. They'd printed out my daily email logs and posted them on the wall of the bar and had a photo of me over the door. I managed to pop in a few times during the stopover, strictly to convey my thanks, of course.

Though there was no doubting Brixham's warmth towards us, the party mood amongst us skippers was partly a façade. Some members of the group had ongoing financial worries that kept them permanently stressed. Every spare moment on land was spent hunting for extra sponsorship or donations to ensure they'd be able to make it round the world. We all had repairs to make to some degree. Koji had major work to do on his keel. Bruce had to fix his boom and his mainsail was in such bad shape that he wasn't sure if it would last the next leg. Simone was evidently happier with the state of *Tiscali*. He disappeared for a week and came back married! His honeymoon would be spent alone at sea.

As far as Team Pindar was concerned, we had our finances just about under control. Barring major structural repairs, we'd have sufficient resources to make it all the way round, assuming I got that far. We did have 'debt' though, in the form of time owed to sponsors and media, which entailed attending events most days and most evenings. I'd also been asked to visit some schools and colleges, which I did, and I spent a madcap day going up to London and back to do a photo shoot that had been arranged in conjunction with Brad's sponsor, Tommy Hilfiger. There were also a number of functions arranged by the race committee, some of which were compulsory to attend, like the first-leg prize-giving ceremony.

Henry and Victoria from Pitch PR ensured that if there were any moments of my time ashore when I wasn't already booked to do something they were soon filled with media interviews or other appointments. I spent one fourteen-hour day in London doing TV, radio and newspaper interviews back to back. I'd never quite realized the extent of the media's appetite for sailing! The funniest situation happened when I'd been supposed to do an interview with a guy from one of the broadsheets. He'd been intrigued by the story of a young British woman sailing single-handed around the world and said he wanted to write a feature. But when he found out that single-handed meant solo as opposed to one-armed, he cancelled! At least that lessened my load, if only by one thirty-minute slot.

Another thing I had to accept was an award at the official first-leg prize-giving ceremony. It was a grand occasion, sponsored by Mumm Champagne, with the food chosen to reflect each of the countries that would be hosting stopovers. Everyone was keen to say their piece and the speeches went on for a considerable time. At least the Mumm was flowing.

When the prizes were handed out I was most embarrassed when Sir Robin Knox-Johnston called me to the stage to collect a prize for being the first Briton home in the first leg. As I was the only Brit in the race, the award had more than a whiff of bias about it. I know it was well meant but was it really necessary? There were no prizes for the first American or Italian or Belgian or Swiss or Kiwi and I didn't feel I had done anything to warrant special treatment. I accepted my prize graciously, though. It was a bottle of Mumm, which was shared and better appreciated the following night with my family and four of my friends who'd come down from Glasgow.

A lot of normal activities, such as spending time with my mates, became huge luxuries during the Around Alone. The availability of a hot shower or bath was treasured, as was the chance to wash my hair and choose food from a menu. Walking barefoot on soft grass or sand after weeks in wet sea boots was bliss. And yet by the end of the Brixham stopover I was champing at the bit just to get back to sea.

The extraneous pressures of the race were clouding any sense of achievement I'd briefly had after the first leg. I had opted for a career in sailing because that's what I love doing and I was confident that my abilities could allow me to be competitive. But I had never envisioned being the subject of so much attention nor how much time and energy it would require to deal with that side of things. I was humbled by it and appreciative of all the interest in the race, and in *Pindar* and me as part of that. But at the end of the day I had a job to do and a race to contend. In hindsight, Brixham was a turning point for me because I actually started to crave being back at sea. My aversion to sailing solo was not markedly diminishing. But being out there on the boat, albeit alone but at least doing the job I'd always wanted to do, seemed preferable to dealing with things that I felt, rightly or wrongly, were suffocating me.

My shore crew had their own headaches. I was reliant on them completing the work needed on the boat during stopovers but the nature of the business is that no length of time is long enough for perfection and no sum of money is big enough to pay for it. Jobs were therefore graded according to what was most important. Essentials such as general maintenance, checks on the safety gear and the autopilots were top of the list. Jobs that increased boat speed or saved weight came next. There was also a 'master list' that evolved from the start of the project, basically a wish list that would lead to the near-perfect boat. You compromise on everything to fit your time scale and budget. Some of the jobs on the stopover job lists could not be done. Most of the things on the master list were never going to be feasible. If you had enough time and money, for example, you'd build a boat from scratch using the best materials and the latest designs. These designs would be improved by endless tank-testing of hulls and appendages, wind-tunnel tests for the rig and sails and exploitation of all the cutting-edge technology that Formula 1 race cars might use. But that's a different world and not one we were operating in.

In our reality we had a chartered boat, a finite budget and limited time. In Brixham, we were able to install the pedestal (grinder) for the winches. And we had to replace the Code 5 (the bigger gennaker) that had been ripped beyond repair when it had fallen over the side in the second of my gennaker nightmares during the first leg. We bought a second-hand sail that was our only option at the time. It was a lot smaller than the original and not an ideal shape for *Pindar* but it was that or nothing. The skipper who sold it to us probably did so because it had been wrong for his own boat.

There was also a problem with the gooseneck, which is the

fitting where the boom joins the deck at the base of the mast. It had twisted and needed to be rebuilt with stronger material. This is not a cheap job because it has to be custom-built but it was essential.

It didn't take long for the buzz of my arrival to subside. I'd been pleased with my comeback to take fourth place after a pretty ordinary start and a shocking display of sail handling. I'd also been pleased at making a few good tactical decisions, sticking to them and seeing them pay dividends. And I'd been looking forward to catching up with people and resting up for a while in preparation for the much longer second leg. How wrong I was about that.

Sponsorship is all about paying back your financial backer, not in cash but in exposure, so in return for me getting to sail around the world and achieve my goals, the interviews were a necessary part of the job. The interviews started soon after I'd got off the boat. There was a press conference inside and some filming outside. Then someone else wanted to film me eating a roast lunch because that fitted best with their perception of what I should be doing on a Sunday. So we did this bit of filming and then I went elsewhere and had something different for lunch. There were more cameras there, and I went through the process again of putting a fork to my mouth and holding it so the photographers could get the right pictures. And then I was asked to take a sip of beer so they could get a picture of that. And then they needed pictures of me holding up a glass of champagne. This all sounds ridiculous, I know, and it seemed all the more so to me at the time. I could appreciate that I should be available and willing to go through these various rituals but I was constantly surprised at the sheer number of people who wanted their own little piece.

I had to smile and get on with it. The alternative was that if I refused to do any part of that, or told someone that I just wanted to go and sit down for ten minutes with my mates, I would run the risk of being labelled difficult. It wouldn't matter if I'd given twenty interviews that day and visited a school and signed 200 autographs and then attended a couple of other functions. The spurned twenty-first interviewee or the 201st kid – the one who didn't get an autograph – would feel I'd let them down. It seemed a little crazy. I really was overwhelmed by the interest. Goodness knows what it must be like to be famous and to have to cope with that kind of thing on a daily basis. If you haven't coveted that kind of attention and you just want to get on with your life and work, it must become absolutely crushing.

I found it impossible to assert myself sufficiently to have any decent period of time to relax in Brixham. Mundane hassles became blown out of proportion because I allowed myself to go along with the pre-arranged plans of lots of people who were trying to help. I didn't want to kick up a fuss and say that things weren't ideal. How could I do that without looking like a curmudgeon? One example was my accommodation during the stopover. I was very lucky to be provided with a suite in a wonderful hotel in Torquay. It was a brilliant place, certainly a few notches above anywhere I'd normally stay, and the people there couldn't have been more welcoming or generous. The problem was that it was a half-hour drive away from where *Pindar* was moored in Brixham and I had no car.

This would and should have been ridiculously easy to fix. I should have hired a car as soon as I'd stepped ashore, a laughably simple solution in hindsight. At the time, it didn't really dawn on me for a couple of days that having no car would be a problem. I needed to rely on other people giving me lifts everywhere. I couldn't just nip down to the boat. I hated imposing on others to ferry me around but the tightness of my schedules meant this little inconvenience became a big headache. I should either have organized a car or else grabbed myself a berth on the *Hatherleigh*, moored near *Pindar*, from day one, although there were so many other people staying aboard that it seemed more like Piccadilly Circus than an old trawler in a seaside harbour.

I ended up just letting the situation continue, being taken back to Torquay each night. On any other occasion it would have been a luxury. By the end of the stopover I decided – again – that next time I'd have to be more independent, more vociferous and less passive. Later in the race I did this to a greater extent, possibly with the result that the team thought I was stepping back and trying to get away from them. In one sense, I was. But I needed some space and time to unwind between legs. The whole campaign was a huge adventure and I was excited about so much of it. Yet I craved quality time with friends and family when I was ashore, and I needed time to put myself back together at each stage. If I wasn't going to be a total physical and emotional wreck when my journey came to an end, I just had to do things that way.

A lot of people had come down to Brixham to see me but there was no way I could spend more than a few minutes with any of them. That left me frustrated and annoyed with myself, but again there were other demands on my time. I couldn't say I wasn't going to visit a school or I wasn't going to turn up at a local event held in my honour because I wanted to hang out with my mates. It wasn't part of the deal. I learnt that pretty quickly and made the best of the situation facing me. Again, it was bizarre, having to cope with pressures on land when the pressures I'd been most concerned with beforehand had been the ones at sea. I was becoming a malcontent and I didn't like it.

On the positive side I was on a steep learning curve. The

first leg had taught me some painful lessons about being more careful with the sails, especially when to reduce sail early. I learnt plenty about the handling of the boat and the electronics and the weather routing programmes. I was also realizing just how powerful *Pindar* could be in full flight and how much of that power I could cope with.

The challenge of the race was in sharper perspective too. I knew it would keep knocking the stuffing out of all of us, all the way round. I took some comfort from the fact that we all had an equal chance of being affected. Bruce's early problems had shown that. Graham had had broken halyards and sail battens. None of the Class II fleet were exactly having an easy time of it. I was developing a better feel for where I should be aiming in the standings, and though the other skippers were doubtless doing the same, I felt my confidence in my sailing growing.

I also took solace from having overcome the hurdles of the first leg, even those that I had placed in the way myself! The truest test of how you can cope is not when everything's going well or you're miles in front. It's when the world is crumbling around you and the sea is giving you a simultaneous kicking for good measure. It's amazing what you can bear when there's no choice and you just have to live with it. Uncomfortable situations become 'normal' quite quickly because your definition of normal redefines itself so fast. On land, sleeping for four hours a day isn't normal. Four hours in a day at sea can seem heavenly. On land, you wouldn't dream of wearing the same pair of cold, wet socks for a week or more without taking them off. At sea you don't worry about it. You relish the chance of a change, when your new socks might stay dry for several minutes. It becomes normal to have white wrinkled feet that look like they're rotting and belong in a horror movie.

At sea, exhaustion becomes a permanent state of body and mind to be battled against. When things go wrong and instant action is required to deal with it, an adrenalin rush usually materializes to help you cope. Otherwise you endure a constant downward spiral of tiredness that takes weeks of recovery on land, if and when the chance arises. You feel low on energy and heavy with fatigue. Of course you look ahead to the next tactical decision and the weather for the days ahead, but the real focus is always on the moment, the task in hand: the next sail change, the next repair or maintenance job on the list, the next meal, the current crisis. It happens and you move on, hour by hour, towards the next nap. The big picture – the finish – is always in the background somewhere. The detail is what allows you to get there.

If the pace of the racing slows it is harder to stay awake as long as on hectic days. If the fatigue becomes really bad, you can also feel a little nausea, and then you have to be even more deliberate about everything you do, or else mistakes creep in. They're inevitable anyway. Even at the time of writing, a year after finishing the race, I still feel as if I'm recovering in some ways from the lack of sleep on the Around Alone. I like my eight hours a night and try to get that every night on land. But such a prolonged period of so little sleep takes time to recover from.

That first stopover was also a first real chance to get to know some of the other skippers. Our Atlantic crossing had been hectic, so there wasn't as much communication between the skippers as there was later on. In Brixham, we were all moored at the same place and spent time in and around one another's boats. We went to a lot of functions together and that only increased the camaraderie.

Undoubtedly the event of the stopover was the party that

Andrew Pindar arranged aboard the *Hatherleigh* for my twenty-eighth birthday on 10 October. Clearly I'm biased but the sheer numbers of people who were still dancing on the decks at 3 a.m. were testament to a pretty decent bash. All the skippers were there except Koji, who was still doing some urgent repair to his keel in time for the second leg. The other skippers' families and friends and shore crews came, as did loads of local people who'd been involved in hosting the race.

I arrived late because I'd spent the afternoon with Graham Dalton at a community college on a visit that was part of the HSBC Global Education Programme. HSBC had put a lot of money into the race and their programme and it made sense for more than one skipper to be involved. On a brutally practical level, if one of us came a cropper, at least there'd be someone left to carry on the work! The race was useful as an educational tool. The kids we visited stayed in touch with our progress via the internet and email and their teachers would use the Around Alone as a basis for various lessons in geography or physics or whatever. I personally got a boost from all the supportive emails that were forwarded to *Pindar* by kids from all over the world as I went on my way. And if even just a couple of them were inspired by our projects to pursue their own dreams then it was worthwhile.

When I did arrive at the party, after the college visit and a couple of meetings, I felt fit to drop, or at least go back to the hotel, watch a film and relax. What a party pooper! But by the time I had a glass of champagne in my hand I began to unwind and we had a fantastic evening. The *Hatherleigh* was moored in the harbour, with a small marquee on the dock alongside. Peter Wilkinson, Pindar's marketing director, had booked a band, The Ambassadors, and they played on a little stage in the marquee. As the evening wore on and the tide went out, the stage gradually rose above the crowds on the *Hatherleigh*. The music ranged from Beatles stuff and other Sixties hits to Queen and Bruce Schwab! Bruce took his guitar up on stage during the band's break and sang a song about the race and in praise of Koji. My abiding memory is being among this crowd of hundreds of people – friends, family, skippers, support crew, local dignitaries, the local lifeboat staff and all manner of Brixham well-wishers – doing the Timewarp from *The Rocky Horror Show*. It left a few people open-mouthed, especially some of the older guests and overseas contingent, when one of the guys from the band appeared in full transvestite gear to lead the dancing. But within seconds everyone was going absolutely bonkers following him. Very amusing!

It was a great party and I had the hangover to prove it the next morning. I left to go back to the hotel about 4 a.m. and I wasn't the last to depart by any means. I stayed up chatting to my best friend Jane for a while. I'd barely had any time to see her during the stopover. And then I got a couple of hours' sleep before getting up for a 9 a.m. skippers' briefing on the Friday morning ahead of the Sunday restart.

There was the usual last-minute rush to get everything aboard for the next leg. I was looking forward to getting on with it, although I did appreciate the chance for extra sleep when the start was delayed by a day. A strong easterly wind made it risky to get the boats off the docks safely and undamaged.* There was no point in sending twelve skippers out into conditions that could destroy the boats on the first day out. That was the ocean's job, as we were about to find out.

* To start a solo race on a lee shore with very strong winds is just plain dangerous.

7

The Bay of Biscay can be a violent, unforgiving place. I'd experienced that a few times, especially during the Transat Jacques Vabre in 1999 when Hurricane Irene hammered the fleet and took the life of Paul Vatine. After the race I saw some video footage filmed from the container ship that rescued Paul's co-skipper, Jean Maurel. As Jean was lifted from the hull of their upturned trimaran, *Group André*, all you could hear above the howling wind was him shouting. He was calling Paul's name. Images like those don't fade easily. In fact they may have grown worse in my head over time.

Paul Vatine was forty-two and had got married twelve months earlier to Mireille, his girlfriend of ten years. He'd been a professional skipper for eighteen years and had made thirty Atlantic crossings, including nine solo. The TJV had been 'his' race. He'd won it in 1993 and 1995 and had finished second in 1997. News of his disappearance and the later confirmation that he had not been found was very sobering. That incident and the images I saw later was the starkest first-hand experience I'd had of the perilous nature of the ocean. Nature always has the upper hand and always will.

When I thought about the number of sea miles Paul had

under his belt, it did make me wonder how long I wanted to make a career of this kind of sailing. Paul was one of the most experienced members of the 1999 TJV fleet and probably the least likely person anyone would have expected not to come back. Sailing has that danger factor – apparently higher with multi-hulls – and you know that it only takes a bad day here and there to increase that danger dramatically.

As we headed towards the Bay of Biscay in the Around Alone, we knew the weather was bad. I didn't get much chance to worry about it in the first two days out of Brixham because so much else went wrong. Within minutes of waving goodbye to the people who'd gathered on Berry Head to cheer us off, I had a problem with the ballast system. Simone sailed past me within a few miles of our departure and shouted good luck. He must have wondered why I was soaked from head to toe already.

To fill the water ballast tanks, which increase the stability of the boat, I had to push a valve down that in turn pushed a tube out of the bottom of the boat. There was a hole in the tube that faced forward when I was trying to fill the tank and aft when I was emptying the tank. The forward motion of the boat forced water into the tube – and therefore into the tank – when the hole was facing forward. When it was facing aft, the water racing past the hole caused a suction that emptied the tank. The faster I was sailing, the faster the tanks filled or emptied.

When I pulled the handle up to close the valve, the whole handle came off and left a gaping hole in the bottom of the boat. Suddenly there was a fountain like the kind you see in the Tom and Jerry cartoons, except there was no Jerry on top, just me getting drenched. I immediately stuck my hand over the hole to try to stop the flow. But there was a jagged edge around the top of valve where the handle had broken. It sliced into my hand, leaving an inch-long cut across my palm. It wasn't particularly deep but it was bleeding quite a lot and stung due to the salt water.

I was still only a short distance from land at this stage. There were still plenty of spectator boats in the vicinity and they must have thought it quite odd that one minute I was on deck 'enjoying the sunny day' and the next, after nipping below, had resurfaced drenched. I realized the only way to get out of the situation was to effectively close the valve off at a lower point.

I stared at the valve I needed to close. I couldn't reach it from where I was and had to take a couple of steps to get there. I went for it and of course the fountain of water shot up again for a few more seconds while I closed it. The flow reduced to a gentle stream until the connecting pipes were empty too. I scrambled back on deck to check I wasn't about to hit any of the spectator boats or fishing buoys. I must have looked in a right state. My hand continued to bleed as I botched the handle back on using tape and cord to secure it in a rudimentary fashion. It would have to stay like that for a while, probably until Cape Town.

By the Monday evening we already had a big breeze and overnight the barometer reading plummeted. Whatever we were heading towards was going to be rough and unstable. One gust came through at 52 knots but I was too busy to be paying much attention to the speed. *Pindar* was pitching like a bucking bronco. With the huge waves and ugly motion of the boat, my compass started spinning round 360 degrees. I only realized there was a problem with it when we changed course suddenly and involuntarily because the autopilot has to rely on the information it is fed. The boom flew over to the other side and I thought we were heading for a tumble. I had no idea which direction the wind was coming from and the waves were pounding us from all sides.

There was no simple solution such as heading down the swell because the sea was so confused. I sailed pretty close to the eye of the tiny low-pressure system that may have been developing off the front of an older system.

As I took down the mainsail while simultaneously trying to redistribute the ballast to give me more stability, the boat went over. Technically this wasn't a capsize because the mast didn't hit the water, although a little more wind would have meant that happening. The four tonnes of lead in the keel are there to make sure the boat rights itself in these situations. She righted herself but the wind blew off my hat and head torch so I was now working in darkness. At least the mainsail was down, albeit in a messy heap on the boom. I went down below to sort out the cabin. The pilot computer had been almost torn from its fitting. I switched everything off and back on again and the gyro compass restabilized. I went back outside and lashed the mainsail to the boom, where it stayed for twelve hours before I rehoisted it when the wind dropped below 40 knots. I then had a chance to make various minor repairs, empty the bilges, charge the boat's batteries and think about sleep. That was postponed for an hour because I spotted a ship that looked like a survey vessel. It was stationary but I was concerned it might start moving and run me down, so waited until I was safely past before heading for the bunk.

The weather we'd just been through was only a precursor of the really rough stuff and I needed to conserve some energy. I wrapped my sleeping bag around the top half of my body, leaving the wet half uncovered in the hope that I might dry off. I kept my boots on in case I needed to make a dash back on to deck if the radar alarm went off or the boat made an unusual motion.

By the early hours of Wednesday the sea had flattened as if

there had not been a breath of wind passing through. I knew it was an illusion of calm and the little monster we'd already encountered had a bigger, uglier brother – Hurricane Kyle – waiting for us ahead. I only found out later that the Around Alone had become a keen discussion point among leading meteorologists at the time. As a 'significant storm', the hurricane was intensely debated, as were the options that were open to the fleet to handle it.

Alan Paris aboard *BTC Velocity* was the first skipper to make the decision to head for the shelter of La Coruña, Spain. John Dennis followed, then Brad, who'd sustained damage to his reefing system. Tim, Derek and Koji all followed, meaning the whole Class II fleet had headed for shelter, a wise move, especially as the smaller boats would be arriving where the storm was later than us and would have no chance whatsoever of outrunning the beast. Of the Class I boats, Bruce also decided to head for Spain, whilst Simone had already been forced to stop in France to make emergency repairs to his autopilots. Each skipper had his own reasons for going ashore, be it lack of experience in that part of the North Atlantic, or delicate sails, or worries that their boats wouldn't cope. I had none of those reasons.

The skippers who opted to keep out of the storm's way had made their decisions by Thursday, 17 October. By then I was off the Bay of Biscay and preparing for the worst. The details had been confirmed. A vast low-pressure system was developing in the Atlantic. The central pressure was predicted at 975 millibars, which is extreme. Winds were forecast in excess of Gale Force. This was going to be one rough ride but I took a calculated decision that I could drive through it, head towards the centre until the front came over, tack on the shift that came with the front and then head south. In the early hours of Friday, waiting for the fringe of this thing to start nibbling us up, I sent an email ashore to explain my decision.

18 Oct I feel as if I am going to battle – I don't know because I have never been and never wish to, and I have been through a few storms before this one, but there has been so much talk about it, it sounds enormous and very much out of the ordianry. It could be very easy to base a decision on others actions but I am in a different situation on a different boat. I have looked at all the information carefully and repeatedly and have made an informed decision as to my tactics so please don't think I am going into this ignorantly. I have a solid boat which I have spent all day preparing for this weather, everything is lashed down, stacked, fixed since the last storm. I have spent the day checking everything – including the backup pilot, backup compass for the backup pilot, I ran them all for a couple of hours today, apart from checking them just to be extra sure of the procedure of changing over under pressure. I have made a mass of pasta in case it is too hard to even make cous cous (which is only boiling a kettle anyway!) topped up fuel so I don't need to in bad weather, made water for a week. I have had lots of sleep and still have a good few hours before it hits hard. I know this storm will be severe, I am expecting that, and Thierry (Solidaires) made a very good point at the press conference that for the first week we are seamen then when we have passed this storm we can race again. I fully understand everyone that is heading for shelter – I am almost jealous simply cause I will miss having a beer with my other skipper mates (and a hot shower, dry bed that doesn't move, food that takes more than 1 pan to make . . . . .). I wonder if they will all decide to leave again at the same time and even have a restart as all the class 2 fleet appear to be heading for shelter. I see that Simone is still in Brest, and Bruce has just written me a note saying he doesn't think his mainsail will hold up to the weather (i have seen it, he has a very good point), I have noticed that Solidaires [I mean

Hexagan here] has wavered from the obvious course but maybe he took a different tactic through the high pressure ridge we have just passed. So it leaves just Bernard, Thierry and myself before we get to the crunch! Psycology alone would have me already sitting in a bar in Portugal but I wouldn't be here if I wasn't confident of coming out of this storm in good shape! Well all thats left is to sleep, wait for the wind to build, reef early and take it easy. . . . . a long way to go! Em x

So that was it, decision made. My options had been threefold. I could have gone to Spain or Portugal and sat in a bar waiting to restart in the tail end of the storm. I could have tried to skirt around the edge, changing course to avoid the centre. That would have meant staying at sea while hoping I could dodge this massive system. I thought the drawback was that I'd end up sailing further in winds and seas that would still be terrible. I reckoned that would mean a greater overall chance of damage than heading straight into the heart of it. I aimed for the centre.

To say I was unafraid wouldn't be wholly true. But I didn't experience fear as I perceive it. I fear not succeeding, not being happy, not being able to support myself. These fears ebb and flow depending on how happy I am with my life and work at any one time. How long can I be a sailor? What will I do when I give it up as a profession? Will I be content one day to settle down, have a family and do all the 'normal' things that my friends do?

My fears in the eye of that storm in October 2002 were much more mundane and based on practicalities. I worried that I might fall or be washed from the deck. That was the likeliest danger, especially when I knew I wouldn't just be able to lock down in the cabin and sit it out. I'd need to be at the helm to hand-steer. But I'd be harnessed and holding on so it was a calculated risk.

I wasn't overly concerned about coping with minor injuries. First aid is important at sea. Being able to keep a cool head to administer it to yourself is even more so. But I was confident of the basics from studying sports medicine. I'd also soaked up a lot of practical medical knowledge during *Royal & SunAlliance*'s Jules Verne campaign and since then. Having seen some gruesome sights on my hospital visits in the run-up to that record attempt, dealing with the majority of sailing injuries was easy by comparison.

Though people die in ocean races, they usually drown rather than sustain wounds that kill them slowly. Horror stories involving self-administered major surgery are thankfully rare, although they do occur. A well-known French sailor, Bertrand De Broc, bit his tongue off in an accident in the Southern Ocean during a Vendée Globe. He sewed it back on. Pete Goss also did an operation on himself, during the 1996–7 Vendée, on a badly damaged elbow. He performed it single-handed (obviously and in more senses than one), using a mirror and instructions sent to him by email.

Fear of the conditions in themselves was never an issue. Screaming winds and big waves don't unnerve me. Or rather, they don't unnerve me if I have faith that my boat is secure and can handle them. I had faith in *Pindar*. I didn't dwell on the possibility of capsizing. These things can happen in much more temperate conditions and often, even in the fiercest storm, you're fine. I suppose somewhere in my mind I held open the possibility that if I did become genuinely fearful for the boat, I would be able to take whatever course would lead me away from the storm, even if it was in the wrong direction for the race. But that was just being practical. You can't afford to waste time thinking the worst. It'll only become more likely to happen.

I worried more about suffering non-fatal structural damage – ripped sails or a crippled rig in particular. I was already placing myself mentally outside the storm, safe on the other side. I wanted *Pindar* to be in decent shape when we got there.

I was also slightly nervous about the chance of a collision. With bad visibility, low cloud, squalls and big waves there's always the chance that the radar won't be as effective as it needs to be. Fishing boats and container vessels were the worry, but then in weather like this they were unlikely to be heading for the centre of a storm anyway.

My last fear was for the safety of the others and I hoped that they were all taking their own precautions. Yes, it was a race and I wanted to come out ahead, but not at the expense of anyone's health or safety. Until we were out of the danger zone, it was very much all for one and one for all.

The storm began to smother us on the Friday afternoon. The almost eerie part was the start, when the big swells came rolling in almost smoothly. They grew and grew and I knew that it was only a matter of time before the tremendous winds that were driving these billions of tons of water would follow. The barometer dropped like a stone and I knew I was about to feel the force.

It built in intensity over a period of eight hours and by that stage it was truly raging. The intensity became apparent when the kettle, which I'd secured to the stove with metal bars specifically for the task, was shaken loose. Then the whole gimballed stove came off. I just had to leave it off and deal with the debris later.

Outside, where I had to spend a good part of the storm, the swells had become full-blown monster waves. They in turn seemed to gang together to form even bigger swells carrying more, still taller waves. Eventually the tops of the waves started getting blown off by the wind and I was into severe gale territory. The sea tried hard to swallow us and the wind was blowing it down again. There was so much water in the air that I didn't know whether it was rain or spray. I had so much salt water pouring down my face that I couldn't even differentiate by taste. Everything tasted of salt. My lips were wrinkly from the stuff. My whole field of vision was alternately grey from the gloom or white from waves and rarely anything in between. At night it all turned black although there was a moment just before sunset on that first evening when I could just make out a small, hazy segment of orange.

For anyone who has never been in a big storm at sea, the makers of *The Perfect Storm* were not that far off. Though the effects in the movie were obviously created by a toy ship on a small wave and then blown up for effect, the fundamentals of scale and noise and violence were pretty close to the mark. I can't say the same about the welding scene, which seems about as feasible in those conditions as a tea party on deck, but then you can't have everything.

As Hurricane Kyle tried to do its worst, I had no option but to stay up on deck for long periods. I needed to steer and watch for other vessels. Besides, there was probably as much danger in the cabin as there was outside. I was thrown forcibly across on more occasions than I find it comfortable to remember. I was also thrown around the deck to the end of my safety line but it did its job and kept me aboard.

At some point in the early hours of Saturday I checked in with the race HQ on the satellite phone to let them know I was coping. I could barely stand up and hold on to the receiver at the same time. A log was kept of all conversations between the race organizers and the skippers. One conversation went as follows.

'How are you?' they asked.

'It's fairly brutal out here,' I said. 'Last night was really tough. At one point I was looking at the wind speed indicator and saw a steady 72 knots. That's one heck of a lot of wind.'

My voice was described in the race report as being 'calm' and as though I were having an amiable fireside chat. I think it must have been my autopilot speaking. The 'heck of a lot of wind' was also an understatement.

'Sometimes it feels as if my arms are going to be wrenched from my sockets as I try to hang on to the navigation table,' I said, apparently not too fazed. 'How am I doing against Bernard and Thierry?'

I did have my anxieties. There's always a concern when a very deep depression or low-pressure system comes towards you. Because I'd been through severe storms before and I knew approximately what it was going to feel like, it made the anticipation worse. It's not fear, more a numbed expectancy. I knew the boat would be thrown around, smashed against the waves and sent diving almost in freefall to the bottom of troughs. I knew that my face would be blasted for days by seawater. I knew that I would only be able to move around the boat by holding on to something for support almost the whole time, even though I also wore a harness while on deck. I knew what these things felt like, and when they happened I wasn't surprised, just uncomfortable. I wore my survival suit throughout, which is a full, dry suit with a hood and a high collar, and I had an extra layer of clothing underneath. But it doesn't stop the water stinging your face.

Such physical discomfort was more distressing than any

mental turmoil. If anything, once the storm was upon us and I was inside it, I felt quite content with my decision. The more *Pindar* withstood – and the first night was atrocious – the more I thought she'd keep holding herself together. As for me, I felt pretty together, mentally at least. I'd called Mum and Dad beforehand and they were fine. Mum told me to make sure I kept my harness on. I'd called Andrew Pindar and he'd told me just to stay safe. I felt safe within the context of the situation. I don't see myself as a taker of extreme risks. I am competitive so will tend to push myself rather than hold back. But I'd made a decision based on risks and benefits, not on any urge to be some brave crusader against a force I could never defeat.

As the storm continued through the Saturday, I began to feel physically exhausted. It was an odd kind of exhaustion. My limbs were aching and tired but the adrenalin was keeping me moving. There was so much to do just to control the boat that there was no chance of rest.

Thankfully I wasn't seasick. I have been sick on occasions but this storm wasn't one of them. There were times when I felt a bit nauseous with the smell of the diesel swilling around the soggy, rocking tip that the cabin had become. But it never got serious.

The cabin was an utter mess. All the velcroed packets had come off the walls, and spares that were secured had come loose. The light switch was dangling. The whole place stank of diesel. Sleep was absolutely out of the question because of the noise and motion. Even if it hadn't been too dangerous for a nap, it would have been impossible to stay in the bunk. I tried raising it so there was only a slither of space in which to wedge myself. It wasn't a great success and I gave that up. At least there was no chance for sitting around feeling lonely. I was just too busy.

My appetite was unaffected and I ate snacks and pre-prepared cold pasta, washed down with water. Hot drinks were a no-no during much of the storm because of the dangers of trying to boil water. When I did chance it, they often ended up on the floor or full of salt water before I'd had chance to drink much anyway. I started to crave a still room furnished with a dry bed and en suite hot shower. The thought of having fresh food and maybe a glass of wine was one daydream. Some chance. Such notions, or indeed any thoughts outside the confines of keeping the boat together and on course, didn't hang around long.

On the Sunday I received news that *Tiscali* had been dismasted. Simone had rejoined the race after stopping in France but had then been hit by the bad weather. Aside from the disappointment, he was fine though, and was limping towards La Coruña for another set of repairs.

Inside the storm, some of us were starting to think beyond survival to racing again. Bernard Stamm had gone further west than Thierry or me and had opened up a lead of about 100 miles. Thierry was still feeling the brunt. He described conditions as 'totally unbearable'. In a dispatch to the organizers, he said: 'The storm is moving slowly from the west and is completely barring the route, so you can't go over it nor through it as it is so big. The only way through is to tackle it head on and tough it through the southerly gale under storm jib alone. Combat gear for this is in the form of foul-weather clothing, well sealed so it doesn't leak water. Energy bars and drinks keep me going for meals right now. I seek refuge in the cabin, but get thrown from the bunk so rest in the sail locker or on the floor, although mostly I am hunched up into a ball to protect my head in my knees.'

By late afternoon on the Sunday, I felt we were through the worst of it. The winds had eased and though the sea stayed big and choppy for quite a while, I was able to put up more sail.

20 Oct The wind has finally died to spend most of its time in the high 20s gusting 30s with the odd 40 as opposed to 40–50 gusting 70, so looking good. the swell is reducing but thats not saying alot, I still have to hold on with one hand all the time and both when I can feel the boat launching, the landing is never very pretty!

This morning the wind died a little, I thought time to go a little more sail, I don't want to lose the place on Solidaires now I have taken him . . . .

Once I have rebolted the stove to the buulkhead, I plan to cook up a good meal if I can hold the pan on it, I have been living on Mum's banana bread, jaffa cakes and nuts for a few days, all very good but I think something more substantial is in order! . . .

Really could do with finding somewhere that does a good massage as my body feels like its been in the ring for a week, but may have to wait a few weeks! Oh oh, I've done it now, after that, a takeaway pizza with my mates, wrapped up inside on a cold miserable day with a huge mug of steaming tea, even the pizza guy gets soaked running from his car to your door so you have to tip him, a few good movies and know that you don't have to go outside til the sun comes out tomorrow! What a thought, I'm not even going to describe the particulars of this place – I have not been out of my drysuit and harness since Thursday, except of course to use the loo but even then you need to pick your moment in case you need to run on deck to ease something or do a major course alteration.

By Monday I was almost back into full racing mode, though the post-storm squalls still had me on edge. By the Tuesday morning, 22 October, I had emerged intact and been greeted at dawn by the incredible sight of Las Palmas in the Canary Islands. I found it amazing that such a high land mass was just sitting there in the middle of the ocean. It was refreshing, almost comforting to see a place where life was going on as normal.

It was the first bonus in a day when the position reports also showed I'd emerged from Hurricane Kyle in second place. My dash towards the middle had paid off. Admittedly Bernard had got out ahead of me and had then shot off like a robber's dog to extend his lead. But I was ahead of everyone else.

The only upset in the day happened late on the Tuesday, just before nightfall. I was sitting at the chart table when an almighty crash stopped the boat dead from 12 knots. I knew it wasn't another vessel because I'd just that minute come down from the deck. I shot forward in the seat, with my pelvis taking the impact on the chart table edge. It was painful but probably better than having been flung from a standing position against the hull.

As soon as I caught my breath, I staggered on to the deck as the boat started to accelerate again. I was just in time to see a massive light-grey object just under the surface, and a wash over it. At the time I was convinced it was a semi-submerged container because I had stopped so suddenly. Whatever I'd hit had definitely been very heavy and very solid. But when we had a chance to look at the keel in Cape Town there was no apparent damage whatsoever, so it could only have been something soft. I may have just woken a whale with a bit of a shock.

My turn for a similar experience wasn't long in coming.

8

The storm hadn't long abated when my nerves and patience were pushed to their limits by a succession of setbacks and frights. The cast of conspirators sent to test me included a Frenchman, several shoals of flying fish, Neptune and the inhabitants of a mystery vessel who scared me witless and brought my vulnerability as a solo yachtswoman into terrifying focus.

The Frenchman was Thierry, who bounced back from the ordeal of Hurricane Kyle to overtake me and move back into second place behind Bernard Stamm. I should have expected nothing less from such an experienced competitor but it was galling anyway. In the evening poll report on the Wednesday, Bernard was about 300 miles ahead of me but I was still some 20 miles up on Thierry, who was third. By 6 a.m. on Thursday, the polls were telling me that Thierry was 2 miles ahead and making faster progress. On the Thursday evening I received an email from *Solidaires*.

'I can smell young blonde English girl in the area!' Thierry joked to mark the fact that he'd gone past.

'Oh yeah?' I replied. 'Well, I'm sure it's better than spending days downwind of a Frenchman!'

It was heartening at least to get Thierry's message. After the eleven days we'd endured since leaving Brixham and with the adrenalin rush from the storm gone, the solitude was coming back to the fore. I tried to counter it by staying in touch with my fellow competitors via brief emails. These involved all the banter you'd find among any crewed yacht in a race. It just so happened that in the Around Alone the participants were each on their own boat, spaced across hundreds of miles. But the communication somehow made the race more real, reminding me that it involved other people instead of being a solitary exercise with just dots on the charts as competitors. It was precisely what I needed to keep my spirits up and take my mind off boat speed and boring food.

Thierry was the most communicative of the other skippers at that stage because we were having a good race amongst ourselves. In the first leg I'd never been within touching distance and we hadn't communicated at all. I heard from Bernard in the second leg too but cyberspace was the closest I'd get to him before Cape Town. I was also in touch with John 'Pops' Dennis a few times as I knew he was having a tough time of it. He, like me, was starting to feel the lack of human contact and our occasional 'chin up' messages were always appreciated. John's stop in Spain, along with the rest of the Class II boats, made his second leg much longer than originally scheduled.

Thierry replied gamely to my accusations that he was a stinky Frenchman by explaining precisely how he'd gone past me. He'd found decent winds of 30 knots and had hand-steered for fifteen hours straight to get the best from his gennaker. I was too exhausted at that stage to contemplate a similar stint myself. I took solace from the fact that there were still 5,000 miles to go to Cape Town and plenty of time to make amends.

Having fought so hard through the storm to keep myself in a good position, I wasn't going to let a little setback stop me pushing again. I'd already proved once that I could overtake Thierry and I made it my mission for the leg to do it again. I'd entered the race for a variety of reasons, one of which was to test myself against some of the most experienced single-handed skippers in the business. If I wasn't going to make an effort to beat them at this stage, when was I?

Bernard and Thierry were very much in the race to win it, as was Brad in Class II. Some of the others had different motivations. Pops wanted to prove to the world that diabetes needn't stop you aiming for the stars. Tim Kent, a good sailor from the Great Lakes, had told his mates at his yacht club he was going to sail solo round the world and went out and did it. Koji was doing the Around Alone in memory of his mentor, Yukoh, who'd died trying. Simone was in love with the sea, and drawn to the lightness and dark it shed on his soul.

I was in it to see what happened. There were benefits beyond the challenge in itself: months on end when I needed just to think about speed, direction, safety, battery power and sleep instead of bills, paperwork, how I was going to replace yet another mobile phone that I'd got wet and where I'd put my keys. These pluses were pretty much balanced by the drawbacks: the solitude, the physical hardships, the peripheral responsibilities. The bottom line was that I was there. I didn't know if I could win. I didn't even know if I'd finish. But then that's the point of sport, isn't it? I was responsible for myself and for *Pindar*. Our results would ultimately tell us how well we'd both worked.

One thing I hadn't anticipated was a brief fixation with flying fish among my supporters. Not long after Thierry had gone ahead of me, the conditions turned tropical (which wasn't a shock as we'd entered the Tropics). What was more surprising was the sheer number of flying fish that seemed intent on jumping aboard.

I started to find them dead on deck and in the cockpit and mentioned this in an email log. Within hours I was being inundated with recipes.

As I got further south into the warmer weather and the trade winds, the flying fish became even more prevalent. Massive shoals of them kept jumping out of the water, fleeing some imminent danger from a predator, presumably. They might have thought *Pindar* was that predator.

These amazing creatures were fairly sizeable, up to a foot in length. They looked like herrings with the addition of butterfly-shaped 'wings', which are actually fins. Their name derives partly from that and partly from the illusion that they fly. In fact they just jump out of the water at speeds of up to 30 mph and then are carried through the air, for 100 feet or more, with their 'wings' spread.

The fish rarely hit the boat or landed on the deck during daylight. But when it was dark they seemed unable to see or even sense where they were going. Maybe they were asleep. It was mostly at night that I'd hear them tapping against the hull or thudding on to the deck. If they didn't die instantly on impact, which normally made their eyes pop out, I could hear them flapping around trying to find their way back into the water. It was always best to go and locate them with my torch and get them back over the side as quickly as possible. They shed big scales at an incredible rate, and all over the place. If they didn't get washed or thrown over the side the fish tended to dry in the sun and then the scales would blow into the cockpit and cabin, sticking everywhere including my feet.

Koji ate the flying fish, which always sounded pretty tasty when he talked about it. But I never plucked up the courage to try them. I love sashimi when it's prepared by someone who knows what they're doing. I didn't. I've only ever filleted big fish for the barbecue and I had no idea what to do with those bony little things. I didn't fancy the fishy smell on my hands afterwards, either!

There were two other reasons why I didn't cook them, using some of the recipes I was sent. The first was a lack of supplementary ingredients. I don't know what everyone thought was in my store cupboard but it certainly didn't stretch to freshly squeezed lemon, onions and fresh herbs. If any of the recipes had included breakfast cereal, snack bars or freeze-dried milk, I would have been fine. The second reason was that I didn't want the cabin stinking of a fishmonger. The weather was heating up and it was getting stuffy down there already. I could happily do without the added aroma of burnt flying fish. I also passed up the chance to eat the occasional squid that landed on deck after being washed in by the waves. I would have boiled a few shrimps after ploughing through a wave loaded with them but there just weren't quite enough big ones to make it worthwhile.

The temperature rose quickly as we got further south during that second week. It was great to be back in the trade winds and warm weather, especially after the storm. I started to dry out my damp clothes. I changed into shorts and started walking around in bare feet. Daily bucket showers became an option again. When it was really hot, I just tipped a bucket of water over my head at regular intervals.

Sailing in the trade winds can be great, with puffy clouds evenly spread across the sky. It's also possible to smell the land or even see evidence of it. Though I didn't get any Sahara dust on the deck during the Around Alone, I had seen it on a previous trip when I'd been within a couple of hundred miles of the African coast.

In general, the sea becomes steadier. There aren't any massive swells due to incoming low-pressure systems. The wind is steady at 20–25 knots so you don't need to keep changing the sails. That provides the chance to rack up some miles and get some of the tasks ticked off the ever-expanding jobs list. So much for the theory. Neptune always reserves the right to change the rules, as I found out on the second Saturday of the leg, 26 October.

At 6 a.m. the world was a fine and dandy place. The polling report had Bernard in the lead. He was due west of Guinea with around 4,600 miles to go to Cape Town. I was due west of Senegal (the section north of The Gambia) and had about 4,900 miles to go. Thierry was about 50 miles ahead of me, further west, but I wasn't losing touch. And as Bernard wasn't showing any signs of hugely increasing his lead, I still felt I had a chance to catch up. It was a beautiful sunny morning and I had the spinnaker up in 10 knots of breeze.

The mass of black cloud came from nowhere. It was moving so fast that I only got the spinnaker down minutes before it arrived. I was quickly enveloped and there was a surge of white water. It was a Doldrums squall. For the sheer unexpected nature of its arrival, it was more frightening than the hurricane. There'd been no warning and I'd been totally unprepared and then BAM! My serene morning was ripped apart by 45 knots raging out of the blue. If I'd had the bigger sail up when it hit, I dread to think what might have happened. The sail would probably have blown down, if not away. Worse, it might have stayed up and exerted so much pressure on the mast that the whole rig would have been in danger.

As it was, I clung to the tiller for dear life and hoped it wouldn't last too long. I had too much sail up, so was having trouble steering, meaning that I couldn't leave the helm to switch on the autopilot. Therefore I couldn't reef the mainsail and decrease the power. I thought it would soon be over so just clung on and went with the flow, downwind and west instead of south, my preferred route.

Five hours later, with every muscle in my shoulders fit to burst and my eyes like saucers from trying to keep control, we emerged from the squall having taken a drastic veer west. We'd been wiped out (tipped over) twice but thankfully recovered. Until I checked the time I had no idea how long I'd been at the helm. The rain had been torrential. Big waves over the bow had filled the cockpit. And there was I, in a thin jacket and shorts, soaked to the skin and numb with cold.

It eased as quickly as it came on and before I knew it I was almost becalmed. My weekend was just about to get sinister.

Sent from Pindar, Sunday 27 October, 1am
I am writing this at 1am, it is still pitch black outside, the moon was out for a short while but is covereed by clouds again and there is only 3–4kts of wind, I'm moving maybe 1–2kts at a good moment in the left over chop frm the squall today, the boom is swinging uselessly around, and I have just been spooked, really spooked. I had sorted out myself and the boat following the squall, checked for damage, mopped up the mess basically. Just about to settle into a napping routine to catch up after a few tough days. literally climbing into my bunk, the VHF bursts into life. not the usual crackle of something far off that you can't make out but a crystal clear whistle, like someone saying, Helllooooo, I'm over heeeeere! Nearly jumped out of my skin . . .

When there's as little wind as there was that night, you spent your time tiptoeing around, trying not to move too fast because you don't want to unsettle the boat. You make minute adjustments to the sails to eke any breath of breeze that might keep you moving.

Everything had been done so quietly that I could hear whether I'd lost any more of my meagre speed. Suddenly to hear the radio screech into life sent my heart pounding even before I began to think about who or what it might be. I went closer to the radio and the signal was crystal clear, which meant whoever was transmitting was nearby.

I walked quietly up on deck and peered out into the night. The moon was obscured by cloud. It was totally dark. I made a slow, 360-degree turn to see if I could pick up the outline of another vessel. In the distance, on the western horizon, I could see one very faint light. It must have been 25 miles away at least. It couldn't have been responsible for the noises on the radio. It was too far away. Maybe I was imagining things. I went back down below to check the radar.

At first I thought it was an error. They happen sometimes. You see an unidentified object on the screen, normally just once, and then it disappears. It's an occasional electronic glitch, usually caused by a wave or a swell.

I thought the blip I was watching was a glitch.

I hoped it was a glitch.

It wasn't a glitch.

The longer I watched the radar scan around the 360 degrees of the boat, the more I felt a tightness in my stomach. Each time the radar went over this particular point the blip was there. It wasn't just a wave or a swell. It was a solid object, a boat. It was less than a mile away and it wasn't moving. Whoever was aboard was on the end of the VHF. I could hear expletives and then mumbled, indistinguishable noises.

Pindar wasn't moving. We couldn't move. There was no

wind. I went back on deck for another look. I knew there was a boat out there but it was so dark I couldn't see it. It wasn't using any navigation lights, which is illegal. Why would someone choose to have their lights off? I was becoming quite anxious.

I went back below. Whoever was on the boat was swearing and then began to sing. I could hear talking in a language I couldn't decipher. It was possibly Spanish or Portuguese but I wasn't sure. My best guess was that it was an unlicensed vessel, perhaps under the control of several inebriated fishermen. But I also had a seed of concern that maybe they weren't fishermen.

Only hours before, I'd received and read the latest NavArea (navigation area) report. All shipping receives NavArea reports on a daily basis with updates on potential hazards. The reports are aimed primarily at commercial shipping but it is useful to read them anyway. Occasionally there are requests asking all boats in a particular area to keep a lookout for a vessel that has failed to arrive at its destination and has gone missing. At other times there is information about changes in buoyage in shipping channels or ports. It is worth looking at.

The latest NavArea report, the one I'd read a few hours before, had included updates on piracy, detailing 'actual and attempted attacks'. Normally I would have skimmed that section because piracy had been most common in ports or against anchored ships that were easy targets. But this particular report had mentioned pirates who had been boarding vessels under way, which marked a change in tactics. The report had opened: 'This broadcast warns ships in passage in West Africa, South America, Central America and the Caribbean waters regarding piracy and armed robbery.'

There was a list of recent attacks by pirates around the world. Six pirates in a speedboat, four armed with guns and long knives, had boarded a cargo ship off Brazil on 29 September. Two pirates with knives had boarded a container ship in Peru on 11 October. A group of seven pirates armed with knives and machetes had boarded a cargo ship in Guyana on 16 October. Under the section headed 'Piracy-prone areas and warnings' there was West Africa, and specifically Dakar, to my east. There was an unidentified vessel sitting a mile away without lights.

With my imagination running riot, I called Robin Gray, Pindar's team manager, who was on twenty-four-hour call for just that kind of situation. He was concerned but did his best to reassure me. It was probably a fishing vessel, he said. They probably didn't even know I was there. Shortly after I hung up, the noises started again. Then one of the people at the other end of the VHF started to sing a kind of love song in perfect, though heavily accented, English. It was littered with expletives. I called Robin back but the singing had stopped by the time I got through to him. He got the coastguard to ring me and ask about the situation. The coastguard didn't sound worried.

By this point I'd turned off *Pindar*'s navigation lights. There was no point in advertising the fact I was there. The noises would last, on and off, for a couple of hours.

All kinds of things were running through my head. What would the people on the blacked-out boat think or do if they knew that I was alone, a twenty-eight-year-old woman with no one else remotely nearby? I briefly thought about motoring away. The way I was feeling, I would have gladly accepted disqualification from the race for doing so if it meant not being approached by whoever was on that boat. But I didn't have much fuel for motoring and in any case, I would have been able to motor at 5 knots when they could have probably done 24. The idea of being chased down and caught absolutely terrified me.

Until that point I had genuinely felt that my status as the only woman in the fleet was of little consequence. I was in the race on merit as a sailor. I could cope technically, physically, emotionally. I'd ended the first leg well, by no means disgraced behind Bernard and Thierry, two veteran single-handed ocean-racing skippers. I was lying third at that stage in the second leg. But suddenly, out there alone, I felt singularly vulnerable. If whoever was aboard that boat had any intention of harming me, there'd be very little to stop them. Of course, a single man in my situation would also have been open to attack. What I felt was different, however, was how I, as a single woman, would be perceived. What if my being there actually provoked an opportunistic attack, unmotivated by robbery? I have no doubt that fatigue and accumulated stress were playing their part in making me worry. But right then, the threat seemed real and imminent. I had my rocket flares out of the safety box and ready to deploy them. I reckoned they would at least temporarily deter anyone trying to board. If necessary, I'd go up on deck and meet an attacker in an attempt to fire a rocket directly at him. But when it came down to it, I knew I was a sitting duck. Despite my best intentions, I was effectively defenceless. If the people aboard that vessel wanted to attack me, rob me, rape me or kill me, there was not much I could do to stop them. It was a dreadful conclusion.

Even now, the thought of walking through any dark, open space, perhaps an unfamiliar park, gives me the jitters. I never put myself in such situations. In many ways, being aboard *Pindar* that night wasn't so different from being any woman walking down any alley out of earshot of other people. If a potential attacker suddenly appears behind you, with no one nearby to see what's happened, what's really to stop them doing anything?

Certainly, that night, I had a head full of 'what ifs' and 'buts' and 'maybes', and there was nothing I could do to shift them.

I went back on deck to check for any signs of life or movement. Nothing. It was cloudy. There was no moon, no stars, no light anywhere. The ship in the far distance had gone. All that was left was the blip on the radar. The sea was almost flat. It was hot and muggy. I was becalmed. The only sound was the odd flap of sails or the occasional small wave slapping gently on the hull.

I was afraid. I was lonely. I would happily have given away all my possessions to have some mates around. I had never been in any comparable situation and I didn't want to be in that one. I had never been required to show real bravery, like rescuing someone from a burning building or saving someone from drowning. I am not fearless.

I did once eyeball a burglar, but that was more through fear than because I'd been intent on willing him out of my house. I was about ten years old at the time. I was at home with my brother Dave and my sister Philippa. My parents were out.

We'd been playing in the living room and I'd gone into the kitchen to get some drinks. A man was trying to climb through the window. He looked straight at me. I was frozen to the spot and met his stare. My mum's handbag was sitting on the table in front of me and this guy was climbing through the window. I don't know how long the impasse lasted, probably not more than a few seconds. I just stared at him. Maybe he thought I was a defiant little kid who was about to scream the place down, bringing adults to my rescue. Maybe that's why he backed off and ran away empty-handed. But I wasn't a defiant little kid. I was petrified. I ran back through to the living room and told the other two what I'd just seen. We didn't know what to do so told the neighbours and they called the police, who came and found footprints in the garden and dusted for fingerprints.

I would have run away sooner if I hadn't been glued to the spot. I certainly didn't want confrontations at that age.

I didn't want one that night at sea, either. I knew I needed to run away, only this time very quietly, very slowly, perhaps without actually ever having been seen.

Email from Pindar, Sunday 27 October
I decide to sail the opposite direction from radar blip with my nav lights off but at 1kt it doesn't do justice to 'doing a runner'! After a series of phonecalls and just speaking to people, my imagination has begun to settle a little, I am now nearly 2 miles from this blip and still 'running' but the voice has not piped up since the song, perhaps in a drunken sleep! I should be thankful that he had no idea I was a 'single chick' on board and I promise not to read anymore piracy reports, and I'm trying to block that horror movie 'Dead Calm' out of my mind, but once its there it's hard to get rid of, I am trying to persuade myself that every creak of the boom isn't a footstep on my deck. Its all I can do to stop myself locking the cabin door from the inside! I know I am just tired with overactive brain but this is not going to help me sleep anymore! Could do with just another 5 kts of wind (not 50)! Roll on the Southern Atlantic trades, and dawn!
Em xx

Within hours of getting away, I felt almost embarrassed that I'd even mentioned the incident. It probably *was* fishermen out there that night. But in my exhausted state, alone, drained and still feeling the effects of the fortnight I'd just endured, I didn't know for sure.

I still don't.

9

My run-in with the mystery ship had given me food for thought but the next week of the journey to Cape Town was marked more by thoughts about food.

I was still fully focused on getting the best from every mile, and my efforts paid dividends with a stream of positive poll reports. But my mood definitely lightened and I daydreamed freely about such weighty matters as cold drinks, fry-ups, hot chocolate fudge cake, jacket potatoes and steak.

During that third week of the second leg I also crossed the equator, which is a significant stage in any voyage. Yet I felt comfortable enough with my progress to be fretting the same day about my biscuit crisis: I was running low on supplies.

News also came through that Simone Bianchetti, whose autopilot problems had stymied his progress before *Tiscali*'s dismasting had threatened his very participation in the race, was back in business and looking to rejoin the fray.

I can pinpoint within a few hours when my upbeat week began to take shape. It was late morning on Tuesday, 29 October. It was during that time that I managed to get back ahead of Thierry and regain second place. The 6 a.m. poll report had put Bernard in the lead, 4,200 miles from Cape Town and with a

130-mile advantage over *Solidaires*. I'd been 10 miles further back. By 2 p.m., my speed had reduced slightly but Thierry had lost pace at a faster rate. I was ahead of him by 17 miles and rising. *Hexagon* was fourth, 100 miles behind Thierry.

It was amazing how life then began to revolve even more around the three points in the day when the updated positions came in – 6 a.m., 2 p.m. and 10 p.m. No matter what else happened in between, I was drawn to the computer just ahead of when I expected the polls to arrive. It was absolutely compelling. I lived by it.

I established a routine in the few minutes before the data dropped, as I explained in an email sent from the boat during that week.

> The few minutes before involve boiling the kettle (assuming all is well on deck at the time), making tea then waiting til it cools enough to drink. Sometimes get the sponge out to make sure the bilge is dry and it s a useful way to preoccupy yourself while thinking how you might have lost a few miles to nearest rivals! Orange light flashes next to the 2 normal green ones on the Satc, receiving message. If the flashing doesn't last long, its just a quick message from someone who doesn't know I'm already on the edge of my seat! but if it continues flashing a long while before it pops up on your screen it has to be the positions or the fleet news report. When we get the reports its just a bunch of numbers and I pick out 4 to start with to see distance to finish on the first 4 boats, quick mental arithmetic to see if I have gained or lost on Thierry, bernard and Graham. then check the longitude to see if anyone has done anything radical in the previous 8 hours to the east or west (Graham, its Cape town this time, not Salvador), then jot the positions and numbers down to plot them on my nav programme . . . no mentions of trainspotting or anorak in following messages. In

fact while I'm on the subject of messages, I have received enough flying fish recipes thank you, and I still have no ingredients! Em x

The poll report at 2 p.m. on 29 October told me just what I'd been waiting to hear. As usual, it gave me my position in the fleet, my latitude and longitude, my speed at the time of polling (SOG), my distance to the finish in Cape Town, the distance to the leader in nautical miles (DTL) and the respective distances each boat had covered in the previous twenty-four hours. With the Class II fleet having stopped for the storm they were even further behind than normal, as was Bruce. Simone was still high and dry. That left me focusing on four boats including *Pindar*.

Class I

Pos	Yacht Name	Lat	Long	SOG	Time	DTF	DTL	24h
1	Bobst Group-Armor Lux	2.5	-24.2	8.7	14:00:51	4145.4	—	148.5
2	Pindar	5.1	-22.2	2.6	14:03:05	4310.5	165.1	149.3
3	Solidaires	5.1	-20.8	2	14:03:05	4327.5	182.1	116.6
4	Hexagon	7.4	-26.2	16.8	14:03:05	4429.7	284.3	212.5
5	Ocean Planet	29.8	-13	6.8	14:03:05	5972	1826.6	133.9
6	Tiscali	43.5	-8.3	0	14:00:51	6799.8	2654.5	0

Class II

Pos	Yacht Name	Lat	Long	SOG	Time	DTF	DTL	24h
1	T Hilfiger Freedom America	28.5	-16.1	2	14:03:05	5831.2	—	144.6
2	Spirit of Canada	30.5	-13.9	5.3	14:03:05	5988.9	157.7	85.2
3	Everest Horizontal	30.3	-12.9	2.1	14:00:13	5996.4	165.2	86.9
4	BTC Velocity	30.9	-14.1	8	14:00:38	6002.7	171.5	108.8
5	Spirit of Yukoh	31.9	-15.9	5	14:03:05	6019	187.8	94.1
6	Bayer Ascensia	32.6	-14.4	7.2	14:03:05	6092.1	260.8	104.5

Although being in the Doldrums at that stage meant frustrat-ingly light winds, the feel-good factor of the poll positions was still a boon. I was enjoying playing the game. My muscles ached and I could almost hear them groaning every time I needed to do something physical, like tack again, but it was worth it. I was, for the moment, seeing payback. My pleasure was all the greater because I was doing fine despite having lost the use of the Sat B system. It had gone down during the storm and I'd been relying on only one type of weather file, received a different way, instead of having multiple sources of information to pick from and cross-check.

For almost a week the numbers stayed good, with a string of consecutive polls putting me between 13 and 42 miles ahead of Thierry. At one stage, we closed the gap on Bernard to less than 150 miles. With more than 2,000 miles to Cape Town, I held real hopes that anything was possible.

It was in this cheery context that I had an amusing encounter with a tugboat, late on the afternoon of 29 October. The tug passed in front of me, not especially close, and then its captain piped up the radio to say hello. We weren't near enough to see each other or tell how many people were on each other's boats but this guy was really friendly.

I said how we'd been struggling with lack of breeze. He said he was delivering the tug from the Bahamas to Monrovia and he hadn't been through a calm patch on his journey yet! He was coming from the west though, not the north.

'Are you guys okay for supplies?' he asked. 'Are you short of anything we might be able to help you out with?'

I knew he must have had a fridge and freezer on board. A cold drink would've gone down very easily in the sauna conditions we were experiencing.

'We're fine, thanks,' I said reluctantly. 'We're racing and it's against race rules to accept any provisions from another vessel.'

'Where are you heading?' he asked.

'Cape Town,' I said. 'And then afterwards on to New Zealand, Brazil and back to Newport, Rhode Island.'

'Sounds like a nice trip,' he said. 'At least you're not doing that crazy shit like those single-handed guys. The stuff they do is insane, eh? Who'd go that far down south in the Southern Ocean by themselves? Madmen!'

'Errr, actually . . .'

I explained that I was sailing solo and that I was in the Around Alone and that my whole journey, not just the bit to Cape Town, was a race. It turned out he was from Cape Town and would be heading back there after making his delivery. I mentioned the fleet would be there in a couple of weeks and he said he might pop down to the harbour if he was around. The tug went on its way and I didn't think much more about it. It'd just been nice to have some friendly human contact. I wasn't too fussed if I ended up meeting him or not. If he did come to the harbour it might actually be quite odd, because neither of us knew what the other looked like.

As it transpired, a few weeks later when I was in Cape Town, working on the boat on the waterfront, I noticed my dad, who was visiting, had started talking to a passerby. He eventually called me over and introduced me to the tug driver! Dad told me later that the guy had been surprised by my appearance. He'd been expecting a strapping shot-putter type of girl, someone he thought would be capable of sailing solo around the world! At 5 feet 6 inches I wasn't quite what he was expecting. To be totally honest, he wasn't what I expected either. I'd anticipated someone portly and perhaps a bit unkempt and hairy after a long time at sea. But he was actually tall, fit and rather handsome. I was most impressed. It was probably a good thing I'd had no idea at the time. It might have broken my concentration! Anyway, he wished me well and that was that. I'd learnt my lesson about stereotyping tug drivers.

After my encounter at sea with the tug, and having dutifully not asked for a cold drink, the weather continued to get hotter. By the Wednesday it was like a sauna below deck, around 36 degrees, too hot to do anything, even sleep. News came through that Bernard had crossed the equator, and that he'd also been talking to the race HQ about the competition. 'Emma has nothing to be jealous about in her position,' he said. 'She is attacking me on a boat which is much harder to manoeuvre. I take my hat off to her.' Coming from someone as relentlessly driven as Stamm, it was a compliment that added a spring to my step. It also made me even more determined to push him all the way to port.

I made my own equator crossing next day. It was my fifth in a year. Three of the others had been the previous November during the 2001 Transat Jacques Vabre, when Miki Von Koskull and we had inadvertently sailed our trimaran back and forward over it. We were meant to cross just the once but having done so we tacked to get better wind and happened to go back across, which meant we needed to make it three to be on the right side again! I suppose that doesn't really count as three crossings but we had technically crossed three times. My other recent crossing had been during the fifth leg of the Volvo Ocean Race in March 2002, *en route* between Rio and Miami.

It is a long-established mariners' ritual to perform some kind of ceremony for Neptune when you pass over the equator. This is done to thank him for a safe journey up to that point and in the hope that he will be kind for the remainder. On a crewed ship, it is traditional that the ceremony is hosted by the crew members who have made previous crossings. There are a number of variations on the theme, often including the 'virgin' crossers being subjected to some kind of trial in the court of Neptune. In those cases, the newcomer will generally be covered with slops and old smelly food as part of the rite of passage before some other gift is offered up to the god of the sea himself.

As is the custom for someone who's been over before, I had a gift ready for Neptune during that crossing. I'd always provided food or drink and it seemed to have worked for me so far. On that occasion the offering was a miniature bottle of Cruzan Estate Light Rum that had been thrown aboard by supporters back in New York.

Email sent from Pindar, 31 October, 1.18pm
Just crossed the equator at 23deg 37 W! I was down below ready to log where I crossed into the Southern Hemisphere when a squall came in, by the time I had eased the sheets, adjusted course etc we had crossed but when I was on deck I didn't see the big yellow line painted so it must have washed away at that part. Let me know if Thierry reports the line or not! Anyway, had a sip of fine rum and gave Neptune the rest, hope he liked it, it burned my throat!
Emma x

I don't generally carry alcohol for personal consumption when I'm at sea. Some of the skippers do. Brad, for example, had a special wine rack in the cabin with just enough bottles for a small glass each evening during a trip. But as far as I was concerned wine meant extra weight, and if I was going to be carrying extra weight in the form of luxuries, I preferred snacks. Unfortunately during that week, on the same day I crossed the equator, I noticed that I'd nearly run out. No biscuits? That *was* a crisis! I'd started eating them – and my power bars and muesli bars – faster than I'd planned during the second week, in the storm. The weather had been so bad that I'd lived off the food I didn't need to heat or prepare in any way. When conditions improved, I'd just continued the bad habit alongside my hot meals. Still, running out wasn't such a big deal. I wasn't expecting any more bad weather. I still had some dry food that I hadn't felt like eating earlier. And it would do me no harm whatsoever to have a forced diet of main meals only. I convinced myself at the time that I might even feel the benefit of my little health kick by the time I reached Cape Town.

My resolve didn't even weaken a few days later when I also ran out of breakfast cereal. Instead I switched to porridge and indulged in fantasy food instead. Once I got started on that there was no stopping me.

An imaginary bacon buttie soon had a soft fried egg added to it, cooked so that it oozed out of the bread as I bit into it. Before I knew it I had one of my mum's full English breakfasts on the go as well: sausages, mushrooms, tomato, plenty of toast, tea in a teapot. After wolfing that lot down, in my mind's eye at least, I was out the door, strolling up the hill above Helensburgh, looking out over the Firth of Clyde and the Gareloch.

And then I looked down. I saw my porridge and came back to reality. Oh well, at least later in my dreams I'd have a jacket potato and a tasty steak. And then maybe fudge cake with fresh cream, and a drink or two and . . . and so it went on.

At least I was firmly in the race though, fighting for what might yet be a win in the second leg, or at the very least keep me on the podium. Simone, for one, hadn't been so fortunate. After his bad luck, he might well have had to withdraw altogether. Instead he was able to get back into the race thanks to some fine teamwork by the Around Alone family, as I was informed that week.

Simone's dilemma was that his mast had broken beyond repair. As masts are custom-built, he had no option of just buying another one and fitting it. He needed to find one already in existence that was suitable – which was a lot to ask – and then get it to Spain where *Tiscali* was undergoing repairs.

Bernard Stamm had been kept informed of Simone's situation. His boat was similar to Simone's and he had a spare mast that might just be suitable to get *Tiscali* to Cape Town. The problem was that Bernard's spare mast was in Caen on the north coast of France. That's where Andrew Pindar stepped in and offered the services of the *Hatherleigh*. Team Pindar's support vessel was already renowned among weary sailors – albeit as a great place for a breakfast, a pint or a party – and there was no reason why she couldn't transport Bernard's mast to Simone. It was loaded on 1 November and Simone hoped to be ready to restart by the 10th. He hoped that he might even make it to Cape Town in time for a swift turnaround so he could rejoin the fleet as we started the third leg. His hopes of winning the race would not be lost because the overall result of the Around Alone was scored on a points system for each leg. He'd lose out by coming last in the second leg but that didn't meant he'd be incapable of doing well enough in legs three, four and five to make amends. I thought it was great news. I also knew that if I'd been in the same situation, everyone else would have rallied round to help me too.

I heard Simone's good news on 2 November, a Saturday. It was a bright spot in an otherwise hot, slow weekend. It was cloudy but so warm that I had to keep drinking litres of water to replace all the fluid I was losing. I was still being bombarded by flying fish and I could also smell whales in the vicinity. I hadn't seen any on the trip so far, unless the object we'd hit had been a whale, and then I only saw a vague shape under the surface. But

I knew they were around. I could smell the air they 'blew', or breathed out, just before they dived when they were upwind of me. Such air tends to have been inside them for a while and it's not hard to detect. It's pungent and fishy. A sailor's nose is often a good early-warning device. If a big container ship or other vessel passes to windward of you in calm weather, you can always smell the engine. As soon as you get a whiff of something in the air, it becomes an immediate priority to find the source because it could spell danger.

None materialized that time and I was able to concentrate on sorting out a problem with the generator engine that I used to recharge the batteries. The engine cut out and I thought it sounded like a simple bubble in the fuel line. But when I went to the bleed screw on the fuel line there was a tiny leak, so I tried to pump some fuel through, hoping I'd watch the fuel and bubbles come out and then tighten the bolt. What's not supposed to happen is the drip turning into a flow, which is exactly what did happen. I got straight on the phone to Brian Harris, who's forgotten more about engines than I'll ever know. He talked me through the potential problems and diagnosed it correctly. I made a makeshift repair to the faulty bolt using sail-making thread. I spoke to Brian again later and he said it would probably have been better to use something else but at least I'd done it and I'd know for next time. With my spirits generally good, I considered it a new fact learnt instead of another obstacle that had marred my day. I know there's a lot of truth in the maxim 'What doesn't kill you makes you stronger' but it's certainly more comfortable to be 'made stronger' in small increments than in whopping great leaps.

My next engineering challenge took all of a day to arrive. At first light on the Monday morning I was making a small repair to

one of the batten ends when I heard an odd creak. I looked down
to see the gooseneck fitting – the crucial mechanism where the
boom joins the deck on an Open 60 – had come clean off. This
was one of the things we'd done work on in Brixham, which
made it all the more frustrating to see it broken now. The work
that had been done was good and would have been indestructible
except for the small matter of a nut coming off the bolt through
the deck. I never thought it would be an issue and I never had it
on my mental checklist of things to look at. It would have been
so easy to solve, just tightening the bolt, if I'd known about it.

Now, left unattended in its broken state, it threatened to
dislodge the boom from the deck altogether, most likely ripping
the mainsail and rendering it useless or worse puncturing and
weakening the bottom of the mast tube. That would effectively
have ended my race. I'd had better Monday mornings.

Email sent from Pindar, Tuesday 5 November
. . . the whole boom was being held on by 2 arms that are designed
to take a little forward-aft load to stop that movement on a strong
vertical pin. Of these 2 arms, (boomerang shaped 12mm Aluminium
plate) one had a crack half way thru it, the other had ripped its bolt
half out of the fixture it was on under the mast. This was all that
was holding the boom on, so I dropped the main to the deck,
resting the boom on a couple of fenders so as not to hole the
coachroof and cause more problems! . . . I had just the small
problem of twisting this aluminium plate back to flat, and inserting
the pin extrusion into a hole barely big enough and holding it there
while I went below and reinserted a bolt and tightened it! No easy
task.

I couldn't even hope to lift the boom on my own, so I used the
lazy jacks that hold up either side of the boom, ropes hanging down
off either side, a sheet hooked round the forward end to pull it

backwards, another round there to pull it sideways, and using all the winches and most of my rope I slowly manipulated the boom back to the right place, and each time I tried to relax one to let it down into the 'socket' it would move to the side as well, so it took as many trips as I can think of back and forth from the cockpit easing or tweaking just mm on each rope. This tweaking is happening under such high loads that each mm moved makes the sounds of a violin string, I was just hoping that none of the blocks explode, I tried never to be inside the 'triangle' of the mechanism, like not standing in front of a catapult, and if I had to, just staying there the bare minimum length to tweak and leave. Eventually it slipped in and luckily seemed to prefer its original position so I didn't need to work out how to hold it there while I ran below to put the nut and washers back in place. At first I thought the whole mission so far had been futile as the threads inside the main pin must be damaged. I couldn't get the bolt to grip, it kept spinning and not catching the first thread, so I couldn't go any further. then its funny what a little adreanline and a whole lot of will can do. It had no choice with a little forceful persuasion and finally got to a stage of pushing all my weight into the spanner to turn it until I couldn't anymore. Had a look on deck, yep the gap was getting smaller, I could ease some of the 'violin strings' around the boom so it could move a little freer. right enough, the bolt had some slack so I tightened that until I couldn't any more, the gap on deck was getting smaller – I eased all the lines from the boom except the lazy jacks so it could swing side to side, and when I went below again to tighten the bolt, it was definitely easier at different parts fo the boom swinging, so I spent maybe half hour sitting there waiting for the easier part to pull on the spanner. I don't know how long I spent doing that but the whole repair took me about 8 hours and that was before I reattached the mainsail to the boom and rehoisted the sail back to full main. My body feels more broken now from exertion than it did after 4 days of the big storm. Typically just after

the sun went down, the wind increased to 24kts and I decided
caution would be a good tactic and reefed again, probably the
slowest reef in the history of reefs, checking and re-checking
everything, my eyes hardly moved from the gooseneck fitting, my
runs back to the cockpit to ease more main etc, had turned into
near-crawls, I just needed to eat and rest. . . . and a cup of tea.
So nearly the worst day turned out not too badly especially when
I picked up the 1400 and 2200hr position repoorts and only lost 12
and 7 miles to Thierry each time! Overnight to the 0600 report I
have regained the 7 miles on him and hope to coninue this way.
I've just heard he has problems with his mainsail!

The Tuesday and most of the Wednesday were comparatively
uneventful, give or take regular checks on the gooseneck, which I
knew had the potential to give way and end my race at any
moment. I'd spoken to Josh, who suggested that I grind off the
bent plate and try to replace the bolt without it. I felt that would
be a longer task than what I actually did and so tried my own
methods of fixing it first. That's one of the luxuries of solo sailing
– you can receive suggestions but ultimately you're the one who
makes the decisions. I was pleased at how I'd coped with a
difficult situation yet lost so little mileage in doing so. It's a very
fulfilling feeling when you solve such problems successfully.

Surely, I thought, after all the hassles of the leg so far, it
wouldn't be too much to hope for a *lucky* break now?

I was about to get a break. There'd be nothing lucky about it.

10

I **was sitting** in the cabin a few hours after sunset on the Wednesday when I heard the dismal thud of my little world falling around my ears. There was a sudden difference in the boat's movement, a loss of power, and I went up on deck to confirm what I'd heard. It was so dark that I couldn't see the end of the boat but I didn't need to look that far to see the mainsail had come down. The halyard had snapped. I knew instantly that I'd have to climb the mast to make the repair. I'd be out of the race standings unless I fixed it. You can't go anywhere fast with no mainsail. It's the main powerhouse of the boat, like an engine in a car.

We were a fraction south of the Tropic of Capricorn and slap bang in the middle of the South Atlantic. Namibia lay 2,000 miles due east, Brazil 2,000 miles to the west. They might as well have been a million miles away, I felt suddenly so isolated.

I would have considered going up the mast immediately if it hadn't been pitch black. Climbing 80 feet is tough enough in daylight and good weather and with help on standby. Attempting it then – tired, alone and effectively blind – was bound to mean a simple error that would only force me up the mast again later. I lashed down the mainsail to the boom that was swinging on its lazy jacks to stop it blowing overboard, and went back inside. I lay in my bunk and was rocked not so gently into slumber. The wind was shifting outside and I was already apprehensive about the task ahead.

The alarm went off at half past five on Thursday morning. I'd slept for four hours, the longest single stretch in almost four weeks since leaving Brixham. My body must have known what lay ahead and persuaded my mind to switch off and let me rest.

I'd planned to go up at dawn, as soon as I had enough light to see what I was doing. I ended up waiting longer to allow some black clouds to blow through. The wind was varying between 15 and 25 knots and I wasn't feeling too comfortable. I needed to make sure I had an appropriate sail setting that would cover the range of winds while I was up there. Obviously I wouldn't be able to alter anything once I'd started.

I contacted the team around 8 a.m. to let them know what I was doing. I told them I'd be going up the mast shortly and I'd let them know when the mission was accomplished. All being well, they expected to hear from me in a couple of hours.

I prepared the gear I'd need to take up. I took a knife to cut away the old dead end. I took the spare main halyard (240 feet of rope). I took some tape, and a spare block in case the one at the top had been the cause of the halyard breaking. I put my video camera in my pocket, strapped on my helmet and psyched myself up for the challenge.

The climb would involve an ascent up a length of rope that was stretched between the top of the mast and the deck. The piece of equipment I used to get up and down the rope was a Topclimber, which consisted of a little platform seat (like a deckchair but with a web strap back and no legs) and two stirrup-like straps, with loops for my feet.

When I was ready to go, I climbed into the Topclimber, which was attached to the rope at waist height with a strap and a one-way jammer. The jammer gripped the rope when you exerted downward pressure on it. When I let go – and therefore exerted downward pressure by sitting in the seat – I could lift my feet from the ground and the seat was supported.

The foot straps were also attached to the rope with a one-way jammer. When I put my feet in them and stood up, I was able to release the pressure on the seat jammer, move it up a few inches and sit back down. Then I was able to release the pressure on the lower jammer by raising my feet, and move that up a few inches. I could then stand again, having moved up a fraction, slide the upper jammer up again, and so on. Basically, you move yourself up the rope – and hence up the mast – by repeatedly standing up and sitting down. To come down, you reverse the process.

It sounds so simple, and if you are trying to do this on a steady platform and with a taut rope, it is. If your platform is unsteady – and my platform was *Pindar* in choppy seas and gusting winds – it becomes a different proposition altogether. The tiniest bit of slack in the rope multiplied the potential for a hard climb, so I wound it down to the deck as hard as I could. I was still uncomfortable with the thought of a big gust coming through while I was high up there. If the boat's motion became too unstable, the consequences didn't bear thinking about.

Scaling the mast when *Pindar* wasn't moving – when she was docked, for example – it took a few minutes to reach the top of the mast and not long at all to reach the first spreaders. (Spreaders are the 'arms' used to hold the rigging away from the mast. *Pindar* had three sets, spaced approximately 20 feet, 40 feet and

60 feet up the mast.) On that fateful day at sea, it took me twenty minutes to get to the first spreader.

I'd lost my footing a couple of times already. The motion, though still relatively stable, was enough to be jolting me around. I was already bruised from being bumped against the rig. I was physically uncomfortable and I was nervous about the weather.

I decided I needed to make myself more secure before going any further. I thought I could do this by tightening the rope between the masthead and the deck so that I wouldn't be swinging so much, if at all, with the motion. But to tighten the rope, I needed to be on the deck. I started to go back down.

Using the Topclimber, I could only move the jammers a couple of inches at a time. I'd gone down about a foot (with five or six up-and-down movements using limbs that were already tiring) when I realized it was a stupid idea to go back. I'd be hurting by the time I got to the deck, which would hardly inspire me to come back up again. The rope was already fairly tight and it wasn't going to get much better. I'd already procrastinated for a couple of hours after dawn about when to go up. I told myself I was just procrastinating again, trying to find some excuse not to continue. I looked upwards. The rope wasn't deflecting from its position too much. I changed my mind again and started to go back up. I reached the first spreader and sat on it while I adjusted my harness. I could already feel my muscles pumped up with the blood flow. I looked around to see if there were any big clouds or gusts heading my way. There were none.

I took a deep breath, put my weight on my feet and pushed up again another few inches. It was starting to hurt and I was still swinging against the rig but I got into a rhythm for a while and was almost starting to feel good about what I was doing.

Then the wind increased. I'd set the autopilot to steer to a certain angle from the wind, so if the wind shifted I would still be sailing with the same angle of wind, just in a slightly different direction, which would have been no great loss for that short period. With the increased wind though, the boat heeled over more.

Each impact with a wave jolted the mast, flicking me like a rag doll outwards and then back into the mast. Ouch. I stopped climbing and held on for a while, hoping it would last only for a set of waves. No such luck. I was going to be bounced all the way and I had to deal with it. I tried to climb an inch or two between jolts, making sure I was holding on to the mast when each one arrived. My arms ached but the adrenalin was pumping and I forced myself towards the second spreader, where I was able to take another break.

The higher I got, the more exaggerated the movement became. Each wave had the top of the mast flicking like a whip. As I rested I scanned the horizon for ominous cloud or squalls on the water. There was not much new to see but the clouds were definitely getting darker. I pushed on to the top spreader. It took nearly all my effort and I arrived there battered, knackered and frazzled. Occasionally I had had to remove my extra safety line – which was preventing me from swinging more than an arm's length from the mast – so I could move it past an obstacle. Several times when the extra line was unattached, a wave hit and I was flung backwards away from the rigging. The violent motion spun me around and brought me crashing back into the rigging. My hips, spine, legs and upper arms all took a thumping. It was at that stage that I began to contemplate the possibility that I might sustain some serious damage. At least I had a helmet to stop direct blows to the head.

I made it to the last spreader nearly broken. I lashed myself against it, rested for a few moments and pulled out the camera. I talked to the camera, explaining where I was and what I was doing, as much to distract my mind as anything else. I was also thinking that if and when I made it down safely, it would be good to have a record of what it was like up there to remind me of the parts of solo racing that I hated.

That was therapeutic, if not for particularly long. I seemed a bit distracted, I thought. I said how tough it was and what the weather was like. Then I panned the camera downwards. Watching it later, I was struck by the way my legs were hanging so limply, even at that stage.

After one more push I almost made it to the top. By that stage the 240-foot rope I'd been carrying around my shoulders felt like the weight of at least a couple of bodies. I was fading and I'd really had enough. I'd been climbing for around two hours already. That's when I saw the black squall clouds coming my way. I didn't know how long they'd take to reach me but I knew there must be strong wind under them.

I drew every ounce of strength I had left to try to hurry up. As I approached the top, movement became almost unbearable and the motion of the boat likewise. With each whip of the mast I grabbed it with a terror-induced grip to try to stop myself being flung around. The g-force was so strong that my hands were ripped away, leaving instant blood blisters. The next time it happened I could feel the blisters burst. The skin on my hands felt raw. I blanked out the pain and carried on.

When I finally made it, I could only just reach around the back of the mast where I needed to do the work. I tied the spare halyard to the mast with more care than I'd ever tied anything. If I dropped it, I'd need to go down 80 feet and get it. The very thought made me feel ill.

I tied myself to the mast so I could work with both hands. I got my knife out and cut away the remaining foot of the old halyard. I put it in my pocket so I could examine it later. There was no sign of damage to the block so I left it there. I tied one end of the halyard to the dead end on the mast with a few hitches and secured it with plenty of tape. Every stage of the task seemed to take an age but I needed to do it carefully. I wasn't going to be coming up again in a hurry. I turned round to check on the black clouds. They were nearly upon me as I started down.

If going up had been slow, descending was more painstaking and painful still. I moved in even smaller stages than when I'd gone up. If I pushed the lower jammer down too far the foot straps would be too low to stand on. And if I couldn't stand on the straps and take all the weight off the top jammer, it wouldn't move. I needed enough play each time so that I could push the jammers up a little before they loosed their grip. Only then could I squeeze the jammer levers and release them to move them down. I was already in agony and in my rush to reach safety I was getting impatient. This only served to make the whole process slower because I was trying to hurry the jammers into working and they kept resisting. I just wanted it all to be over.

I was somewhere around the top spreader when the first big squall came in. *Pindar* heeled over and the autopilot struggled to keep her heading where she was meant to go. Each time the pilot tried to force the boat at an angle further from the wind, she heeled over more.

When she heeled, I was incapable of making upward progress. The mast was leaning over too much, with a more violent slamming motion than before. At points I was hanging over the water, urging *Pindar* with every fibre of my being to straighten herself back up. I remember hoping that if I was going to be thrown from the mast, I wanted at least to fall 60 feet to the deck and take my chances with the bump. I wouldn't be in good shape afterwards but I'd have a better chance of survival than if I landed in the water and then watched the boat sail away from me on autopilot. *Pindar* had turned into something more like a powerboat, bouncing off every small wave.

Trying simply to hold myself against the rigging was no good. I was taking a full-body battering. The skin was being scraped from my knuckles each time I used the jammers and my hands were becoming numb. My arms, ribs and legs were being pounded. I could feel my back and shoulders bruising. My head cracked against the mast. Thank God I was wearing the helmet.

On a calm, stable sea I'd have expected to go up, do the repair and come down in less than an hour. That day, it was close to two hours before I wished I was anywhere else in the world but then somewhere in the region of four hours I stopped thinking properly at all.

I desperately wanted not to be there but I was and I had to deal with it. Mentally, it was like being a nervous flyer on an aeroplane as it hits terrible turbulence. There was the same sense of intense discomfort and stomach-churning uncertainty. If being thrown around at the top had been the seatbelt sign coming on, then being tipped and shaken and hammered by the squalls was like hearing the pilot start to weep.

At times, I so craved respite from being thrown around, just needing to rest my burning muscles, that I lashed myself to the mast merely in an attempt to be still. But in those moments of 'rest', when my mind was given a moment to think about the situation, darker thoughts stole in. And beyond the fear of broken bones or serious head injury or being thrown into the sea I was ultimately most chilled when I thought about Mum and Dad.

They were waiting back in Scotland for a phone call that hadn't arrived. The image of someone telling them their daughter was dead crushed me. I was breathless thinking about it.

I untied myself and started inching down. I went through the motions and after what seemed an age I reached the deck. When I got to the bottom I was still tied into the climber but I just lay down on the deck and stayed there for several minutes. Then I took the camera from my pocket and told it I was okay but I'd had a nightmare. Then I unhooked myself, untied the new halyard, fed it through its own jammer on the mast and tied it around the winch so that it wouldn't go anywhere. Next I scrambled across the deck, adjusted my course and sails and went downstairs to make some calls.

My first calls were to Andrew, Robin and my parents. It was about 1.30 p.m. by the time I got on the phone. They hadn't heard from me for five hours. None of them answered and I left messages. I found out later that they were all on the phone to one another, wondering where I was. When I did get hold of them, it was Mum I spoke to first. I think it's safe to say she was relieved. Subsequently, in the still, warm safety of the living room at home, she's said that if I were ever to die at sea, at least she'd know I'd died doing something I loved. After that trip up the mast, I knew I didn't ever want that to become true.

When I'd pulled myself together a bit, I stripped off some of the layers I'd worn up the mast for protection. The heat was suddenly very apparent. I finished rigging up the main and then started winding the mainsail up the rig very slowly. I got it up, trimmed the sails and slumped back down on the deck again. It took all my remaining energy to go below and cook some food. I ate three-minute noodles.

After lunch I checked the computer to see what course I'd

23. *(above)* Bernard and Thierry greet me into Cape Town. (Billy Black)

24. *(below)* Laurent and Brian working hard as ever. (Billy Black)

25. *(right)* HSBC Education Trust children we visited. (Billy Black)

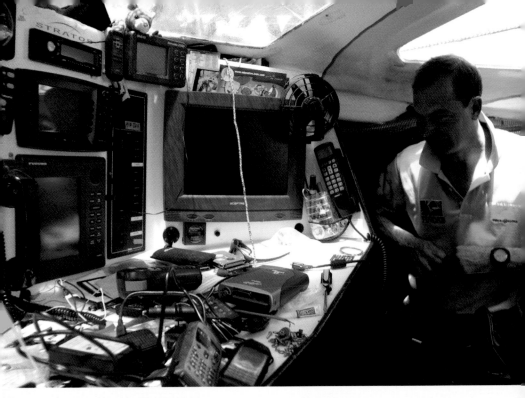

26. Mark Wylie in the nav station – did I say he was messy in his work? (Billy Black)

27. With my parents, collecting my prize in Cape Town. (Billy Black)

28. *(right)* Josh and I in the shade going over the job list. (Billy Black)

29. *(left)* Saying farewell to Tom and Margery Pindar, Andrew's parents, just before I departed for the Southern Ocean. (Billy Black)

30. *(below)* Just a hint of what the Southern Ocean can throw at you! (Billy Black)

31. *(below)* Arriving in Tauranga, New Zealand, with Mount Manganui as the backdrop, what a welcome sight. Note my repair across the mainsail . . .
(Ray Riley, Marine Pics)

32. *(left)* Looking at my repairs on the sail loft floor, with Fraser, Rodney, Mike and Robin. (Billy Black)

33. Peter Harken, thanks. (Billy Black)

34. Finally caught a whale on camera!

35. Dad, Daisy, Mum and I, just arrived on the dock in Salvador – refreshing! (Marc Turner)

36. The final few hours of the Around Alone, almost becalmed. (Billy Black)

37. Crossing the final finish line, with the Castle Hill lighthouse in the background. (Billy Black)

38. Jane and I returning to Helensburgh Sailing Club, where we learnt to sail.
(Marc Turner)

39. Start of the TJV 2003 on *Pindar* with Mike Sanderson. (Thierry Martinez)

40. Mike and I on the new *Pindar*, summer of 2003. (Marc Turner)

41. Dawn finish for Mike on *Pindar*, end of the Transat 2004. (Billy Black)

taken. Thierry had overtaken me. I know I should have been glad just to be in one piece but I felt demoralized. Never mind, I'd just have to catch him for a third time.

I checked my emails. There was one from Thierry asking where I'd been! He'd been hoping to wave as he overtook me. The following day he sent a message to the race HQ. It was posted on the race website and made me laugh out loud when I read it. It said:

There was only one charming creature on the Atlantic Ocean yesterday, and it was fate, destiny, chance – some force of attraction? – that I crossed her path. Perfect or what! No dream or hallucination after several weeks at sea on my own, not a siren sent by the Swiss gods to lead me astray, but a real woman, girl, a beauty . . . the charming EMMA on her beautiful boat! I steered towards her, hoping that I would surprise her in the middle of sunbathing session on the deck in a skimpy bikini, instead there's no one about and nobody answers the VHF. Musing that she was frightened by the approach of a big bad sailor, recognizable by his beard and his smell, she had to hide herself in her cabin, I told myself. Disappointed, gutted even, I sailed off on my route against my will, on my own . . . I'm a lonesome poor skipper! Once out of sight, at a good distance, I receive a message from her: what cheek! She was taking refuge up her mast! She was inventing terrible excuses on the lines of 'I was busy replacing my main halyard' . . . well it was too late by then! But then, I imagined the terrible scene of jealousy that I would have with my wife. Thank heavens for those little ARGOS beacons that track us wherever we go! Some consolation that the wind picked up from behind and the sea calmed so I could accelerate off again – nearly perfect!

Such cheeky banter was welcome. In the immediate aftermath of a situation like my mast climb, the race was all about morale and keeping in good spirits. I was just hoping that with all Thierry's expectations of seeing me in a bikini, it might have disturbed his train of thought about racing a little. It hadn't seemed to, unfortunately.

Another message I received after getting safely back down came from America. It never failed to surprise me how many people were following our progress and how many took the time and trouble to drop me a line. I was later told that more than 137,000 emails had been sent to me via the various websites during the trip. It was staggering. The email on 7 November from the States had come from a guy called Scott Kennedy. He owns an AlphaGraphics store and I'd met him on occasion and visited it. He'd been following the race. His message said: 'Unbelievable, Emma. The last time I was this glued to the news of an unfolding event concerning a single craft so far from home was the Moon landing in 1969!' It was simultaneously humbling and hard to believe that our day-to-day progress was gripping people in the way it was gripping us.

For all the relief of being safe, by the evening of 7 November I was toast. I was ready to climb into my fantasy king-size bed that didn't move and go to sleep for a week. But I had to keep going. If I didn't, Graham would get past me as well. And I wasn't going to have that!

Email sent from Pindar, 8 November, 6.20am
Anyone Got Any Arnica? Ouch, black and blue, and keep finding new bruises from yesterdays escapades, not only on limbs but back, shoulders ribs etc. Night of squalls and rain, wind every direction, just gone from downwind hardly making East to on the wind just west of South, hope its a cloud effect and will go back to 'normal soon. Its nothing like my weather chart, so 'patiently' awaiting new one to come in this morning. New halyard holding, gooseneck bolt looking

OK, fuel line leaking again but just a drip. the skipper is hobbling like shes 100+ or on deck stumbling like a new born giraffe trying to stand for the first time (only her legs aren't so long and thin!). More later, need to do some kind of wind dance, intrigued to see if Thierry had such a windless/changeable night on the position reports – cant afford to lose another 50 miles like yesterday!

I maintained my hopes of catching Thierry again and kept on pushing to do so. I was still feeling fragile, as I would for several days, but simply being safe again did wonders for my spirits. On the Friday evening they were boosted further when I rang Miranda Merron for our weekly chat. She was in France, preparing to do the Route du Rhum. She was attending a pre-race press conference for the skippers when I called. Luckily for me, she'd left her phone switched on.

'Where are you?' I said.

'Under a table,' she whispered.

'What?' I said.

'Under a table. I'm in the press conference for my race. I don't want to disrupt proceedings so I'll have to whisper.'

We'd developed a ritual of phoning each other every Friday when one of us was at sea. The other would generally be in a pub somewhere, so it was always good to hear the background noise and be reassured that life elsewhere was continuing as normal. We had a bit of chat about our respective races but kept it brief. I spoke to her later when she'd got to the pub and she passed the phone around to various people who were there that I knew, including Fraser from the *Maiden II* crew. I even heard him order me a pint. It was good to talk, and then I got back on with my race, taking consolation that at least I wouldn't be waking with a hangover.

The 6 a.m. poll on the Saturday morning confirmed that Thierry was still ahead of me, by about 40 miles. Bernard's lead ahead of Thierry was some 200 miles. I still had a reasonable margin of 100 miles or so over *Hexagon* in fourth place. I kept on pushing, using blaring music to keep me awake and pumped up. The weekend passed peacefully enough otherwise, with Mother Nature finally granting me sight of some wonderful wildlife.

On the Saturday I had a big, beautiful albatross flying over the boat most of the day, gliding over the waves just behind me. On the Monday, I finally got my first confirmed sight of the ocean's biggest creature during the Around Alone.

Email sent from Pindar, 11 November, 11.36am
Luckily I was on deck handsteering this morning when I just avoided, with a quick reaction and only metres to spare, what I have been dying to see all trip – from a distance! The most enormous whale I've ever seen, maybe just because it was so close, but the curved part of its back that showed was the length of this boat, 60ft, so it must have been way bigger with its tail, as I passed it closely it took a dive and I saw most its tail curling into the sea but missed its fluke (if it showed it) as I was looking forward again to check he didn't have a mate with him close by, or if there were lots in a feeding ground. Beautiful, fascinating, huge, scary and again nearly race-ending for Pindar.

It really was an awesome creature and I was glad I got to see it so close up. But it also set my heart pounding because it reminded me again that I was only ever a split second from the next potential disaster. Having come through so much in almost a month since leaving Brixham, I really wanted to get to Cape Town and do so as high up in the fleet as possible.

I saw the first sign that I was in coastal waters on the Tuesday evening. A huge container ship passed a couple of miles in front of me. Luckily, I'd taped my emergency navigation lights to the bow earlier in the day. My masthead lights and strobe had been blown off by the storm and I'd only noticed they were gone when I went up the mast. I hadn't been using them mid-ocean with no shipping around.

When I first caught a glimpse of the coast itself, it was quite magical. Cape Town was illuminated and Table Mountain seemed to have back lighting. To get into port I had to cross some incredibly busy shipping lanes and it would take a day to get in. I had problems with my charts and had to use my radar to gain a more accurate and real idea of the coastline. Then the wind died in the shadow of the mountain. It wasn't until Wednesday evening that I was within touching distance of the finish. Bernard and Thierry had already secured the first and second places but at least I'd seen off a late dash by Graham for third place.

I closed in on Cape Town at 14 knots of boat speed, with two reefs and the staysail, then slowed to a halt under the shadow of Table Mountain. There was simply no wind there, I thought about just drifting slowly to the finish, but I was still racing and plain impatient to cross that line. I used the last of my strength to pull the whole mainsail up and pull out the solent, and made my way to the finish line with better speed, just as the sun was coming up on the Thursday. A few boats came out to greet me but there was one last surprise in store.

As I emerged from the wind shadow, we were hit by 25–30 knots of wind, seemingly from nowhere. I'd seen a dark gust on the water but wasn't expecting a 25-knot increase. It was something I'd never seen before and as it was my first time in Cape Town, I didn't know enough about it.

Seconds later I crossed the line, dropped my mainsail in a hurry and slowed down to allow Laurent, the sole member of my shore crew in town at the time, to board. The others were due in later that day. Despite the storm, the leading boats had arrived earlier than expected.

Bernard and Thierry both came out to greet me too and jumped aboard. Neither of them had stopped celebrating since their arrivals so they were in flying form and a lot of fun. I opened and sprayed and shared the bottle of champagne I was given before we headed off for a breakfast of beer and croissants, followed by a second breakfast an hour later when another place opened.

The rest of the day was a bit of a blur, what with the rest of the shore crew arriving, various meetings and a few bits and pieces of press stuff. By 1 a.m. on the Friday, when it was time to get on a support boat and go out to welcome Graham in, I was ready to drop. Apparently we motored out and had to wait for a while as he was becalmed in the wind shadow, and then decided it was best to come back later. I missed all that. I'd fallen fast asleep under a blanket in the cabin and didn't wake up until we got back to the dock.

I was going to need all the rest I could get before we hit the Southern Ocean.

11

One legacy of Hurricane Kyle was that the restart from Cape Town was delayed. The fleet had originally been due to depart for New Zealand on Sunday, 8 December. If there had been no storm and no enforced stopovers in Spain, that would have given me three weeks to prepare for the third leg, with somewhat less for the last boats in the Class II fleet. As it was, an 8 December restart might have meant that some of the last boats would have not even arrived in Cape Town before the race got under way again. The race committee made the decision to delay the restart to 14 December. That gave Team Pindar a month in South Africa.

The delay worked both ways. On the plus side we had more time to do repairs and get *Pindar* in better shape for the trials of the Southern Ocean. There was also a longer period than anticipated to recover from the physical effects of the second leg. It had taken its toll on all of us.

The postponement had its downsides too. It would mean entering and leaving the Southern Ocean later, which increased the chance of bad weather and icebergs, and we might spend more time down there overall as well. The delay also meant more hectic weeks than expected dealing with land-based activities.

Just because we'd been handed an extension to our time ashore didn't mean I had a free week to go and relax.

From a recovery point of view, the month's hiatus was long enough to start feeling physically comfortable again – and start slipping towards 'normal' sleep patterns, which didn't really help – it wasn't enough to recover totally. In fact my strength and power actually began to decrease soon after arriving on land because I was no longer being so strenuously active every day. I needed to address that. I also needed to boost my cardiovascular fitness because that tends to decrease at sea. Although you're engaging in physical activity, you're not exercising the heart intensively for prolonged periods.

I went swimming a few times in Cape Town but it took a while to get from where I was staying to the pool and I decided to concentrate on cycling instead. As soon as I arrived in Cape Town, I resolved to join some of the other skippers' shore crews in some mountain biking. We developed a regular circuit that started at the boat every morning and took us around the Lion's Head and Rump, which are the two hills that lie immediately behind town, in front of Table Mountain. At one stage the cycling posse had eight or nine members, including shore crew, organizers and media. I really looked forward to that part of the day. I also attempted a game of tennis with Andrew Pindar during the stopover. Suffice to say he looked very glad he wasn't sponsoring me for my proficiency with a racket.

I know some purists believe that the stopovers in the Around Alone somehow negate the challenge, as though sailing around the world alone with breaks makes it easy. I have to beg to differ. I can appreciate the hardships of a race like the Vendée Globe in terms of leaving a port at the start of winter and arriving back there three months later having barely seen land in between. That doesn't seem at all inviting to me. But not having to cope with five starts, five finishes and four interim periods of shore-bound hype, hassles and bodily disorientation has its upsides too.

Just reaching land at the end of the second leg proved a long struggle for several of the boats in the Around Alone. After the first four of us had arrived in Cape Town within the space of a few days, the rest of the fleet finished in dribs and drabs from the last week of November. Brad arrived as the Class II winner of the leg on 27 November, almost a fortnight after I'd arrived aboard *Pindar*. Bruce was the penultimate Class I skipper to finish, on 28 November. Tim Kent arrived on 1 December and then Derek and Koji on 3 December. Five days later Alan was next to finish, pipping John 'Pops' Dennis by twenty-three minutes in the very final stages of a leg that had been a struggle for both of them and taken them the best part of two months. Finally, on 10 December, Simone sailed *Tiscali* into port, fifty-seven days after leaving Brixham. With the restart for all of us on 14 December, it was going to be an uphill struggle for some of the boats to get ready to head back out to sea. Most of the Class II boats had shore crews that consisted of only one person, who would travel between stopovers and help their respective skippers with the turnaround. The 'host' yacht clubs in each place tended to provide extra volunteers to help out when necessary. Visiting family and friends would muck in and help. The generosity was amazing at every stopover.

Compared to the skeleton teams of some of the smaller boats, I was very fortunate to have Team Pindar behind me. The shore crew were in attendance at every stopover, which meant several people working flat out solely on *Pindar*.

Busy though we were, I did have chances to taste a bit of South Africa, a country I had never previously visited. I went up

Table Mountain by cable car (the easy way) in the first few days with both my parents, who were out visiting. I later went up again with my dad and Billy Black – we climbed. The views were incredible, as was the heat by the time we got to the top. It was even more sweltering working down in the marina, inside the boat. The temperature in the cabin reached 40 degrees one day. It was bizarre to think that within weeks, down in the Southern Ocean, it would be so cold that I'd have to remember not to sleep with my arms bent otherwise they would take minutes to straighten again as the blood flowed back into them. After periods of sleep in the intense cold weather, it always took a little while to get the circulation going again when I woke, even after a nap of only twenty minutes.

Cape Town was a great place to visit. I especially enjoyed the outdoor lifestyle while I was there: the cycling and walking; a visit to a safari park; a day out at a winery. I'd been warned about the dangers of the city, particularly night-time drivers who don't slow down at traffic lights. There were a few accidents on the busy road outside the apartment but we all steered clear of trouble. We'd also been told not to walk home in the dark, especially on our own. There wasn't the remotest chance that I'd be inclined to do that anyway.

One of the highlights of the stopover for me was a string of visits to schools as part of the HSBC education programme. They consisted of a kind of 'roadshow' visit to one of the townships, where the truck that had been carrying us around turned into an impromptu stage complete with DJ booth, giant screen and 7-foot inflatable globe. Graham was at the centre of the HSBC campaign although Bruce and I were also there. There was a huge crowd of kids and I had no idea what they'd make of our bits of film about sailing but the message, as always, was follow your dreams. The

MC, a local guy called Sky, soon had the party started, and at one stage Graham was wandering around with a microphone asking the kids what they dreamt of doing when they were older. One little girl said she wanted to be a rapper so she was ushered on to the stage and did an incredibly confident impromptu rap all about herself and her family and her teachers. I'd gone along hoping I'd do whatever I could to help. I came away having been inspired myself. The day ended with a mass of people dancing in a huge circle. I can still clearly picture Robin Gray, Pindar's team manager, jigging around in the middle, leading the conga!

The stopover flew by. Within two days of the last boat finishing the second leg, we were into the final countdown for the third. Two days before the off we all had to attend a refresher course on survival. The Southern Ocean holds a special place in the world of sailing and the race organizers wanted us all to be in the right frame of mind for it.

The main reason for extra caution is because when you go deep into the Southern Ocean, you quickly become isolated. All the other oceans in the race were used by regular shipping. That offered a degree of safety and usually guaranteed that another vessel was within a day's passage if need be. In the Southern Ocean you can find yourself in situations where you're a week from help, if not more. There's also a landless band around the bottom of the globe where the wind and waves can build up quite dramatically.

In the Atlantic even the deepest low-pressure systems eventually reach Europe and slow down. In the Southern Ocean, the waves just keep getting bigger and the weather systems keep spinning around the bottom. They keep growing and building before they're funnelled through the gap between the Antarctic and Cape Horn. That's why the Cape has such a bad reputation.

The wind accelerates through that gap and waves build as they try to get through.

Though some of the wildlife is stunning, not least the stately albatross, there are plenty of hazards. There seem to be more whales. There's a danger of ice. You often have days on end without sun and it becomes chilling to the bone. The constant damp increases the discomfort. It is such an isolated place that it can feel eerie on a less than stormy day.

There are benefits too. The Southern Ocean can provide wonderful sailing, certainly some of the best I've ever done. On a good day in fine conditions, you can surf the same wave for hours on end.

I had done a survival course three times previously. They invariably contain the same information but it's worth being reminded, if only to keep you on your toes. We were reminded always to step *up* into a life raft. When your boat is sinking beneath you, you should never step down into one as your boat is then still floating and therefore safer than the life raft. We had a session in the pool with survival suits and lifejackets and an exercise to practise getting into a life raft and righting one that had tipped over. We received instruction on how to fire off flares, how to conserve warmth when you're in the water, how to administer basic first aid and how to treat someone for hypothermia. During the first medical briefing at the start of the race, we'd also discussed the possibility of carrying a supply of insulin in case any of us needed to assist John in a diabetic emergency. I believe all the Class II boats decided to take some as they would be the most likely to be around him at any given time.

On the Saturday of the restart I woke early but lay in my warm, dry bed for an extra half-hour before getting up for a breakfast of muesli and a mug of tea. I went down to the boat at 7.45 a.m. and there was hardly anyone around. *Pindar* looked spotless, as good as she'd looked all trip. My parents had already gone home so there were no prolonged goodbyes, just quiet last-minute preparations and then a routine departure. A rib from the Royal Cape Yacht Club towed us off the dock. Next stop New Zealand.

The start was good. Everyone was jostling for position and I was second over the line but then lost ground. I was being fairly conservative with my sails and when the wind dropped suddenly I didn't have enough up. While I was trying to increase the sail I was getting knots in everything by trying to work too fast. It was very frustrating but I had no excuses. I couldn't shake out the reefs quickly enough and I fell off the pace. I wasn't too despondent. We were under way, there was a long time to catch up, and the weather would be warm for a day or two yet. I was still wearing a T-shirt, albeit with foul-weather bottoms.

The first day was fine, with more chances to nap than I'd expected and some beautiful sailing at 10–12 knots. I was starting to feel ready for some bigger winds. The first scare came not from the weather, however, but from a fellow competitor.

In the 2 p.m. poll report on the Sunday, Bernard and Thierry had rushed off to dispute the lead and Graham, aboard *Hexagon*, was in third place. *Tiscali* was fourth, 5 miles further back, and I was fifth, another 5 miles behind. I hadn't plotted our positions so I had no idea that I was directly behind Graham and on his path. Shortly after receiving the positions data, I spotted a yacht on the horizon in front of me. Although I was only going slowly, about 5 or 6 knots, I was getting closer.

I used my binoculars to check who it was. It was *Hexagon*, evidently sailing some way below her potential. Within two hours I'd almost caught up. I could see on to the deck but there was no sign of Graham. I thought he must be sleeping and decided to take advantage and nip past. He'd be able to find out when he saw the next poll report. But the closer I got, the more I became aware that *Hexagon* had virtually stopped dead. She almost looked abandoned. The sails were flapping.

I used the VHF to try to make contact and check that everything was okay. There was no answer. I tried the satellite phone. It rang but Graham didn't pick it up. I drew up almost alongside and shouted at the top of my voice. Still nothing. When I tried my foghorn to no effect I began to get quite concerned. There was still no sign of life. I called the race committee to tell them and ask when they'd last had any contact. Not recently, they said. They seemed a bit worried.

I felt a surge of panic that maybe Graham had fallen overboard and drowned. There was no sign of anyone. I sailed on slowly as it was easier than gybing and tacking to stay in the area but kept checking back to see if he'd materialized.

He eventually appeared on deck, stretching and yawning, and waved at me! He had apparently caught a bug in Cape Town that had become much worse soon after departure the day before. He'd been in a deep sleep, he explained a few minutes later via the VHF. So deep, in fact, that even a foghorn hadn't woken him. He was fine, he said. I was relieved but still a bit freaked out. What if he *had* fallen overboard and I'd been hovering nearby, too late to do anything to help? I'd never been in a similar situation before and it underlined again for me that a new crisis could happen at any moment.

The Monday and Tuesday were a bit of a struggle as I experimented with my bigger sails in anticipation of higher winds. I was nervous about having too much sail up in case I couldn't cope, though. When the winds dropped I ended up under-powered a lot of the time. But then I didn't want to be over-powered either.

If a twenty-minute squall came through, that was fine. I could just about hand-steer through those in the knowledge they'd end soon enough. But I was also feeling a bit too low on energy and confidence to put myself in a situation where I might find myself struggling for control for hours on end in winds up to 50 knots. The poll reports reflected my reticence. On the Monday afternoon I'd fallen further behind Simone, who was third, while Graham was less than 30 miles behind me and had Bruce on his heels. By the Tuesday, Simone had extended his lead over me by 36 miles, Bruce had gone ahead by 6 and Graham was only 2 behind.

Overnight I passed through the most intense lightning storm I'd ever seen. I was on tenterhooks expecting to be struck down and frazzled to a crisp at any moment. The 'rumbles' of thunder had nothing rumbling about them. They were deafening cracks, simultaneous with the light. I didn't so much tense up as gape at what I was seeing and hearing. And there was absolutely nothing whatsoever I could do to get away or take shelter.

The storm broke while I was trying to cope with a 46-knot squall, and I was therefore unable to switch to autopilot. Normally in thunderstorms I'd let the autopilot steer so I wasn't gripping on to a carbon tiller that was attached to an all-carbon boat. I worried that the lightning would hit the boat and go right through me. I was, after all, attached to the main conductor in the form of the carbon mast.

On that occasion I had no choice but to keep hand-steering because otherwise we would probably have broached while trying to set up the autopilot in such strong winds.

Email sent from Pindar, 18 December
When the big one came with 46kts it was a white knuckle ride, made worse by those little white knuckles holding firmly to a carbon

tiller of a carbon boat with an 80+ft carbon stick, and the most intense lightning storm you've seen/heard!!! the thunder claps almost the same time as the light, so it was right above me, no forks fortunately, just an intense flash that leaves you blind for a few seconds! When that squall finished, and my heart rate returned to normal and I handed steering responsibility back to the autopilot, the boat was still static (electric, certainly not still) so everytime i touched anything I got that little shock!

When the storm passed and the winds were back down to a steadier 30 knots, I was thinking about preparing some soup when the autopilot started playing up, skewing towards the wind and tipping the boat on her side. I thought I'd made an error in the setting but I checked it and reset it and it happened again. I knew no one would be awake back at home (it was 3 a.m., UK time) and anyway my electrician, Mark Wylie, would be on a plane at that moment flying between South Africa and England. After an hour at the chart table, where I'd been sitting making manual corrections to the pilot every few minutes, I called Sharon Ferris in New Zealand. I'd raced with Sharon on *Royal & SunAlliance* and *Maiden II* and I knew she'd be awake. I didn't think she'd be able to help me with my problem but at least she'd be able to laugh at my predicament and cheer me up. She couldn't offer a solution to the autopilot error but we did have a good catch-up chat, which was just as much of a morale boost. I eventually got hold of Mark when he landed and he said he'd work on it and get back to me. After the winds had calmed down a bit I was at least able to switch to the back-up pilot, something that hadn't been possible earlier for fear of not having any control of the boat during the changeover.

By the Wednesday afternoon, the polls had me back in fourth place but I wasn't closing the gap on Simone and I was now 210 miles behind Bernard, who was leading from Thierry in second place. On the Thursday, by which time I'd dropped back again to fifth, I received a message from Thierry. 'What are you doing?' it said. 'Don't you want to play with us?' Such Gallic charm.

It was always disappointing if I was doing badly when the position reports came in. They were easier to deal with when I had a very obvious problem that I knew I could fix, allowing me the chance to make up the ground. But this time I didn't have any massive problems – certainly not anything over and above what the others were experiencing – and the loss of miles was harder to take because I couldn't really connect it anything. At times like that I'd go round the boat and check to see there was nothing dragging on the rudders or keel, some kelp or something, that might be slowing me up. I wondered if I had dramatically different sails up compared to the others. In the end I had to conclude that the boats in front of me had maybe caught a better system first and hope that I'd find one soon and catch up. In the meantime, conditions were become increasingly 'true Southern Ocean'.

Email sent from Pindar, 21 December
Grey, cold and windy – yes, typical Southern Ocean, but quite amazing at the same time! Birdlife everywhere, the deep grey sea is streaked with foam from breaking waves, the grey sky is all different shades depending how thick the cloud cover is there, and even the birds all look grey through the drizzly damp air! had some rain this morning that was threatening to snow, but it must be just above freezing outside, I have the cabin up to a cosy 8deg at the moment . . . i have two hats on and fleece gloves when I'm not typing! To go outside, if I plan to steer for a few hours I take 15mins to make sure there is no way water and cold will get through my clothing, although I'm always set to pull on my jacket in a second! I have been sleeping in my bunk which makes a nice change, for up

to an hour at a time, and wrap my sleeping bag round my dry top half, but never remove my foulie bottoms so I'm ready to go on deck in seconds! It would be easy to go weeks without taking your boots off! Mmm . . . nice Christmas thought for you! I had a thought for all of you last night, last friday before Christmas, might have been a big night so hope you had a beer for me! I have tinsel up in my cabin, but otherwise its not too festive yet here.

On the Sunday before Christmas, 22 December, the sun came out for the first time in a week. It was a bright spot in a ninth day at sea otherwise shaded by grey, literally and metaphorically. The afternoon poll put me sixth in Class I, although at that stage Simone, Bruce and I seemed to be shuffling between fourth, fifth and sixth every few hours. The wind was all over the place and the waves had become real rollers. The risk of getting knocked down increased exponentially when I raised more sail to take advantage of the higher winds, as I soon found out.

Email sent from Pindar, 23 December
I had just sat down at the chart table when I could hear the roar of a big wave about to hit my starboard side, having no time to do anything, I held on for dear life and was tipped beyond 90deg. I only know this because things that are lashed so the only way to get out is directly up. . . . got out! i am still finding things in odd places, and the smell of tomato soup that liberally spread itself everywhere is still haunting me although I've cleaned up the mess. One of my hats got the worst of it which has been rinsed in sea water and discarded til the end of the leg! – tomato soup might be good for the hair or something but its pretty revolting (maybe that'll become a fashion like beer shampoos did) . . . dreaming of Mum's mulled wine out of a huge pan on the stove at home, Em x
PS it snowed too while I was out there and my hands are just thawing out now!

Christmas Eve was like Groundhog Day: a bad day repeating itself. I had another wipeout and more frustrations with faulty autopilots. There was no tomato soup incident, however, which meant at least I'd learnt a lesson about hot liquid food in rough weather.

Email sent from Pindar, 24 December
Just to top it off, in 24 hours I went from 4th to last place, quick enough to get messages from both Thierry and Bruce to see if I was OK! SO if you were wondering how I managed to lose so much, so quick – there you go! Not sure I like this position much, so once I am up and 100% again, and this xmas storm is passed, I'll have to settle, rethink my tactics and hopefully repeat my leg 1 performance. Its far from over yet – Ok, back to my worklist . . . . Em x

My own troubles were put in clearer perspective when I received news that John 'Pops' Dennis had retired from the race due to technical problems and was on his way back to Cape Town. If only his boat had had as sturdy a constitution as he did. He had a problem with his alternator and his ballast was frozen. With no power and no ballast it would have made no sense for him to continue deep into the Southern Ocean. His own safety would have been hugely compromised and if he had got into difficulties later, he might have been too far from help for a rescue effort to make any difference.

John talked of 'defeat' in a statement to announce his withdrawal from the race. Nothing could have been further from the truth. I knew myself that even being young and in good health did not protect you from the sea's moods or your own or the multiple obstacles that are thrown in your path during an ocean race. John had been an inspiration simply by being there. He had had a good sponsor but, like the skippers who took part with inadequate funding and no corporate sponsorship, and spent the longest time at sea and the shortest time making repairs, his participation had helped to keep the real spirit of the race alive. I wished we could rally round to magically effect all the repairs he needed doing and then turbo-charge him by willpower to catch up with us. But the fact was he'd lost too much time and distance and it simply wasn't possible.

Christmas Day aboard *Pindar* was not as long or as lonely as I'd expected, maybe because I'd anticipated a bad day but actually ended up with a bit of sunshine and a decent bit of breeze. With my head full of numbers and my attention firmly on the race, I didn't dwell too much on life away from the confines of the boat.

Of course I would have loved to be at home with my family. Christmas Day was always a special occasion as I grew up, with a house full of relatives and games. As we were an engineering family, these would inevitably involve Lego or Meccano or some kind of construction puzzle. Mum liked to receive difficult jigsaws and we'd usually help her start a new one on Christmas Day. It would often lie on the dining-room table for some months afterwards as she pieced it together in her spare moments.

We'd all eat too much for lunch in the afternoon and then have turkey sandwiches while we stayed up far too late playing board games or cards or watching a movie. The noise level in the house was invariably louder than even our normal four-kid volume. I remember one occasion in particular when all of us were in Dad's study asking him things at the same time, talking away and not listening to him or one another. I was about seven or eight at the time. Unknown to us, Dad pressed the record button on his dictaphone and let us all babble on. He then played it back to us, which we thought was very funny and kind of embarrassing to hear how noisy we really were!

As we got older, Christmas involved joining our parents in a glass of sherry while opening our presents. When we were allowed wine with lunch, Christmases just got better. We had fewer toys and more stories and Christmas became a good time to catch up. With the next generation arriving and Mum and Dad having their first grandson, the cycle is starting to repeat itself, just as enjoyably.

I didn't dwell on this in the Southern Ocean because quite frankly there was no point. It wasn't as if I had been suddenly transplanted there and my situation was a great surprise. The sacrifice had been made and I got on with the day before me.

Henry Chappell, with one eye permanently on PR, had encouraged me to take a Santa suit for that leg of the trip and told me to film some 'Santa footage' and take some seasonal pictures. I also had a few decorations, party poppers and streamers with me. I can't honestly say they made a bit of difference. I felt about as Christmassy as a desert.

Opening my presents from family and friends made me think of home – and miss it – rather than rejoice in tidings of goodwill. My gifts were thoughtful and practical, though, and I thanked everyone, if only by telepathy. Socks and lip balm have never been so genuinely welcome.

My main meal consisted of freeze-dried roast lamb and minted potatoes, provided by Graham Dalton's shore crew. They told me Graham only ever ate a fraction of what he was given and they'd amassed a supply of spares. After eating the lamb I had a better idea of why Graham ate so little. The taste stayed with me for three days and had a peculiar effect on my digestive system. Pasta and couscous might not be the most exotic staples in the world but I'll take them any day over freeze-dried food. The real treat of the day was a little Christmas cake my mum had given me in Cape Town. I thanked her when I made a brief call home and got to speak to all the family. I also had quick chats with my best friend Jane, with Andrew Pindar and with Miranda Merron. They all assured me that life was very much as normal. It was just what I needed to hear and I turned my attention back to the race.

I just wanted to get on with it and reach New Zealand as quickly as possible. I wanted to see my brother Dave and his girlfriend Pippa, who'd be coming out to visit. I wanted to see some of my friends who were in New Zealand as part of Britain's America's Cup challenge and others who were just out there surfing.

Most of all I wanted to hurry up.

12

After spending Christmas alone in the Southern Ocean and getting through it without feeling too despondent, I had high hopes for the remainder of the third leg. No doubt New Year would be another occasion when I'd miss home but it would also be a time for resolutions: to enjoy whatever the race handed me, to redouble my efforts, to leave aside the doubts and fears and move forward with optimism. On Boxing Day, full of such intentions, I had no idea of the erratic weather and moods around the corner, nor how close I'd come to having my very participation thrown into doubt again. The despondency would return, with my only refuge being the finish line.

On Christmas night I'd made a tactical decision to head south to avoid a windless high-pressure zone to the north of me. The sea soon became choppy and uncomfortable but at least the sun was out. I spent much of 26 December hand-steering. This eased the effects of the slamming motion on the boat and also allowed me a better chance of dodging the kelp that kept getting caught on the rudders and keel.

Over the next day, as I waited to see whether my southerly gamble would pay off, the sailing became nervy. The wind was all over the place and the autopilots were playing up again. The boat was being pushed sideways across the waves, putting her under incredible strain. But we were making progress. The decision to go south, if only temporarily before heading back through a more northerly 'gate' as required by the race committee, was paying off.

I could relax a little more again, at least in relative terms for a sailor on a single-handed Open 60 flying through the 'growler'-infested icy cold Southern Ocean waters at high speeds. I had taken the gennaker down, safely and perfectly rolled and not, luckily, in my normal manner, too late and out of control. When that happened the gennaker always ended up in a mess up forward in the sail locker!

Also, the risk I had taken in going south had paid off. When *Ocean Planet* went north and I went south, Bruce was in front of me, but by now he was still 180 miles behind. And *Hexagon*, 220 miles in front on Boxing Day, was now only 90 miles in front. Thierry and Bernard were both about the same distance in front but at least they hadn't taken the usual 40 miles out of each of us in each position report. *Tiscali* was already south when I made that decision and if Simone had stayed south instead of following the route that he took, I was convinced he would have been streaks ahead of *Hexagon* too. With that excitement over, strong nor'westerlies were due in the next few hours and the wind was going to stay in that quadrant for three or four days at least. I was anticipating some good speeds again to make it through the 'gate' at New Year. I had broken the 4,000-mile barrier to the finish and from the gate there was a mere transatlantic race to go!

The deeper south I went, the colder it became and the more I craved sleep, though I wasn't getting much. The boat was crashing around, which didn't make for easy napping, and the lack of sleep as well as the lack of its quality was getting to me. I was dreaming, while partially but not quite awake, of a big dry bed and soft pillows and a huge duvet. I was drawn to my bunk, a rather more austere place, and wrapped my sleeping bag around my top half in the hope that at least I'd be able to build up some warmth inside it. With the wind so unsteady though, I couldn't rely on the autopilots maintaining control, so I kept a remote control for the pilot within arm's reach of the bunk. When the boat intermittently slowed, the deceleration was sufficient to wake me if I'd nodded off. That would force me off the bunk or at least mean me sticking a hand out into the cold cabin air to reach the remote control. I'd adjust the steering and quickly wrap up again so as not to let too much accumulated warmth escape. My feet never got warm.

In those dying days of 2002, my mind began to wander as it tired. I was cold but was almost feverish mentally. There were periods when all I wanted to do was slope away and keep dry and warm, but couldn't. That only intensified my desire to sleep. I'd hold the thought of sleep as I did whatever needed doing to build on the gains I was making, like check for weed that was impeding progress, and then go back and try to sleep again.

The kelp around *Pindar*'s prop even had the cheek to flaunt itself, streaming out of the back of the boat at one point. I was sure it was laughing at me. I'd perform some sharp turns to shake it off, then having failed in that tried to sail the boat backwards, which cleared a lot of it. Some still remained, causing the engine to vibrate, a sure sign of something still wrapped around the prop. To make matters worse, the sea was so choppy that we'd build up speed only to be slammed by a wave and slowed right down again. Conditions were erratic and my mood likewise. I couldn't seem to get a clear run on anything, be it progress through the water or holding an idea and following it through.

A couple of days before New Year I had a day when my thoughts alternated rapidly between 'Hooray, nearly half-way around the world' and 'Oh no, only half round the world.' These were invariably followed by 'What am I doing here anyway?' My perspective was as skewed as the conditions.

I felt a sense of achievement at having made it so far and through a variety of challenges but it never got any easier. I was exhausted, physically and mentally, and not just with the adventures at sea. I think I was probably already contemplating the next stopover in New Zealand, and imagining that I'd have no let-up on land, that as soon as I arrived I'd be back into the next round of questions and attention and too much other stuff. I was feeling a little isolated and couldn't really see a way out. Even the good days of sailing seemed to have the opposite of a silver lining attached, such as 30 December, when I went from low to high after eight hours of steady breeze and good conditions when I had an average boat speed of 17 knots for the duration.

I don't think I looked at the position reports all day because I was so busy and feeling 'up' again but I assumed I must have made some miles on the rest of the guys. However, when the poll report came in at 2 p.m., though my twenty-four-hour run was better than anyone else's, I was still in the same place in the Class I fleet – fifth. Bruce was behind me but I was trailing the leader, Bernard, by more than 700 miles. Thierry was 440 miles ahead of me. Graham and Simone were both within range but also seemed to have been enjoying good days at the office. It was easy to feel that everyone was having a better time of it than I was, right down to the amount of protection their boats were affording them from the sea.

In the very wet surfing weather, the whole time I was on deck was a bit like having a firehose right on me and there was nowhere in my cockpit I could get away from it. During the Cape Town stopover, I had had a look down below on some of the other boats, and on most of them there was at least a little shelter from an extended 'roof' from the cabin past the hatch into the cockpit, with a small hammock seat or something similar. Thierry even had a wheel inside so he could hand-steer the boat while standing below, without even bothering with his foul-weather gear. So while I was being pounded by icy water on deck, I had images of Thierry all snug (and smug) below with a good view out of his leeward window to see his sails. And just to rub it in he had showed me how easy it was to heat up the kettle and pour his coffee right next to the wheel, without even going on autopilot! I knew this was possible because I often had to make my tea one-handed while I held on for dear life with the other. Anyway, the tea probably tasted better after an icy-cold wake-up from the south.

For Hogmanay at sea, I'd taken a small bottle of champagne to welcome in the New Year. Conditions were so bumpy and required so much attention that I postponed opening it. *Pindar* was regularly being flattened and at one stage we were pinned to the water and it was possible for me to walk on parts of the cockpit that were normally vertical. I was a nervous wreck and with winds of 35 knots expected around midnight on 31 December, I wanted to keep what was left of my wits about me.

I don't know anyone who manages to keep all their New Year's resolutions, but I made some of my own anyway. These were: to appreciate the good weather more; not to let any Italians or Kiwis beat me in any races in the coming year; to get my tactics right and stick to them from the beginning of each leg, not half-way through when I had given myself more miles to catch up already; to eat better, and to enjoy the local vineyards more when I got to each destination; to enjoy every moment of people's company and stories on land, and somehow save it in a box so I could open it up at sea when I was feeling a bit too alone.

It was an unusual way to start the year, alone on a 60-foot yacht in the Southern Ocean, surfing up to 28 knots of boat speed in up to 40 knots of wind. Lonely? Yes, I was a little lonely, but I had some fantastic messages and a few short phone calls to hear everyone, and the sun was shining, and in a couple of weeks I hoped I would be able to celebrate on land, in company.

The sun wasn't shining on 2 January when my hopes were torn apart. The wind was up to 40 knots, the seas were huge and we were surfing down the mother of big waves. I was sitting on the deck, babysitting the autopilot, when we took off on this thing at incredible speed and started hurtling into the trough in front. As we plummeted downwards, the wind speed dropped because we were in the shadow of the wave. The pilot brought us back on course but we'd lost speed dramatically by the time we reached the bottom.

At the peak speed, the boom had moved half-way over, when there was no pressure in the sail. The sail had moved too. But as we slowed the boom crashed back into the right place, twisting the sail as it went. I couldn't believe what I was seeing. It almost happened in slow motion. I couldn't rewind it but wished fervently that I could. The sail ripped halfway up, all the way from the leech to the luff (from the aft to the forward edge). I was willing it not to be happening, hoping that my eyes were deceiving me. They weren't.

I knew within an instant that the rest of the leg would be spent fixing it, if indeed it could be fixed at all. My next thought, within seconds, was that I'd have to stop somewhere and repair it. I was overcome with a surge of despondency. Why me? Why now? I felt utterly deflated, almost hopeless. I'd already been feeling run down from the last leg. That had been obvious from my vacillating moods. Unlike earlier in the race, I hadn't felt able to pick myself up each time I'd had a setback. My energy had been slowly draining to nothing and wasn't topping itself up. I wasn't ready for anything major to go wrong. At that moment, as the sail tore itself apart, so did I. Why couldn't I have just one piece of good fortune? Or one easy run? I knew in my heart of hearts that it doesn't happen that way, not for me or anyone. I was shattered. I wondered if maybe my race was over. And then I went to look for a needle.

By the Friday morning, 3 January, I'd already spent eight hours working on the repair. It was going to be a long, difficult job but I'd gone beyond the stage where I was even thinking about it. It didn't bear thinking about. I'd just have to make an attempt to sew the sail together and then hobble to New Zealand. I still had more than 2,200 miles to go. Right then, it seemed an awfully long way.

I sat on the boom while I was sewing. It was bucking like a bronco but it was the only place to do the job. I couldn't take the mainsail off and even if I'd had the strength, it was only wetter on deck and the sail was too big to take below into the cabin. My fingers quickly became so numb that I couldn't feel it when I accidentally pricked them, which I did, time and time again. They looked like pin cushions within hours but there was no way I could wear gloves because then I wouldn't be able to wear the sailmaker's palm, hold a needle or feel what I was doing properly.

I was freezing cold and wet. The sewing lasted for days. Every stitch seemed to take an age and there were 1,500 or more of them. The mainsail was made from a fabric called Kevlar, which among other things is used to make bulletproof vests. The sail was laminated, with millions of Kevlar threads sandwiched in between two layers of Mylar-covered polyester that made the sail strong and limited its capacity to stretch. It was tough to push a needle through it once, let alone thousands of times. The mess in front of me was made harder to handle because I had to line up the sail where it had torn and glue patches of spare Kevlar sail cloth into position before sewing them tight. The spray glue got everywhere in the strong wind, including my hair. It took a while to dry and so I couldn't move on to the next section until that had happened. By the weekend my hands were a horror show, punctured and red and sore beyond belief.

Bizarrely, my mood had improved quite soon after the sail ripped. Once I'd actually dragged myself metaphorically from the floor and started work on sorting out the sail, I'd decided that things *could* be worse. I was only in a yacht race, not in some struggle for my life. I was safe, if uncomfortable. And my mission right then had become an immediate one to repair the sail, something that was vital before I could look again at the bigger picture of gaining miles, or rather, regaining miles I had lost.

I'd started the Around Alone in September aiming to finish and had already proved to myself that I could make the podium in individual legs. Indeed, even as things stood, I was still holding an overall top-three placing. I might still be able to finish, as long as I somehow got safely to New Zealand and then had time to get the boat ready for the fourth leg. This would include having the sail repaired by someone who knew what they were doing – my sail-making knowledge was basic, to say the least. Yes, seeing my mainsail tear in half had been an awful sight and another blow that I could have done without. Yes, it had been the harshest reminder yet that my original aim, of simply completing the race, was not a foregone conclusion. But I was still hanging in there. I would respond, however wearily initially, to whatever was thrown at me.

Andrew Pindar emailed to reiterate that my priority, in his eyes, should always be safety. He told me to remember that whatever else I did. He said my second priority should be getting to New Zealand, but only as long as it didn't compromise my first priority in the process.

As I sat there sewing for days on end, I knew there was no guarantee that the repair would hold when I finished. I had no choice but to keep going. Maybe it was that lack of choice that improved my mood. Maybe, at some level, I was rising to the more dramatic challenge of survival more enthusiastically than I had to the challenge of simply trying to gain a couple of miles here and there. This was encapsulated for me in a message sent by Tim Kent at the time. It contained a copy of a note that he had aboard his boat, written by his ten-year-old daughter, Whitney. It said: 'The difference between an adventure and an ordeal is attitude. You are gonna finish the race!'

Certainly, before New Year, my race had become more of a habit, worrying about the pilots while waiting for the poll reports as I tried to keep warm and maintain my basic needs. When the mainsail tore before my eyes, the race became still more of an ordeal. I was faced with decisions on how I was going to react, how I was going to repair the sail and whether it would be quicker to stop in Tasmania. A change in perception went some way to altering that. With my attitude changing to cope with the situation, the ordeal changed to an adventure, or a new added challenge to be overcome.

By 6 January, I'd made enough progress with the repair to raise the mainsail partially again. The wind until then had luckily stayed strong enough – near 40 knots for days – to keep me moving at a pace with just the staysail up, so that reduced the massive potential loss of miles I might have suffered if there had been just a little wind. I'd lost track of time, confusingly so, but that was more to do with passing through so many time zones than anything. Whenever I was aboard *Pindar*, I always used GMT for consistency's sake so that I remembered to pick up the poll reports and weather information at specific points in the day. But because we were now in the southern hemisphere, my day was upside down. It was getting light at 7 p.m. and dusk began settling about 9 a.m. In my constant tiredness I'd find myself momentarily forgetting whether the sun was about to go down or come up, not that I could see it often in the permanent grey. I'd be having my breakfast cereal and notice that my clock said 8 p.m. or 9 p.m. At least, by that stage in the trip, there were signs that I was getting closer to the end of the leg. I'd had to change both my satellite communications systems from the Indian Ocean region to the Pacific Ocean region. I was also working from a chart where my position was on the same page as the top corner of New Zealand, even though the end of the leg was still some 1,500 miles away.

Though it was still so cold that I kept a hat on at all times, the weather had warmed sufficiently for me to stop closing the hatch to sleep. I was also cheered by the stunning sight of the Southern Lights, which manifested themselves as streaks blazing in the sky. They were so vivid they looked supernatural. Watching them reminded me how fortunate I was, to be witnessing this phenomenon that many people will never see in their lifetime. I remember thinking, 'And this comes free!'

I'd just watch in awe. Better, I could do so without losing boat speed, sailing along underneath nature's light show until it disappeared. A different show might come along then, like the dolphins that swam in the bow wave at night in the phosphor-

sescence, leaving sparkly tracks behind them like magical creatures from a Walt Disney film.

As the sewing continued into the second week of January and
I edged closer to New Zealand, I saw more proof that I was
heading towards an inhabited part of the globe. My radar picked
up the first ship in a fortnight, the first since before Christmas.
The same day I picked up an email from the message board on
our website. It had been sent by a wellwisher, who only gave his
name as 'Doug'.

> *There once was a sailor called Emma,*
> *Who sailed through all kinds of weather,*
> *Her sail ripped in 2,*
> *But she did not get blue,*
> *No, she just stitched it with her hands made of leather!*

He was right about the hands, anyway. My mood was up and
down again, depending on how much or how little mileage I was
doing between poll reports. I was still tired. I still had more than
1,000 miles to go. Though the mainsail was partially raised and
the repair was holding up, I was getting frustrated again by the
lack of pace and my inability to do anything about it. When
Bernard won the third leg on 9 January – after a twenty-four-
hour mauling during his run-in that left his boat battered and
had caused the tiller to fall off in his hands – I was still 950 miles
away from Tauranga.

Email sent from Pindar, 9 January
While Bernard has been finishing, in very tough conditions i hear
(Bravo Bernard!!) its been a long day in the office here, the wind has
died and the sun has come out, and the only good thing about this is
that I have now repaired the solent and I think it's in good shape so I
at least have a bigger headsail. I would normally be tearing my hair

out in this weather, but I haven't stopped working on the solent and main since shortly after sunrise, and my fingers are burning from the sewing after they have had a few days off. In fact I might have sunburn too as I am out of the practise of applying suncream! We're in slip slap slop country now! It definitely feels like the Tasman sea and not the Southern Ocean now that the waves have reduced, the sun is out, alot less birds around and I have to admit if I keep travelling at 3.5 kts I will wish to be back in the depths of it asap! Since the sun came out and warmed the place a little the boots came off! yes, after 3 weeks in the southern ocean the feet are free, I finally peeled off the socks – no description here, it is up to your imagination, and yes it was that bad, I was going to throw the socks overboard but I wouldn't be that mean to the sealife!! I am still in thermals, midlayer bottoms and foulweather gear, but maybe by tomorrow or the next day, another layer can come off! Better get back to a little more stitching before the sun sets (about 0800ish now), Em x

When Thierry crossed the line in New Zealand in second place, Graham was lying third with almost 600 miles remaining, followed by Simone, me and then Bruce in sixth. Bruce had also lost the use of his mainsail but was still managing to close the gap on me, as was Brad at the front of the Class II fleet. *Hexagon*, *Tiscali* and *Pindar* seemed to be in a battle for the lowest average speeds and counting down the miles was a painful process. Saturday, 11 January offered some respite in terms of stable weather and a leisurely feel to the day yet I was still conscious of the need to be going places faster than I was. I had to hold back, though, because pushing would only risk damaging the mainsail and setting me back again.

Email sent from Pindar, 11 January
If this wasn't a race, today would have been the most pleasant yet. smooth water over a long slow swell, 5–6kts of wind, all the hatches

open and the boat airing, while I have spent since first light sitting at the helm and simply sailing the boat, no repairs, no maintenance, haven't needed to bail the boat out since yesterday, just short breaks to eat or make tea or dare to look at the positions (and my feet had another airing – but its still not warm enough to shed more layers yet – still thermals and mid-layer). My mainsail is still holding, if under will power only. I have a stiff neck from the habitual twitch I have towards the repair after every wave we go over awkwardly. the sun was shining behind the repaired part for a few hours today and its amazing how much daylight comes through, not very reassuring, but it doesn't look reassuring at the best of times. I am a little dissapointed today that neither Bruce or Brad want to join our 2kt contest we have going on, they insist on keeping up the boatspeed and somehow have dodged this parking lot that we have found! the 0600 poll just came in and I'm afraid that may be the last one I see with Bruce behind, only a few miles, at least he has slowed a little! a couple more hours of pleasant evening sailing to go, and squeeze every 'knot' out of this baby! Em x

On 13 January, a month after leaving Cape Town, we rounded Cape Reinga, the northernmost point of New Zealand. It was a gorgeous sunny day and I had my first sight of land since leaving South Africa. I could smell it: bracken and ferns, which, after a month of nothing but salt air and occasional whiffs of ships and whales, was like music to my nostrils. There were still 300 miles to go to Tauranga but at least the endgame had begun. It proved a struggle.

On 14 January I looked at the 6 a.m. report expecting the worst because I'd done only 20 miles in the previous eight hours. The sea was awful to sail on – not dirty but short, sharp waves, each one crashing over the boat or pushing it sideways, each one from a different direction, up to 30 knots of wind. I had tacked maybe four times and my tacking angle was terrible. I finally made a choice to go further east to catch a shift in the wind that I was supposed to have had by then. It was a bit of a risk but I appeared to be slower than Bruce at that moment anyway so it was really my only choice, and somehow we were still equal in terms of miles to the finish, so I had only lost one. I knew I'd find out soon if the risk had paid off.

My run-in was made more uncomfortable when I took a tumble in the cockpit in a wave. There was no bad injury but I was stiffening up so I felt like a crooked old lady. (Not that there is anything wrong with crooked old ladies, but it wasn't practical right then.) The fight went on.

The light winds were followed by stormy weather, the effects being compounded by autopilot failure. Bruce and Brad had been catching me due to better winds before I rounded Cape Rienga and then the three of us starting beating upwind southwards, down the east coast of New Zealand, to try to get ahead of one another before we reached the line.

Email sent from Pindar, 15 January
In the last 24hrs we have seen all types of different weather. Last night we had up to 40kts on the nose, and now, with 48.6miles to the finish Bruce, Brad and I are within spitting distance of each other, absolutely becalmed. Not a breath of wind. So again, the race restarts for the 2 crippled 60s amd the fast 50! I have my full main up, still holding together despite it flapping occasionally. Last night when we still had 25kts beating, one bad slamming wave destroyed the wind instrument at the top of the mast (I guess, they don't work now anyway.) and that was the spare one. This and a compass fault basically took out my pilot so I was sitting there handsteering in these 'filthy' waves wondering how to dash below and spark up the back-up. Finally built the courage to do that, lashing the helm while

I did, hoping a wave wouldn't crash tack the boat. Back-up didn't work either, totally different fault with a feedback unit down the back hatch. Being as stiff as I am at the moment, a dash to jump down the back hatch and then clambering out wasn't looking like a good idea so it was a case of running repair on the first pilot, which I managed getting on the phone to Mark Wylie again – what a star. So that was the beginning of the eventful night of 40kts trying to tack numerous times to get down the coast . . . no sleep except for a half hour this morning so I might take a nap on deck and wake with an alarm every 10 or 20 mins to check nothing has changed. I have just had a look on deck now after writing all this, and I think the only thing to report is that Bruce has rolled his headsail in and his bow has turned a bit but no movement otherwise. . . . I wonder if we will finally break the 2kt contest down to 0.4kts average in a position report . . . hmm, Maybe we'll finish this leg tomorrow if any wind fills in. Time for a nap, Em x

I was so close to the finish yet so exhausted. I was wishing it was over, all over, not just the leg but the race. I'd had enough of fire-fighting all the time. Then I was terrified when the pilots failed again. I was in my run-in, among rocks, islands, shipping and pleasure craft, not to mention 50-knot squalls. I don't know how I got through it. I didn't know how I'd got through a lot of that leg. I eventually arrived in Tauranga on 16 January, in last place in the Class I. I received a great reception. I disembarked. I sprayed champagne and spoke at a press conference.

After all that was done, I had only one urge left: to get as far away from *Pindar* as possible, and stay there.

13

I was determined to leave New Zealand refreshed. If I didn't manage that I thought I might really struggle to get through the fourth leg of the race, which was to include our second crossing of the Southern Ocean. I'd sailed between New Zealand and Brazil a year earlier, as part of the crew aboard *Amer Sports Too* in the Volvo Ocean Race, and knew what a hazardous trip it could be.

Although *Pindar* and *Amer Sports Too* were both 60-foot ocean-racing yachts, they were different species. The VOR 60 was designed to have twelve people sailing it and carried more sails than *Pindar*, despite a limit in the Volvo on the number of sails the rules allowed the boats to carry. There were no restrictions on the amount of sails on the Open 60s in the Around Alone – that was down to the discretion of the skippers – but the need for the lightest boat and ease of changes meant we carried fewer. Open 60s like *Pindar* would actually be quite difficult to sail with more than six people, let alone a dozen, because they are usually set up for one or two people. They have smaller cockpits and cabins and the set-up is based around more time using the autopilot.

Each crew member in a VOR 60 has a specific role, so you're

very much focused on one task. On *Amer Sports Too* I was a helm and trimmer, sharing the responsibility of steering the boat and trimming the sails in between shifts.

The team dynamics aboard *Amer Sports Too* were great. We were racing against teams who had accumulated up to four times the number of previous round-the-world races. It would take a very long time for a women's team to have such an experienced crew. Some of the other teams had skippers who were on their fourth or fifth round-the-world race. The most experienced women on board our boat may have been doing their third and perhaps a couple of the girls had completed two races, with another couple having achieved one or part of one. More than half the girls were on their first race. For the time and money that our team had, and for how well they actually fared against the guys in real time, I was proud to be sailing as part of such a team and look forward to it again in the future, hopefully on a mixed team where the physical limitations will be eliminated almost completely.

Prior to the Around Alone, the last time I'd left New Zealand by sea had been as part of that *Amer Sports Too* team. Once I was at sea aboard *Pindar*, the team was me. I didn't want to leave for Brazil wishing I'd spent more time recovering or full of regrets that I should have been more forceful in demanding time to rest. On the day of departure I wanted to actually feel like getting back aboard *Pindar* rather than reluctantly dragging myself back out there.

The three months of the race so far had already taken their toll. Keeping focused for so long during the race was draining in the extreme. I needed the New Zealand stopover to be a proper break. Of course I expected to devote my first week on land to fulfilling media and sponsors' commitments. Similarly, I knew I had to be around to make sure the guys on the shore crew had understood the job list and knew my priorities. But with a little over three weeks until the restart, I was keen to take up some of the opportunities to have some fun. I wanted to do things that didn't involve *Pindar*, team politics or pleasing other people. We had a shore crew to take care of the boat so that I had time to fulfil other commitments – most of which involved media and sponsors' work – so why not make the most of it? I felt I almost had to disappear to do that, though, otherwise my proximity would mean I'd be drawn in to doing something or other. Every skipper felt different about what they had to do. Some wouldn't leave their boats to anyone else, some couldn't as they had no choice, but as I had a great shore team, I took the opportunity to spend some much-needed time with friends and family.

An invitation to disappear arrived almost as soon as I stepped ashore. The America's Cup was due to be staged in Auckland from the middle of February and the precursor event, the Louis Vuitton Cup, was in its final stages when I arrived. In the Louis Vuitton Cup, all the 'challengers' to the reigning America's Cup holders (then Team New Zealand) race against one another for the right to compete in the America's Cup proper, a best-of-nine match race series. The Alinghi team from Switzerland were engaged in a battle with Oracle BMW Racing in the Louis Vuitton Cup final. The America's Cup is the Formula 1 of inshore yacht racing and I was intrigued to see it at first hand. It's less about coping, which is what I'd spent so much of the Around Alone doing, and more about seeking perfection.

I had friends who'd been involved with GBR Challenge, who had been representing Britain in the Louis Vuitton Cup, and on the day I arrived in New Zealand they asked me whether I'd like to go out on a hospitality boat to watch Alinghi versus Oracle

BMW the next day. It was the only chance that the members of the GBR crew who were still in New Zealand would have to be treated on the corporate vessel in question and I jumped at the opportunity. Tauranga is only 130 miles south of Auckland by road, so I'd be able to get up there quite easily. The racing was taking place in the Hauraki Gulf, just offshore.

My brother Dave, who was in Tauranga to greet me when I arrived, was driving up to Auckland on the Friday morning. Though I was ready to drop by the Thursday night, I got up early the next day to go with him, and slept the whole way. When we arrived, I went straight to meet Leslie, a friend who had been working with GBR Challenge, and she showed me around the GBR base before we boarded the luxury launch to go out and watch the racing.

We had a great view of the boats from the deck and if we were ever too far away to see them properly we had big screens with live TV coverage inside for a better view. It was wonderful just to be spending time with friends. The fact that this was a major event where I could just fade into the background and not attract any attention was great too. In the evening we went to a party hosted by One World, another of the teams who'd been contesting the Louis Vuitton Cup. The contrast between how I spent that day – having fun in comfort in the company of other people – and how I'd spent the previous month couldn't have been more marked.

On the Saturday morning I went back to Tauranga, did some more interviews, caught up with the guys and had an early night. On the Sunday I went back up to Auckland with some of our shore team to see what proved to be the final day's racing in the Louis Vuitton Cup. Another of my friends, Sanna, with whom I'd shared a flat in Glasgow for two years during university, was working on the Alinghi team and we were offered a place aboard Alinghi's support boat, *Pure Adrenalin*, for the day. That meant watching from the race course itself. The views were fantastic. Again we had live TV pictures screened below but could also watch via cameras onboard Alinghi, and then look out of the window to see the action unfolding right outside!

It was a great day out, made better by suddenly finding myself among the team who'd just won. The atmosphere was euphoric – lots of hugging and kissing and crying – and this went on into the evening when Alinghi had a massive party that lasted until the early hours. (Alinghi famously went on to win the America's Cup. Goodness knows what the celebratory bash for that was like!)

On the Monday morning it was back to *Pindar* business. One of the reasons for going to Auckland on the Sunday was I had an appointment at a sail loft on the Monday. I had a big decision to make about my mainsail. Either I had to get a new one made or have the torn one repaired. My shore team had talked with different sailmakers about the best thing to do before I got to shore. Most sailmakers would have preferred that we paid for a whole new mainsail. But when we laid the sail out on a sail loft floor, another sailmaker advised us that it was not necessary to build a whole new sail and that actually the repair would not be too expensive, and they could also strengthen it in obvious places. That would work and was considerably less expensive and so we got on with that. We left the sail with the North Sails loft in Auckland. It was the best decision I could have made.

We headed back 'home' to Tauranga, where I was asked if I'd like to go kayaking that evening. I did, enthusiastically, although I was so tired that I must have looked quite bedraggled at that point. I sat in the back of the leader's kayak, put my paddle up and crossed my feet on the top of the kayak. What a relaxing evening. The water was quite still and we saw glow-worms covering the sides of a rock face in the dark.

Tauranga was a superb place to be based. We were only a few minutes from a great surf beach, there were natural hot saltwater pools nearby and Mount Manganui was on our door-step. While we were there some idiot started a fire on the mountain that lasted for two days. A lot of native bush was destroyed but the local community responded by fund-raising to replant it.

The local gliding club took each of us skippers gliding and I also bought some flying lessons. If I was going to unwind, I might as well do it properly. The gliding was awesome. I even got to steer for a while although I was more intrigued to sit back and watch how it was done properly, playing in the thermals. My first flying lesson began with forty minutes in the classroom, learning how a plane moves. It wasn't that dissimilar to sailing. Once you reach a certain speed, it's all about small adjustments. I spent forty-five minutes undergoing checks and taxiing round the airstrip and then away I went. It was great to be allowed to take off and land on the second run.

I also took a surfing lesson. I hate learning things from scratch when I know I won't be any good so I asked the instructor beforehand whether if I paid my $50 for a lesson I would be able to stand at the end. He said only if I had good balance but he would try his best. I stood a couple of times, not for long, but it was an encouraging start. Unfortunately the three hours I managed during the stopover weren't enough to transform me, but it's something I'd like to take up one day, when I've got more time.

I went down to the boat now and then to check on things but

I really felt that I wasn't needed too often. I was finding plenty else to keep me occupied. I found I could spend more leisurely time thinking about the race and the next leg instead of squeezing thoughts and mental lists into the spare hour before I went to bed as on the other stopovers.

One day I tried kite surfing with Sanna and some other friends from the Alinghi team who came to Tauranga. I called my lesson on a kite surfboard to a quick halt right after one of the guys shot some great 'air' and landed in a tree. He was eventually discharged from hospital with a cast on his ankle and a few broken ribs. I didn't think I'd be too popular if my Around Alone participation had to be scrapped because I'd smashed myself up while kite surfing.

One of the more leisurely things I undertook was a pedicure, although it did serve a practical purpose. My feet had been a terrible mess after the third leg and were in dire need of some attention. It took the beautician some time to cut away all the dead skin. My feet were revolting, not the kind the beautician usually dealt with, she admitted. I certainly got my money's worth, even after I tipped her!

Our local hosts for the stopover were incredibly generous, staging all kinds of events and dinners and barbecues in our honour. We were treated to all manner of local dishes (smoked baby snapper, sea trout and the best steamed mussels I've ever tasted) and experiences, including watching a haka (a Maori war dance).

The race never wholly left my thoughts, but I was happy with the distractions. Even the reminders of the struggles of the race somehow seemed less burdensome. Alan Paris, for example, finished the third leg a full twelve days after I'd arrived. I watched him come in. Despite his rough trip, during which he'd had to stop in Tasmania, he looked completely unfazed, as fresh as when he'd left Cape Town.

A few hours after we'd had a celebratory breakfast, my sails arrived back from Auckland, mended and fit to go. The start of the countdown to the fourth leg began. More and more items on the job list were ticked off, including the removal of *Pindar*'s toilet. This had been on the list for some time but we finally got round to it as a weight-saving job. The weight wasn't in the toilet as such but because it was located so far from the water inlet and waste outlet, all the water-filled piping added weight too.

The toilet had been installed by Josh, who did a lot of corporate sailing. A genuine toilet was more appealing to clients. I'd rarely been able to use it. The way that *Pindar* moved when I was trying to sail as fast as possible made it much more difficult than the traditional 'bucket and chuck it' option. The toilet did have handles to hold on with, but they were too badly placed to make using them easy. I'd only used it once in the whole of the third leg.

With a little more than a week left until the restart, we put the repaired sails back on the boat. Things were looking pretty good. I was keen to stay relaxed during that final week and not let too many things put more pressure on me. I disappeared for two days with friends, returning to Tauranga on the Thursday before the start. I was ready to go to sea again.

During that final week's countdown, I got back onto *Pindar*, we did some great sailing, and I felt revived to go back into the gloomy grey of the Southern Ocean – it takes some motivating. I am fully aware that some people would have done things differently and spent 100 per cent of their time on the boat, going over everything with a fine toothcomb. But after more than 20,000 sea miles already, I felt I wasn't going to learn much more about her in two weeks in dock. I had spent evenings on the boat with Mark, working on the electronics, after the others had finished jobs on board during the day. The electronics were the most worrying part for me and often led to other things that could go wrong. I was happy with the boat, and as far as I was concerned, that was all that mattered. I wasn't tearing my hair out because of media commitments and the shore crew knew what they needed to do and did a great job doing it. It meant I did not have to be there on a full-time basis.

So to the final skippers' briefing ahead of our departure. The emphasis was on the threat of icebergs. The race committee imposed a 'way point' in the lower latitudes to prevent us from sailing too far south into the ice fields. They also told us that if any of us spotted any growlers we were to report them immediately to race HQ so everyone else could be informed. The briefing was a good way to make us refocus. Within a day we were on our way.

My send-off was touching. Tauranga had been a great stopover. It had been advertised as offering the 'warmest welcome' and it had lived up to this. Being out of a big city, we had had the advantage of the whole community, not least the local Maoris, getting involved. A race village had been set up with stands from all the local establishments including tented cafés, and there had been a social area in the middle with tables, chairs and sun shades.

Hector, a local Iwi elder who'd 'adopted' me during the stopover, presented me with a pounamu jade and sang a Maori prayer for my safety. We left the pontoon at 9.30 a.m. and were towed off the dock and into the Bay of Plenty. There were about 300 spectator boats watching us, but then New Zealand is sailing nuts.

At just after midday there was a five-minute warning and then a pleasant shift in the wind saw us head off. I was happy with my start over the line and with the way I left the Bay of Plenty but over the next twenty-four hours I was caught in several wind-free patches. I had problems with the autopilot that I couldn't figure out – nothing major but enough to worry me a little. I decided that I'd take fewer risks early on and not put myself in any situations where I had too much sail area up.

I was soon sailing with Brad, who was leading the Class II fleet by a long way, and spent a while in the same breeze as him. The other Class I boats were taking some distance out of me already. It didn't feel good, but it was only the beginning of the leg and I knew there was a long way to go. So much always happens that I didn't feel too disturbed by it. There were bound to be chances to catch up, if only because the boats in front of me would have their own problems and breakages later. That was inevitable. I wanted to sail a steady, consistent race and maintain a good average speed rather than sprint too early and break something. I reckoned that would only cost me more time in the long run, as it had done previously. I also wanted to conserve my energy to be ready for any problems.

As usual, I'd switched to using GMT as soon as I'd stepped back aboard *Pindar*. Within a day or so of leaving Tauranga, and having crossed the international dateline, the merry confusion of clock time and nature was under way again. My surroundings were telling me it was night but my watch said it was coming up to lunch. Local time said it was the early hours of the morning. In New Zealand, where my body clock was coming from, it was the early hours of the following day. At least by working to GMT I didn't have to worry about what day it was.

The position reports of the first few days weren't too bad. On the Tuesday afternoon, Bernard was in the lead (as usual) and had an 8-mile advantage over Thierry in second place. Bruce was only 7 miles further back, then Simone 10 miles behind that, and me 10 miles behind him. Graham was lying sixth in the Class I fleet, 23 miles behind me.

The pack shuffled slightly by Wednesday, with Thierry taking the lead, Bruce in second place, Bernard third and *Pindar* up to fourth. Graham was still behind me but so was Simone. By Thursday afternoon it was all change again, with Bernard back in front, followed by Thierry, Simone, Graham and Bruce. I was back to sixth but there were fewer than 100 miles between first and last and still 6,500 miles to Brazil. That kind of margin really shouldn't have concerned me too much at that stage. We were chopping and changing at regular intervals, each having our own mini-rallies and setbacks. Nothing was going badly wrong and I was clocking off the miles while feeling I still had something to spare. Yet at the time, probably because I was at the back of that shuffling pack instead of at the front, I was castigating the conditions daily for not having the grace to give me a fortuitous break.

Email sent from Pindar, 13 February
Having a shocker! I really thought that by now the wind should have come aft a little more and we could ease onto an easier and faster course, but the wind insists on teasing us and keeping us just low of course, still hard on the wind. I say 'we' as I still have had Brad (TOMMY HILFIGER) in my sights all day. He has been good company to talk to and I don't really want to lose sight of 'the dude' but no matter what I adjust to gain a little boatspeed, he is attached to me with elastic! I wouldn't normally mind so much – BUT HES NOT 60FT! Again I keep reminding myself it is a long leg, but that's already a broken record in my head and I could really do with being

a week down the line already after a few really fast days so I didn't have the whole leg in front! Its amazing how the whole psych of this leg is different, there has been a bigger build up maybe, more focus on it. I have images of how much ice we saw down here on Amer Sports 2 (Volvo Ocean Race) a year ago, and it really isn't good to dwell on but it's hard not to! Also today been looking at a few nasties that the weather has in store for us further down the line . . . but I'll leave that for another day, the really long term forecasts are not very accurate anyway, hmm. Time to put on some loud music and wash away those thoughts, sing along like you do in the car at the top of your voice when you think no-one is watching, til you realise you have stopped at the lights . . . at least I won't get caught out this time! Em x

My concerns about icebergs intensified the same day when the Around Alone fleet received news from another sailor, Olivier de Kersauson, that there were potential dangers for us ahead. Olivier was in the Southern Ocean aboard his maxi-trimaran *Geronimo*, making an attempt to win the Jules Verne trophy for the fastest circumnavigation. His shore team had contacted the Around Alone organizers with a message headed: 'Urgent – growlers and iceberg.' Although Olivier was further south than us by several hundred miles, it was still rare to be encountering ice where he was, and even rarer in such a relatively warm temperature (9°C). 'Never seen ice so high,' ended the message.

What was also alarming was the size of the main iceberg, which was apparently huge, and the fact that it was breaking apart, shedding 'growlers' as it did so. Growlers pose a bigger threat than icebergs simply because they're harder to spot and thus harder to avoid. They're easily hidden by the swell but if you hit one it still has the potential to sink you.

I'd experienced the dangers of ice during the Volvo leg

between New Zealand and Brazil. We'd sailed quite far south and the icebergs had drifted much further north than normal to meet us. They were monsters. Some were so big they appeared to be only a few miles away even though they were actually 20 miles away. But we knew we still had to be aware of growlers.

We could see them in the waves when we were surfing at 25 knots and they were a terrifying prospect. Every angry white surf in the ocean started looking like one after a while. So each time we sailed over a wave and were heading for the broken surf, we weren't sure whether it really was a broken wave or a lump of ice. Growlers can be the size of a fridge or car or bigger than a house. If we'd hit one it would have been the equivalent of hitting a brick wall in your car doing 30 mph. Our race would certainly have been over and our safety would have been far from assured.

We saw so many growlers during daylight hours from *Amer Sports Too* that all our efforts were spent spotting them and sailing around them. At night this was impossible. It was pitch black and we were barely able to see beyond the surf of the wave breaking in front. We had no idea where the growlers were. We had three days and nights of that and it was nerve-jangling stuff. The fact that we avoided a collision at night was more by luck than through any kind of skill. I think the only reason it didn't seem worse was because there were twelve of us on board and mentally I felt that twelve people dealing with a problem made it much easier to handle.

Still, having experienced the stress of what we went through then, I was determined not to find myself in that position again and definitely not when I was by myself. I didn't have a navigator telling me exactly where the icebergs were or guiding me to safety if I came across any. I didn't have twelve pairs of eyes taking turns on lookout to spot growlers. I had no desire whatsoever to be dealing with the stress of such a situation on my own. And after Olivier's warning I was convinced we would have a lot more ice and ice warnings.

So when it came to making a tactical decision about my route during the fourth leg, I took the cautious approach. Or rather, I bottled it. I stayed further to the north than any of the other Class I boats, therefore sailing more miles. I knew it was a gamble. No one would have a true picture of the ice situation until they got to it.

As it transpired, very few of the Around Alone fleet, even those who went furthest south, saw anything but a few scattered growlers. There weren't any major mishaps with ice. Ultimately my decision to stay north was not only cautious but unnecessary. It was a bad call, meaning I ended up sacrificing miles and ultimately put myself at the back of the Class I fleet. But faced with the same situation again, I can't honestly say I'd do anything different. I had had to make a decision I could live with. I made it. I lived with it. I lived.

My priority became to get through the Southern Ocean safely and get around Cape Horn in one piece. If and when that was accomplished, I hoped to get my mind switched back to pushing myself and the boat harder.

Email sent from Pindar, 14 February
Well, what to say really, I have decided to sail my best course I can without being pushed way south by the fleet, especially with Olivier de Kerhauson's ice report that came in. I need to keep reminding myself that my race begins at the Horn and I must get there with the boat in one piece to race the second half!! I have just had the perfect days sailing, beautiful sunshine, 12kt average boat speed, I wouldn't mind one bit if we had this weather all the way to Salvador but I am not kidding myself it will be! Time is a little

confusing since we crossed the date line, so I have continued to work on UTC and NZ time which has extended my Valentine's Day a little. I just had a call from Graham and I'd like to tell you what a romantic man he is under that rough exterior, but actually he just called to talk about ice. I spoke to Brad too but he is working on Local time so its still the 13th and his Birthday! Never mind, the bright side is that this year I have a very good excuse for the dozens of red roses not turning up. . . . . I really don't think the postman can make it this far out!!! I did however open some small gifts from my best mates, a reminiscing CD, some chocs, lace undies with a note I can't repeat, sheepskin insoles for my boots to keep them warm, a gift I haven't opened yet that's labelled, 'in case the next door neighbour pops in for dinner', and another gift I haven't yet opened, 'in case I get a 'snog', i think it is a chapstick/lip balm. . . . . what are friends for. . . . . thank you very much to Jane, Fi, Vic and Sanna, you are great. Oh, and a shell from Main beach by the Mount where we just left as a great reminder of surfing – thanks.

Back to the helm where I belong, With Valentine's Day thoughts, Em x

PS Happy Valentines Day Dad!!

14

Cape Horn holds an almost mythical status for mariners. It is the southernmost point of South America, on Horn Island, part of Tierra del Fuego in southern Chile. The route out of the Southern Ocean around that jut of land has claimed countless lives and scarred many more. Some sailors who have been within sight of it, feeling confident that they were only hours from the 'homeward' stretch north, have had their boats wrecked before getting there. Others have disappeared amid the mist and waves, never to be seen again. I knew on Valentine's Day 2003 that I was probably still a fortnight away. Yet my past experience – and my preoccupation with not becoming another statistic – meant there were few moments in those two weeks when the Cape wasn't already casting its shadow.

On the Friday, I had a call from Simone aboard *Tiscali* to see whether I was okay and to say not to hesitate to call him if I was worried. It was pretty unusual for him to get in touch while we were racing and I thought he must be anxious about the conditions too. Graham called, to talk about ice again. The same day I also spoke to Miranda Merron, who was in England and about to leave for our local in Hamble, The King and Queen. I asked her to have a drink for me.

The weekend weather was unusually clement, almost warm, and I had a couple of good days that culminated in a positive mood on the Sunday.

Email sent from Pindar, 16 February
I'd like to tell you how extraordinarily tough it is out here at the moment, how bitterly cold, constant physical demands are so extreme and we are just on the edge the whole time. . . . but I'll tell you the truth instead. . . . We're having a 'Blinder'! For three days now I hve been on the same tack, with the wind just aft of the beam so travelling at a good constant cruising speed, I did pull out a reef yesterday going to full main and put it back in this afternoon, other wise, the extent of work on deck has been occassional fine trimming as the wind has changed slightly, which has only been between about 18–25 kts.

In fact, it is as close to perfect sailing in perfect conditions that I can remember. I handsteer every so often for recreation but the autopilot has a bigger concentration span than my goldfish one . . . they say 3 seconds . . . and with the new true wind software on the pilot it has been almost perfect! The bonus is the warm wind coming in from the North so I still haven't got my full Southern Ocean kit on and we should have this another 36 hours or so now as the boatspeed has been better than I anticipated, so that front that has been threatening still hasn't caught up!

The 2 p.m. position report put me sixth of six in the Class I fleet but the data had its pluses. I'd had the best twenty-four-hour run, covering 367 miles, which was at least 30 more than any of the others. Bruce wasn't too far ahead, with the gap between him in first place and me at the back still a manageable 227 miles. With some 5,500 miles to Brazil, there was still everything to play for.

The winds rose on the Monday to 35 knots and the ride

became bumpy again. News also came through that Bernard had spotted a big iceberg. I knew where I preferred to be. My stress levels were rising again due to the weather but they were nothing compared to what they would have been dodging ice. And although my napping opportunities were becoming rarer again, I preferred that to sitting at the helm peering into blackness for growlers.

My pilots began malfunctioning on the Tuesday. Whenever the seas were bad, as they were becoming, this was always an added headache. I didn't have time to keep on top of everything while I was trying to diagnose and fix the problem and I quickly became agitated. With Mark Wylie's help I sorted it out and relaxed again. But days like those played havoc with my nerves. No problem ever seemed to start and end in isolation. When something went wrong, it invariably took my attention from other things, like keeping the boat in good racing trim. And if I wasn't keeping the boat fast and I still hadn't fixed the problem, then I couldn't nap properly. That made me more tired and more hassled. When something else went wrong, the pile stacked up. Maybe I'd miss a meal. Routine repairs were left to wait. Small worries grew and nagged at me. Before I knew it, a good day had gone bad.

The Southern Ocean had the capacity for its own swift metamorphoses, as I'd been reminded by Wednesday, 19 February. This was the Southern Ocean I remembered. The seas were mountainous, from varying directions, so there was no gentle swell, just masses of peaks that moved fast so they kept breaking and everything was white. In fact the water was so aerated I was sure that the boat was sitting lower in it than normal and kind of sticking to it a bit more than usual. I had spent six hours at the helm waiting for a lull so I could go on to autopilot and drop the staysail. I only had that and the three-reefed main up, but that was still too much for the constant 40-knot wind and gusts reaching 49 knots. The sea state wouldn't allow too much speed otherwise I would break the boat up. Every time I gained momentum, the wave behind picked us up and threw the boat nose first into the next one before the rudders could do anything about it. Sometimes I would be concentrating hard on taking some speed and working it over the next waves when I'd hear a massive roar and look back to see a mass of white water about to engulf me and fill my cockpit! That's when I wished I hadn't bothered looking around. One thing more terrifying than tonnes of water about to collapse on you is when this happens in the pitch-black night and you are on your own of course. It took until it was dark with squall clouds all around before I had the opportunity to go forward. I saw the wind drop to 30 knots once and just went for it. I was sure the wind was back up to 40 even by the time I reached the foredeck as the boat was screaming at top speed already. I just blew the halyard then spent about half an hour trying to control the mass of flapping sail on the foredeck and eventually lashed it down. It was amazing how big that little staysail could seem when there were 40 knots filling it. Where were the crew mates when I could do with a hand?!

I was in the kind of sea found in movies like *A Perfect Storm* or documentaries about rogue waves. It was building into a force that seemed more a sum of its parts. It was no longer something we were floating across, it had vertical factors in it. The tops of the waves were rolling over and crashing down so that the surf covered the surface. It was an angry, awesome sight and it was literally in my face the whole time.

Sometimes the Southern Ocean can be cold, wet, grey, miserable, isolated and exposed. At other times, like then, I wished it were just that and not a freezing maelstrom hurling hailstones as I panicked about icebergs and growlers and not being able to see beyond the bow.

Conditions stayed bad into the next day. The waves were huge and lumpy and there was no pattern to their form or movement. The wind, up to 40 knots, was in competition with the water to see which of them could be the most erratic. There seemed to be no relation between what the clouds were telling me that the wind should be doing and what it actually was doing. Big black clouds came and went with relatively small gusts and then a little white one, apparently harmless, would balloon to engulf the boat and bombard us with more hail.

Just before dark, I noticed a small new tear in the mainsail. It was in a no-stress area, fortunately, and I was happy to leave it temporarily. It didn't take long to repair the next day. The fact that the mainsail had been repaired in Auckland actually stopped this new rip becoming worse before I fixed it because the repair to the original damage had been so sturdy it had prevented the new tear from going further than might otherwise have been the case.

The second weekend at sea after leaving New Zealand saw the wind ratchet up again. It was sustained at 40 knots and gusting at 50. Every time *Pindar* took off on a surf and slammed down I was nervous about us breaking up. I was having trouble finding enough time to go to the toilet (or, to be more precise, to the bucket). Even for that apparently simple task, I needed to find a small lull in the wind, switch to autopilot, wait to see if it was happy and then dive below. Then I needed to remove my rubber-sealed gloves, my harness, my smock top (with dry seals at the wrists and neck) and my salopette foul-weather gear. Then there was a midlayer jacket, a salopette midlayer and three layers of thermals to come off while I kept an eye on the pilot knowing that if anything did go wrong there'd be little I could do about it but fall over. Then everything had to go back on before dashing back to the helm. At one stage I wasn't drinking enough fluids simply to minimize the number of times I had to go through the procedure. For all the questions about what it's like to be a woman in a sport dominated by men, perhaps that's the key difference: it takes longer to go to the loo!

Conditions such as those just had to be endured. They weren't comfortable and I couldn't sleep – all I could do was get on with it. I kept everything well stowed in case the boat broached in a freak wave and was laid flat. Getting through it was ultimately about coping at the helm, hand-steering to increase speed and using the conditions to my advantage.

The weekend saw dramatic developments elsewhere in the fleet. Bernard became the first boat to round Cape Horn and leave the Southern Ocean. Soon after doing so he reported that he'd suffered serious damage to his keel and was contemplating a stop for repairs. In the rough conditions, Graham had broken his boom on *Hexagon* within hours of Bruce doing the same on *Ocean Planet*. Koji, aboard *Spirit of Yukoh*, had suffered a knockdown and although his boat had recovered he had had to undertake a bruising climb up his mast to make repairs. Elsewhere in the Southern Ocean, not far from the Kerguelen Islands, which we had passed on the third leg, Ellen MacArthur's *Kingfisher 2* was dismasted that weekend as Ellen was making an attempt on the Jules Verne trophy.

I hated hearing bad news about anyone. Everyone in the Around Alone wanted to see everyone else make it safely to the next port. We all went through highs and lows and knew what the others were experiencing. Having said that, once I learned that all the other skippers were safe, I knew their misfortunes would at least give me a chance to make up some ground. And I felt vindicated in the cautious approach I had taken to the leg.

Since deciding to opt for a more northerly course and making a conscious decision to keep *Pindar* free of a hammering wherever possible, I'd wondered about the wisdom of my actions. I'd questioned whether I should have been pushing harder and taking more risks. But I kept coming back to the same answer. No. My decisions had been about getting to Cape Horn safely, and I couldn't bear the thought of another major repair to the sails or another climb up the mast. I just wouldn't have gone up in those conditions. It was too wild. It really would have been deadly.

Hearing about Ellen, my heart went out to her. I knew the frustration and disappointment she must have been feeling. In 1998, aboard *Royal & SunAlliance*, we'd also been dismasted in the Southern Ocean during a Jules Verne attempt. It felt like an unbelievably cruel blow of fate at the time. The memories of it came back that weekend in the Around Alone, not only because of Ellen but also because I was then not that far from where our *Royal & SunAlliance* dream had ended.

Aged twenty-three, I'd gone into the Southern Ocean without a clue about what was really in store. I'd heard so many stories about it – mountainous waves and terrible weather – and I couldn't imagine how we'd cope if things really got that bad. I'd never been there, so how could I imagine it? But everyone else had seemed pretty confident so I figured I didn't have anything to worry about. The only thing I was nervous about was the unknown. But just because it was unknown I didn't really get that nervous. I should have been a bit more afraid but ignorance was bliss and so I just went about my work as the medic, camerawoman and sometimes helm.

I wasn't involved in tactical decisions or decisions about how hard to push the boat at all, apart from when I was at the helm. When the dismasting happened I was down below. We'd been through some atrocious weather, then some relative calm and then more rough stuff. We'd just hit a couple of waves that had been bad enough to throw us from our bunks. I was getting dressed. It was about half an hour before my watch and I was stepping carefully from my bunk where I'd pulled some water-proof Gortex socks over the socks that were already on my feet and still drying out after the previous watch.

I stepped into my boots and tried to move down the cramped cabin without touching the condensation-drenched sides of the boat. I reached my foul-weather gear, pulled it down from the peg and then dried the bench with a chamois so I had somewhere dry to sit while I got dressed. I pulled off one of my boots and put that leg into my wet drysuit, pulling it up to my knee before replacing my boot and doing the same with the other leg. I pulled the drysuit up to my waist and then put on my midlayer jacket because I could feel an icy draught coming down through the hatch. This was routine but exacting, the kind of thing I'd done several times a day for more than a month.

As I was zipping my midlayer jacket the boat hit a wave and stopped dead. I grabbed at the shelf in front of me but had absolutely no chance of holding on. I shot forward, my ankle hitting the seawater pump on the bulkhead as it went past. I was thrown down the cabin, through the foul-weather gear storage area and into the furthest forward compartment. It took a second to register what had happened, but almost as quickly I was flying back the other way as the boat accelerated again at an amazing pace.

I held my ankle for a while, holding on to the shelf for stability with my other hand. My ankle and hand were both throbbing. Then I continued pulling my drysuit over my head. A few minutes had passed when I registered a lot of shouting coming from outside. But the main noise I could hear from there in the starboard hull was the loud twanging of the metal rod rigging as it hit the deck. And then there was silence. The rushing of the water ceased, as did the whistling of the wind. There was just the sound of the waves slapping against the hull. We'd stopped dead. A massive sea anchor was holding us in one place.

The off-watch girls came staggering out of the bunk cabin wondering about the commotion. 'The rig's down,' I said. I pulled on my harness and ran up on deck. There was just a void where the rig and sails had been.

Shit. It really was all over.

We spent a couple of frantic hours cutting away what was left of the rig with hacksaw blades and trying to remove the danger of the hull being punctured as each wave made the rig slam near it. After the boat was free of the rig we addressed the practicalities of building a jury rig (makeshift mast). We'd be safer again sailing down these waves in control as opposed to drifting around.

As the boat was 42 feet wide, when the mast fell over it had snapped on impact with the edge of the boat, leaving the bottom 20 feet of mast intact. Once we'd cut all the dangerous bits of rigging away from the boat, we adjusted what we had left and hoisted our new mini-mast. We strengthened the top of our new rig, which was a mass of splintered carbon, by putting a horizontal section in there so it would hold its shape and be strong enough to take some stays to hold the rig upright. Once the mast was in place, we pulled up a staysail on its side as a makeshift mainsail. The base of the staysail was now the height of the jury mainsail. Somehow we managed to get 19 knots out of the boat at this point but we already knew our destination was never going to be further than Chile.

The whole operation from the big rig coming down to our new dwarf rig going up took twelve hours. After a day or two we ended up taking the rig down to adjust it. It was an almost welcome distraction to the disappointment of having to end our adventure in South America.

As the onboard camerawoman, one of my tasks was to go around and record the crew's reaction. I've had more uplifting experiences although I still take pride in the documentary we made using the footage from that voyage. Among those dog days after the dismasting, several images still stand out in my head. One is of the various girls lying in their bunks trying to find the words to describe what they'd felt as the mast came down. The total disbelief at what had happened – through no one's fault – and the descriptions of willing the mast to stay upright in one piece were hard to film. Goodness knows what it must have been like to experience on deck.

There were lighter moments in the aftermath, as in the days after an RAF Nimrod had come to visit us and drop a package of beers and magazines and other morale-boosting gifts, such as the board game Trivial Pursuit, to while away the days *en route* to Chile. One day I was filming Adrienne Cahalan, our navigator, as she was working on the computer, planning our route to shore. She confided that she kept being distracted by the girls asking her to use the internet to find answers to questions for Triv!

And then there was Miranda, who was resolute in her requirements as soon as we made landfall. 'Steak,' she said. 'And red wine, and beer, and steak, and red wine, and red wine . . .'

•

Back in the Around Alone, not so far from where we'd been hit by that fateful wave, the bad news weekend of 22–23 February gave way to a more routine new week. *Pindar* was bobbing in a large swell but not so uncomfortably that I couldn't catch up with some maintenance tasks including topping up the diesel, charging the batteries, filling the stove with fuel, checking the position reports and preparing something to eat. I was more than ready to leave the Southern Ocean.

Email sent from Pindar, 24 February
Roll on the Atlantic, climbing towards home and the North Atlantic that I know so much better! The last leg us taking back into 'The Pond', it seems like years ago almost that we left Newport, and New York, and Brixham and so much has happened since! Hmm, 700miles til the corner. Em x

The storm hit me soon afterwards.

Email sent from Pindar, 25 February
Can't write much now, been on the tiller for almost of 10 hours now, been gusting to 56kts, now between 30 and 45, nearer top end most of the time. Have deliberated taking main down a few times, but have kept it up. The quicker I get round The Horn the better. Gybed a couple of hours ago in 40kts, went smoothly somehow. . . thank you. . . . white water and spray everywere, big waves from the side knocking us sideways, in the dark. It's just a mad sleigh ride that you can't get off, even when you want to. . . Hopefully the wind will die soon so I can get some naps in –

exhausting and quite stressful, but only 380miles to The Horn now.
A day and half and counting. . . . em x

By the early hours of Wednesday 26 February, I was 150
miles away from Cape Horn. The weather had eased and I was
already planning to give Neptune most if not all of a bottle of
champagne for his kindness.

Email sent from Pindar, 27 February
Rounding the Horn, finally, has been every bit as good as I imagined
and better! And the best part is my final memory of the Southern
Ocean, Surfing on some perfect waves, 2reefs, Solent and Staysail,
35kts gust and my highest speed on this machine – 32kts! Just
Fantastic!! I opened my bottle of Champagne as I cruised past the
island, the rain stopped, the wind died, the sea flattened out and
some rays came through the clouds over the islands! Quite awesome
and such a contrast between the two oceans! Wow, I have been
looking forward to getting back into the Atlantic, it feels almost like
'home turf'! I spoke to the lighthouse keeper who took the yacht
details, I believe he logs all vessels that pass. He asked about 3 times
how many people were onboard, didn't confirm and went onto the
next question, I thought I spoke good English to him, I even tried
'uno' – nevermind. I saw a cruising yacht rounding the other way,
and a ship – quite civilized after weeks of seeing nothing, its pretty
special sailing past after having done the hard slog across the
Southern Ocean. The jagged islands and rocks were stunning and
quite daunting, I was happy the wind died to 15kts so I sailed in very
close to them, not sailing any extra miles than I need to – afterall,
my race has just started for real!

I had less than 3,000 miles to go to Brazil, where we'd have a
stopover in Salvador. The distance was equivalent to a mere
single crossing of the Atlantic. I felt better than I had at any stage

in the leg. I was clear of the most obvious danger it would throw at me, had moved up to fourth place and thought third was attainable. The boat was in good shape and I was looking forward to warmer climes. What could possibly go wrong now?

15

The way I saw things after rounding Cape Horn, I had two home
straights to negotiate. The first, to Salvador in Brazil, would give
me a chance to consolidate my overall position of third in the
race. The second, which was the fifth and final leg of the race – a
relative 'sprint' of 4,000 miles from Salvador to Newport, Rhode
Island – would be all about faith and hope. The faith would be
imbued in *Pindar*, that she would hold together and help to hold
me together, and that nothing dastardly would befall us at the
last. There was little chance of winning, with the top two boats
never being outside those positions, but the hope was not only to
hold together but to show some great form at the end and break
Bernard and Thierry's habit of coming first and second. We had
all shown potential at some point to be able to give them a good
race but never quite separated them. Maybe this would be my
chance to do just that. A big hope, but I thought it was feasible.

From here on in it was all about numbers, and not just boat
speed and twenty-four-hour runs but the bigger picture – points.
Because in the way that the Around Alone had been structured in
2002–3, it was each skipper's points total that would decide who
won.

The system was straightforward enough. The winner of each

leg scored 10 points, the second skipper scored 9, the third skipper 8, and so on. Whichever of the skippers had completed all five legs and had the most points at the end was the winner. Obviously, if a skipper didn't finish the whole race, they were out of the equation. It was no good having four great legs and then smashing your boat on the fifth and failing to finish. The scoring system was designed not only so that completing the whole course was a pre-requisite but so each skipper on each leg had an incentive to keep pushing to improve their placing every mile of the way.

Bernard had started the fourth leg with a perfect 30 points, followed by Thierry with 27 and me with 20, the same as Graham. I was ahead of Graham on the overall podium because my total elapsed time was quicker than his. (Elapsed time would always be the 'tie-breaker' when two skippers had the same number of points.) Simone had 18 points and Bruce had 17. All of us still had everything to win or lose. Any of us, as I'd rounded Cape Horn, could still have won the race or ended up last of the finishers, or failed to finish.

Failing to finish wasn't in my thoughts at all, not after safely exiting the Southern Ocean. Coming last of the finishers wasn't getting a look-in either. It couldn't be ruled out but it wasn't palatable. Which left me looking upward and forward. I wanted to get past Simone to increase my overall advantage on him. And as for Bernard and Thierry, I'd just have to wait and see. It wouldn't be over till it was over. That had to be my mantra after turning the corner.

The wind began to shift on the Friday, 28 February. This wasn't in my favour because I wanted to bear away at a point north of the Falklands and then gather speed as I moved north. The shift was disrupting my plans. On the other hand, a shifting wind meant we were all relying on tactical acumen to steal an advantage. I thought this levelled the playing field despite making life physically harder because of more frequent sail changes. If the wind was steady and stayed that way, the race risked turning into a procession to Salvador, with all of us heading steadily forward in the same order.

> *Email sent from Pindar, 1 March*
> In answer to some recent advice on our website for me to sail a straighter line so I would get there quicker and beat the others; I really wish it were that simple – you hold the wind steady, I'll hold the boat steady. . . . . I promise! In fact you have written that advice just as I have taken a detour slightly to the east so I don't try sailing through the middle of a high pressure system in a couple of days – there normally is a reason for my squiggly lines – honest! Talking of sail changes, winds up again, time to reef! Em x

The fatigue from the Southern Ocean was starting to set in but I had to keep pushing to maintain my podium placing. The more I pushed, the more tired I became. It didn't take long for the psychological boost of rounding Cape Horn to start wearing off. A day or two without any decent sleep quickly eroded my relief, opening the way for different frustrations.

Instead of worrying about *Pindar* staying in one piece, which had been the most important thing before Cape Horn, I had new worries about not making the best of the safer conditions. I think that's natural enough, to escape one set of circumstances and be heartily grateful but then find fault with the next set. It was a sapping experience, however, one where mercies were accepted but quickly forgotten in the hope that more might follow. But that's just not how it seemed to be happening.

Yachting and most sports are futile if you look at their direct meaning in life. Sailing is my passion and I want to excel in it. I know the risks and I know what I am doing and wouldn't go out there if I thought I wasn't going to come back. Yachting is not dangerous compared to some sports – it is just a perceived risk that some people have. I believe there are a lot more dangerous sports and I would easily be convinced that ocean yacht racing has quite a low real risk.

As I was entertaining such thoughts my emotional roller-coaster was set off on another lap by breaking news. Behind me, Graham Dalton had suffered a dismasting. One minute I'd been fretting about losing miles, the next I was in shock wondering if he was okay – details were still sketchy. Then came word that he was safe, which was a relief. Next came the realization that just because we were out of the Southern Ocean it would be stupid to start assuming conditions wouldn't turn nasty. Then there was more relief that at least it wasn't *Pindar* floating around with no mast. Gut instincts are all well and good, and my gut instinct, my first reaction, was 'I hope Graham's safe.' But in a race situation it's not only water that hits you in awkward waves. Just what *is* the appropriate reaction to hearing that a rival has had a setback? I'm still not sure I have a definitive answer to that.

I knew that before the dismasting Graham would have been pushing hard to catch up. He'd been so far ahead of me through most of the Southern Ocean that he'd wanted to get back there. I knew how competitive he was and how keen he was to catch me and overtake me again. And I was quite relishing the prospect of a good race and staying ahead. But the last thing I expected was his dismasting. It happened, however. And he was safe. Time to move on.

(Graham made it to land, slowly, and later announced his retirement from the race. He was hugely disappointed, as anyone would be, but there was no way he could continue without a mast. A replacement was one requirement too many.)

By the fourth Monday of the leg, 3 March, the bite of the Southern Ocean conditions had finally started to ease. The grey skies and sea had turned blue. The air temperature was still too cold to shed much clothing but at least one top layer of foul-weather gear came off. My mood was enhanced immediately, and improved again when I saw the afternoon poll report. By dodging the high-pressure zone that had been impeding the boats ahead of me, I had closed a 200-mile gap between *Tiscali* in third and *Pindar* in fourth to 70 miles. For the first time in a long time – probably since the second leg – racing felt like a great pleasure again. That continued to be the case through the Tuesday, and by that afternoon I'd closed the gap on Simone to 31 miles.

Email sent from Pindar, 4 March
Another good day on the fine ship Pindar! The evening was finished of with a stunning green flash as the last of the sun dipped over the horizon – what a great sight. I have only seen a couple in all of my sea miles . . . perfect!

The weather has warmed up nicely, down to just thermals under the foul weather gear, and the breeze, even now its dark, is still warm which makes a nice change! As it got dark, I was fortunate to be sailing away from some quite amazing thunder clouds behind – clear skies except for a couple of these clouds which looked quite ferocious. So I am feeling exceptionally lucky at the moment! I also finally took my hat off which has been on (one of three or four hats) for basically 3 weeks – nice!

On a more serious note though, I only have about 100 miles ahead of me before I hit the 'no breeze' zone near the centre of this long barrier-like high pressure. It is slowly moving north but really not that quickly; so it looks like the end of Pindar's turbo-catch-up moment! Shame, I was beginning to enjoy it! I'll soon be joining the frustrations that the others must be feeling at the moment, and when it comes upon me, I must remind myslelf of the couple of hundred miles I have just made up! Off to enjoy the last of this breeze. . . . Em x

By the Wednesday, I'd gained on Simone again. The afternoon poll put me 12 miles behind *Tiscali* and at one point I was as close as 6 miles. I was on a roll. I felt vindicated by the tactics that had kept me safe in the Southern Ocean and were now propelling me home. I felt, for a short while, invincible. Even when a discarded fishing net and ropes became tangled in my starboard rudder, I had little hesitation in performing a balancing act over the back to cut them away with a knife. Okay, so holding on with one hand wasn't too clever and my heart leapt a few times as images flashed through my head of me slipping into the water and *Pindar* sailing away from me. But I was wearing a harness and the fear factor kept my mind sharp as I completed the job and got safely back to the deck.

Somewhere out there, just over the horizon, were *Tiscali* and Simone and I felt I was reeling them in. I'd been in a good weather system. I was so near. I was determined to get in front. I did everything I could to eke the last knot of speed from the boat. I was willing the wind to pick me up and throw me forward. I was going past them in my mind. I was on to the next target. This was dreamland, surely? It was. I hit a windless zone and stopped dead.

Email sent from Pindar, 6 March
Long frustrating day as you can see from the position reports. I hope I don't lose all of that 250 mile catch-up in the same 'turbo'

fashion. . . . . . let me out of this high pressure. . . . . what more
can I say . . . Em x
PS wish I had a good fishing line, there have been some big fish
jumping in the becalmed waters!

Tiscali had opened the gap to 88 miles by that afternoon. Worse, Simone's twenty-four-hour run had been 150 miles and he still had some wind. My twenty-four-hour run had been 69 miles.

It's hard to describe just how frustrating it was to be sitting becalmed, knowing the three boats ahead were tearing more miles out of me by the minute. There was absolutely nothing I could do about it. It wasn't even the case that I could work harder to go faster. There was no wind, full stop. Patience became a virtue. I didn't feel very virtuous. There was no guarantee when the breeze would arrive. I knew I'd done the same to Simone only a few days before, torn miles out of him while *he* suffered his lull. But who wanted to be fair about things? It was yet another situation where I would have paid all the money in the world just to get out of there. Except I didn't have any money on me. And Neptune doesn't accept cash.

I stood around grinding my teeth. I always grind my teeth when I'm stressed, especially in my sleep, and never realize I'm doing it. It's something I'm very aware of though because dentists always tell me to 'reduce the stress, Emma'. The last one who'd said this had been back in New Zealand. The problem had got worse during the race.

Email sent from Pindar, 7 March
Well I was hoping that this would be my last Friday at sea, but after
a couple of very slow days I will have to average faster than 6 kts for
that to be true. Looking at Thierry and Bernard's speeds, that does
not look very possible!!

Nevermind, the last 48 hours have been pretty tough and it has taken alot of self-counselling to get through the days. About every 20 mins when I get frustrated at doing 2 kts and I can't stop my brain from calulating how long it will take to get to Salvador at 2 kts (painful); or each time I was stopped dead with no wind, watching a little dark patch of breeze slowly creeping up, when it finally gets to the boat with 4kts and a wind shift, it promptly puts the boat into irons (directly into the wind), by the itme I sort it out, tack back, the 4kts has reduced to 2kts, lasts a little longer then dissipates completely and there are various other scenarios just as frustrating like the full length battens not popping through with a tack, trying for 2 hours to get them to pop, finally get fullboatspeed from the 3 kts on the good shift, then it shifts back and you have to tack again!. . . . . well it has taken this long just to be able to write that down without grinding my teeth more than I already do . . . Well, every 20minutes or so, when another frustration shows itself, I have to remind myself that, all the miles I am losing now, at the moment amouts to half af what I gained in a couple of days; I am in a 60ft boat not class 2 so will spend less time out here than most (unless Brad skirts this high pressure and flys by); I am not in Graham's shoes at the moment which would be the ultimate dissappointment/frustration and my heart goes out to him, hang in there Graham!! . . .; also I am not in Derek's shoes, he has had a very long, very tough leg and I hope he gets to Salvador in good shape after his Falklands stop that he is planning. . . . keep going Derek!!

So after these thoughts in succession, I feel better about my drifting around until the next frustration arrives, then i go through the whole thought process again! I now have 7 kts and want to continue spending all my time on the helm to make the most of it, but the reality is I have had about 2 hrs sleep in the last 24, and need to nap during these dark hours – each time I have left the helm to the pilot doing 4 kts (abuot the minimum boatspeed the pilot copes with) within minutes the wind has died or shifted faster than the pilot can react to so I slow down again!

Anyway, enough of my wingeing, this message has been more therapy for me, so I know I am in good shape really, off for a nap, with my fingers crossed, Em x

As I emerged from the light winds, huge, dark clouds filled the skies and I was engulfed by the harshest thunderstorm I can remember at sea, with claps like bombs accompanied by torrential rain.

I recall big thunderstorms on land as a child when we'd hide indoors in the warm and listen to the rain bulleting against the house and then see lightning and count until the thunder rumbled to see how far away it was. Out there that dawn I was wishing I was tucked up in a warm bed, listening from the refuge of a house.

The lightning was so close I could smell it. Imagine standing in a field with lightning hitting other parts of it not far from you, and hearing and smelling the sizzle as it hit. I was imagining.

I still don't understand how I could see the lightning hitting the water within a stone's throw of the boat and yet it didn't hit the top of the mast, more than 80 feet up in the air. I thought lightning was supposed to take the quickest route to the surface. I was mightily relieved it didn't and just grimaced and bore it but I felt isolated and vulnerable. Even my thick, rubber-soled, Southern Ocean sea boots didn't diminish that feeling.

Email sent from Pindar, 8 March
There was one squall that looked like it had more wind than the 22kt gusts I had been getting. Standing next to the mast and dropping in the 3rd reef, a white wall of water, spray, rain, wind just hit us, knocked the boat flat and the sail that had just dropped

into the lazy-jacks on the boom just got blown back up the mast as the boat was on its side and my poor mainsail just got flogged for what seemed too long, but was probably just a matter of seconds.

The boat eventually popped upright again, dropping the sail back into the boom; and I have to admit that I'm feeling lucky the mast is still in place, but the mainsail did get the worst deal again. Another small tear, different place, but not as big as the one during the Southern Ocean leg a couple of weeks ago!

Once again, the sail repair kit and drill has been put to good use and I am now back to sailng with 2 reefs, upwind, not quite making course!

830 miles to go and just trying to get there in good shape. Too many people have had a rough time this leg; the latest being Derek who really has had the worst of it now. He has seen the Cape Horn conditions that the rock is reknown for!! I wish him well into the shelter of land, safely and quickly!!!. . . . . . at the moment, Rio is only 160 miles NW of here and looks very appealing! A year ago, on Amer Sports Too, we sat off Copacabana beach for about 8 hours becalmed, and even that sounds like a great thing at the moment!!! Better get back on that helm, the waves are not making it easy for this autopilot. Happy I'm up and going again, EM x

For a day after the worst of the storm had passed I could still hear the distant rumble of thunder and see flashes on the horizon. The air was electric but at least I was through it.

Behind me, back at Cape Horn, Derek had been dismasted in winds of 70 knots. His boat had pitchpoled (suffered an end-over-end capsize) and he had briefly been trapped underneath. His mast had snapped. The boat had righted itself but some of its electronics equipment had exploded and the keel had been damaged. Incredibly Derek vowed immediately that he would head for land to make repairs and then rejoin the race, which he eventually did, with Andrew Pindar coming to his rescue.

My weekend passed peacefully enough, although the cogs in my weary brain were doing overtime trying to work out the permutations of how I'd stand in the poll if various situations unfolded. Bernard was ahead of me but would incur a forty-eight-hour time penalty for stopping for repairs back in the Falklands. That meant I still had a chance of finishing ahead of him in the points in the leg as long as I finished less than two days behind.

I also knew that as long as I stayed where I was relative to Simone, I'd enter the final leg ahead of him on points, but I wanted to give myself a cushion before then, not see my advantage eroded. That would only add stress to the run-in. I kept pushing, onwards and north, right through the heart of the Pampo oilfield.

That vast area – some 120 miles long and 40 miles wide – was packed with rigs, support boats, tankers and other vessels. As I began sailing through it I had plenty of wind and I really thought it would only take a few hours, maybe half a day. I'd planned the shortest route through and when I first got in among the rigs I had good speed. Then the squalls came through, big winds from different directions that dramatically altered my course. It became tougher to control the boat. I had to be careful not to hit any number of rigs, tankers, security boats, maintenance vessels and supply ships. It was like a buzzing but malevolent city from some different kind of world.

It got dark very quickly that night. The rigs had burners on top that threw massive flames into the air. It all looked very surreal and futuristic. The wind was all over the place. I was tired and wasn't ready for a full night awake dodging obstacles. I was all over the place just trying to stay safe. I kept trying to head upwind and towards the finish. But then hard-earned distance would be wasted as I had to bear away round the back of some vessel or other.

I tried to go for pure speed and get out quicker but it just wasn't that easy. I wished I'd stayed outside the oilfield altogether. The reason I hadn't was that I was on the wrong side of it when a big shift in the wind came through and that made it hard to justify sailing up to 50 miles out of my way on a bad shift.

If I'd known how difficult it was going to be though, I wouldn't have hesitated to go the long way, around the outside. Too late. I was amongst it and there was plenty more to come.

When dawn broke I realized just how many obstacles were around me. Dozens of towering rigs. Hundreds of vessels. It was a vision from hell. Then the wind died so I was sailing at about 5 knots. With maybe 2 knots of current against me this made it even harder to sail around obstacles. I couldn't sail to windward of anything because I ran the risk of drifting down into a ship or into the security proximity of a rig. I knew that if I did I'd instantly have security boats all around me within seconds, and they wouldn't hesitate to ensure I left the area immediately.

At one stage I sailed close to one large vessel that was about to drop its mooring and motor away. I was just about to sail past its stern so it waited for me. I could feel the eyes of the guys on the ship watching me, just waiting for me to go past. I wanted to shout to them that I had a big crew down below but they were all sleeping just now. I didn't. I just got out of the way as quickly as possible.

I'd been in regular contact with Brad since Cape Horn. What he told me around that time only made me want to move even more quickly. He wasn't too far behind and would call up daily. I'd told him how awful and frustrating the Pampo oilfield was and not to bother going through. But he must have encountered similar wind patterns and decided it couldn't be so bad as to throw away a bunch of miles. He went through, and the next day I got a call from him.

'You were right,' he said. 'This is totally hellish. I shouldn't have come through and now I've got some boat that's been following me for ages. I'm heading away from it at the fastest speed I can go. I've changed direction and it's still following me. I can't get through to the race committee but I just want someone to know what's happening. Can you try them again for me? I'm going back on deck.' He told me his position and signed off.

I called the committee and let them know what Brad had said. I called him a few hours later to check he was okay. He said his pursuers were further behind but still following him even when he changed course. A little later that day, he was nearly out of sight of them and was just ready to be as far away as possible from that oilfield. I don't think anyone else went through after that. I wish I hadn't. Brad wished he hadn't. I wish Brad hadn't. I'd had enough of a fright with my own mystery boat back off the coast of Africa and I didn't even want to think about it any more.

Email sent from Pindar, 11 March
Well, if i didn't laugh i'd cry!! finally out of pampo oilfield, the afternoon held one setback after another. Problems with the auto pilot . . . wind instruments . . . ballast . . . water maker . . . [but] my luck is turning as I had a wind shift a few hours ago that has allowed me to head north, but is that a mixed blessing as it will allow Simone to pack in some miles and keep up a high average? – nail biting stuff! I'm off for a nap now while everything appears balanced! Em x

Bernard had crossed the line first, on the Monday afternoon, 10 March, followed by Thierry, who actually won the leg due to

Stamm's time penalty. That meant I needed to finish by the Wednesday, 12 March, to 'beat' Bernard in the leg. That wasn't going to happen. The conditions and my mood had both improved but I simply wasn't getting the wind I needed to propel us to the port.

When Simone finished on the Thursday, I was still out there, frustrated. I couldn't even find it in myself to enjoy being warm and dry. It was actually too hot for that, pushing 40 degrees in the cabin. I was constantly near the helm to keep the boat moving, adjusting the sails with every little puff of wind. Then as the boat speed increased slightly, I'd need to adjust the sails again. But while I was doing that the pilot kept steering on a slower course, which meant the wind changing again. It was a battle to keep the boat moving at all. If I left the helm for more than a few minutes at a time, I risked stopping altogether. In those few days drifting towards Brazil, I wished more than at any stage in the race previously that I was sailing double-handed. I just craved an extra hand onboard.

I was still at sea throughout the Friday, by which time I was longing for the finish. I had visions of Salvador within my sights but no wind to carry me the final miles. That little stretch of Brazilian coast became purgatory.

Email sent from Pindar, 14 March
I had a call from Brad earlier today in obvious frustration, and by the end of the call he was laughing and told me he always feels better after our phonecalls which I was quite flattered by. . . . . until he told me it was only because every time he has called I have been going slower than him. . . . . maybe not that flattered (today I was doing 0.8 kts when he called). Better go and squeeze a little more boatspeed out of the mighty fine Pindar while I have the end of the night's breeze, Em x

By the time I crossed the line, on the Saturday afternoon, I had almost got over the fact that Simone had beaten me. That's how long the last few days felt.

I felt absolutely knackered but a fireworks welcome perked me up. I didn't even feel too stressed by waiting an extra half hour for the spectator boat carrying my parents. They'd broken down offshore while following me the last few miles in.

When we docked, I took my first steps on land for thirty-four days. My legs didn't really understand what was going on but I managed to convince them to hold me up while I was handed champagne and a caiphirina cocktail. I thought I'd earned it. The local hospitality was refreshing.

I knew anything could happen in the last leg, and probably would. I also knew I was still on the overall podium. I could even afford to finish behind Simone in the run to Newport and still beat him overall. As long as no one else came between us.

16

Brazil was a blast, certainly the most sociable stopover for the skippers. I think this was partly because we had a de-mob mentality, knowing we were only one leg away from the finish. The casualty list meant Graham wasn't there and Derek didn't arrive until after we'd left but the rest of us made the most of Salvador. The nautical centre where we moored our boats wasn't open to the public so that also meant there were fewer outside distractions. The hotel was just a short taxi ride from the boat so access was easy. I had my parents there for a while and my good friend and team photographer Marc Turner. There was us skippers, our shore crews and supporters. A few hammocks dotted around added an air of relaxation.

There was an organizing committee at each stopover that worked closely with the overall race logistics manager, who basically ran the race on site and communicated back to the race headquarters office in the UK. Daisy was the local Brazil stopover organizer. She also worked for customs and would check us in and out of the country after we crossed the line and before we left.

When I arrived on the dock in Brazil Daisy gave me a string bracelet, tied in local fashion with three knots. I was told as it was tied on to make a wish for each knot. The idea is that you keep the bracelet on until it falls off naturally, and then the wishes come true. I wished that I would finish the race safely, that I would continue living life as I chose, and that I would be able to spend more time with friends and family in the future than I had done in the previous five years of sailing and travelling.

Salvador had a good feel to it, especially Pelourinho, the historic part, known as 'the city within the city'. It was full of old colonial buildings, cobbled streets, markets, cafés, restaurants and clubs and was a good place to unwind, especially during evenings spent there with the other skippers. Still recovering from the fourth leg, I was so tired on one occasion that I didn't even fancy a beer, let alone going out late. But I found a bench next to our dinner table and had a twenty-minute nap while everyone else finished dinner. It seemed perfectly acceptable behaviour to everyone, including the restaurant staff, and I woke up refreshed and raring to go. We ended up going dancing all night and then walking home at 6 a.m. as the sun came up.

That night also stands out for an incident in one of the bars where we went dancing. A big, friendly local guy approached Tim Kent and me as we were on the dance floor, not exactly moving like the locals but giving it our best shot.

'Do you speak English?' the guy asked.

'Yes,' I said, expecting some articulate revelation about where exactly we were going wrong. I'd overestimated his grasp of the language, which turned out to be about as good as my Portuguese. For the next hour he stood next to us, saying, 'One, two. One, two. One, two.' As though we couldn't feel the bass moving the bar stools!

By the time we left, Tim and I were in absolute hysterics. Like I said, we were de-mob happy. Everything we did seemed to have a lightness to it. For the rest of the stopover, and during the final leg, Tim and I would pass the odd 'One, two' to each other. Even now, if I wrote Tim a letter (or vice versa) that said 'One, two' and nothing else, I know it'd raise a laugh.

The stopover wasn't devoid of work. I was out of bed and down at the boat by 7.30 a.m. on the Sunday after my Saturday arrival. We needed to do some filming in the cabin so we had footage for some of the activities that I hadn't been able to film myself doing at sea. This included climbing into the bunk in my foul-weather gear, which felt faintly ridiculous in the searing heat of a sunbaked, stationary boat. Then I had to do some cooking shots, which only increased the temperature more.

At least having access to a swimming pool at the host yacht club was a bonus. Whenever there wasn't any need for me to be down at the boat, I'd go for a swim or test one of the hammocks. Lying around never lasted long though. Not doing anything is fine for a few minutes but I've never been good at lazing in the sun. I was soon finding other things to fill the time.

I went away for a couple of days with my parents to a nearby island, Itaparica. We caught a 'taxi' from the ferry slip. The taxi was actually a wheelbarrow, pushed by a local guy. He ferried our bags and we all walked along the beach – lucky we each just had a small overnight bag! During the break I did nothing but stroll down the beach, eat, drink, sleep and read. It was exactly what I needed and good to spend time on my own with Mum and Dad with no other commitments. They returned to Scotland shortly afterwards.

I spent an evening in Pelourinho watching a display of capoeira, which was part dance and part combat and seemed to be one of the most popular local entertainments.

•

Two weeks after arriving in Brazil, a lot of the skippers already in town took an excursion to meet Alan Paris, who aside from Derek was the last person to reach Salvador. As Alan sailed in, the skies opened and we were all drenched by torrential rain but he couldn't have been less bothered. He was as light-hearted and as full of smiles as usual, despite another tough leg. He'd taken it all in his stride, again.

A couple of days after that, and with a fortnight to go to the start of the last leg, work on *Pindar* was progressing well enough for me to make a quick trip to England and back for a day of meetings that Pindar and Pitch had managed to schedule. I arrived in the UK at lunchtime on Tuesday, 1 April, and went straight to Southampton to surprise my sister Philippa. I hadn't seen her for six months and it was her birthday. She almost fainted when she came home and found me sitting on the sofa with a mug of tea. She had no idea I was even in the country.

That evening I went up to Canary Wharf in London for the official launch of HSBC's massive new forty-four-storey HQ in Canada Square. I'd been invited to attend because of working on the HSBC Global Education Challenge and I was well looked after by HSBC's chairman, Sir John Bond, and the then chief executive, Sir Keith Whitson. I found it amazing how these people in such prominent positions were so down to earth and friendly and just plain interested in what I was up to! John and Keith were both keen recreational sailors, and I'd met Keith before during the Brixham stopover, when he'd kindly invited us to a reception at his house in Devon.

At the launch I was introduced to Sir Jackie Stewart, who runs Jaguar, the Formula 1 team sponsored by HSBC. The evening seemed a bit surreal at this point but I invited him to come sailing with me sometime. He turned me down, citing seasickness as the reason! But in return for my offer, Sir John Bond invited me to attend the British Grand Prix once I'd finished the race. I said I'd love to as long as I didn't have to get in one of his cars. 'I get road sick,' I joked.

The following morning we had some team meetings about future Pindar projects. It seemed a bit strange because I was still steeped in the Around Alone, but then if we didn't plan ahead, there wouldn't be a next project. Pindar was in negotiations to buy *Hexagon* from Graham Dalton. Aside from the *Hatherleigh*, which didn't really count, the company had never owned a boat outright. Andrew Pindar wanted to change that so that Pindar's racing team could move forward without having to lease boats in the future. *Hexagon* was a modern design and fitted the bill. Despite its dismasting it would be fine after repairs. We also started talking about future races, possibly that year's Transat Jacques Vabre. I already had a tentative idea that I wanted to sail in that race with Mike Sanderson, an outstanding New Zealand sailor who had heaps of racing experience, including two Volvo Ocean Races and two America's Cups. Mike had been competing in the Louis Vuitton cup final for the Oracle BMW team against Alinghi when I was in New Zealand. He'd also been thinking about trying to buy *Hexagon* from his fellow Kiwi, Graham, to pursue his own projects. Mike had known Graham's brother, Grant, for a long time and if Andrew Pindar was going to buy *Hexagon* it made sense that Mike might also be involved.

By the Wednesday evening I was back on a plane to South America. If nothing else, the two-day trip to Britain and back, a lot of which was spent in the air, was a great time to catch up on some sleep. And when I wasn't napping, I could watch movies.

On my return to Salvador, it was straight back to work on the boat and the countdown to departure. We spent a few days sailing and testing. We had Mike out there as an unofficial advisor. He is a sail-maker by trade and had worked for years at the sail loft in New Zealand that had mended *Pindar*'s sails. He came up with some great tips and also pointed out plenty of things that he thought might individually slightly improve our boat speed, adding up to a good amount overall. Where had he been 23,000 miles ago, when it would have made more difference?!

Somehow the prospect of the final leg began to feel slightly less daunting than the others. It didn't loom ominously, it didn't fill all my waking hours or cause me to fret. It was simply going to happen, and then its end would also mean the end of the race. By mid-March, my life had been consumed for six months by the race-stopover cycle of the Around Alone. I was looking forward to that coming to an end. I have no doubt I would have been gutted if I'd been forced to abandon the journey – like Graham, who officially announced his retirement while we were in Salvador – but that didn't mean I wanted the race to go on for ever.

In the final couple of days before the restart, I buried myself in weather studies again and started to think about tactics. I had high hopes. I was keen to push hard and do my best. Above all I wanted to get the job finished.

On the morning of the restart, 13 April, I got up early and had a long breakfast, eating as much fresh fruit as I could manage. I packed, headed to the marina and media frenzy, boarded *Pindar* and cast off. There was a spring in my step. Let's get this done. We were towed from the pontoons and led into the bay. The start gun was fired into overcast skies and we were off.

I had a great start, first across the line. The opening stretch was downwind and most of the other skippers pulled out their gennakers. I was taking too long to furl my sails and was worried about dropping the gennaker to the deck after turning upwind, as I'd need to do soon. I sailed downwind with just my solent out and lost places but at least I knew I'd be ready for the longer upwind stretch after I'd turned. A sense of frustration started to nag at me though, even that early on. Since New Zealand I'd felt very much on my way home and it seemed to be taking an awfully long time to get there. Every little bit of extra time it took meant another pang just to get finished. For the leg overall, I had a tactical plan in my head based on the interpretations I'd made of the weather information I'd seen in the days before departure. I wasn't to know that conditions would change pretty dramatically and I wouldn't pick up on it.

Everything was still going fairly smoothly by the Monday afternoon, with the gap between Bernard in first place and Bruce in last standing at only 11 miles. I was fourth, less than 10 miles off the pace. But by the Tuesday the fleet was splitting in two very different directions. Bruce took *Ocean Planet* in the same direction as Bernard and Simone, off towards the coast. It seemed the three of them intended to hug the coast before sailing a direct line towards Newport. I headed north-east on a route where I expected conditions to favour me if my interpretation of the weather was right. It was a tactical decision based on the premise that it would be the shortest route through the Doldrums, which had the potential to stall any of us indefinitely. I thought that heading along the coast, as Bernard, Simone and Bruce were doing, would mean running a risk of less wind for longer. There's often less wind there. I was nervous about my decision but I was also comforted that Thierry had taken the same decision as me.

We were both mistaken. I thought I was in good company even when we started going through the Doldrums but it slowly became evident that we'd both been dramatically wrong. We didn't just lose a day's sailing, we lost hundreds of miles within a few days. It was a deflating feeling. It was so early in the leg but I felt at such a disadvantage already that I knew the rest of the run-in would be spent playing catch-up at best. In short, three boats had gone up the coast and found wind. Thierry and I had gone a different way and found ourselves almost becalmed. There was absolutely nothing I could do about it. Once I was stuck, I was stuck. I couldn't just back-pedal into better winds.

Worse, from the point of view of our overall positions, was that Simone was not only ahead of me but there were boats between us. As things stood then, he'd be winning at least two more points than me for the leg. And if Bernard and Thierry both finished – no matter where – they'd be either first or second respectively, followed by Simone in third place. If I'd only wanted to sit back and enjoy that last leg, bask in the sun, play safe and nurse myself to the line, I would have been in clover. The weather right then was gorgeous, if a bit hot, and the sea looked picture-postcard blue. But that wasn't what I wanted. I wanted to hurry up, get back into the fight for places and make sure that the whole escapade didn't tail off into some damp squib of a finale.

Email sent from Pindar, 17 April
This could be perfect if I was just cruising, and enjoying the very peaceful gliding through the water. Perfect sunshine and crystal clear water in the day, then at night slipping through the water under the full moon so everything is lit like day light. I had a pod of maybe 30 dolphins playing around the boat today and no matter how many times you see them, you could still be fascinated by them for hours! BUT, I am in a race with the front runners getting further and further ahead while we sit in no wind! It is most frustrating and the worst thing is there is nothng we can do about it except watch the others sail away. It is now only a couple of hours from daylight,

I've had a couple of small fans going all night which has barely cooled the cabin, and soon it will be heating up again soon in the heat of the day, I saw 36deg c down below yesterday which is up there, i have been drinking lots of water to keep replacing the fluids I am losing. We are now only 3 degrees from the equator so getting close to my more familiar sailing grounds of the North Atlantic! I am going to try a couple more naps while it is bearable to sleep down here. . . . . . . Em x

Each time I woke from a nap and there was no sign that the wind was about to increase I got more frustrated about my bad decision. Until that point I'd been confident in both my navigating and my tactics. What had happened was a blow to my confidence. I had little or no breeze, so spent a lot of time steering by autopilot and just staring at the water ahead or the sails or the horizon.

It gave me plenty of time to think about life after the Around Alone, like what I'd do next and what the rest of the fleet might do next. Would they all go back to whatever they'd been doing before or take steps to another race? Thierry had already announced that he was going to retire from ocean racing. Brad had promised that he would never do another solo round-the-world race because he just didn't enjoy it enough. Bernard was unstoppable. But would Alan be able to go back to Bermuda and just pick up where he left off in the hotel business? Would Tim, the Great Lakes sailor who had now raced across all five oceans, want to do something even more spectacular and be able to repay his ex-wife? Would Bruce be able to repay his debts? Who knew what Graham would do (apart from sell his boat to Pindar, hopefully) or what adventures lay ahead for Derek (if he ever finished) or Simone or Koji, who both seemed perpetually drawn back to the solitude of the sea. They'd disperse to their various corners of the world and do their own thing. *I might even do my own thing, when I decided what it was.*

By the weekend, the poll reports had become no more encouraging. At 2 p.m. on the Saturday, Bernard was in the lead, 2,600 miles from Newport, ahead of Simone (80 miles behind), Bruce (300 miles behind), Thierry (455 miles behind) and me (465 miles behind, and with 3,062 miles to go).

Email sent from Pindar, 19 April
Well, I have crossed the equator, reached the trade winds and am sailing now at about 9 knots. Staying east of the fleet turned out to be about the worst decision yet, so I have cut out my work for myself. Overnight I could see Thierry's Stobe light (white masthead light) as he crossed in front of me, he is now about 7 miles from my bow! At least I have company in my error. Starting from scratch, the aim is to pass the two open 50s now in front, then work our way towards the Class 1 fleet. Just to let you know that my gift to Neptune when I crossed the equator this time was some wine from a very fine bottle of Dry Creek Vineyard, 2000 Heritage Clone Zinfandel! Thank you Brad for that. . . . I have to admit that I cracked it open the evening before last and enjoyed a glass (mugful) with my last couple of dinners. . . . very pleasant, and eased the frustration slightly! Em x

On the Sunday – Easter Sunday – I'd just left the Doldrums. It was still hot and I was still going slowly. I called home and tried not to imagine the ice clinking in their drinks. On the Monday, there was little wind and more pondering. On the Tuesday, after Thierry and I both had brief rallies to record twenty-four-hour runs better than the others, I had a few hours of optimism.

Email sent from Pindar, 22 April
I have caught a few miles on every boat which feels good, I just
need to continue doing that all the way to Newport! . . . As you
can see though my work is still cut out for me, so I must go and
concentrate on that again and stop my mind wandering past
this race which it is tending to do now the end is drawing closer.
2300 miles to go and for the first time would want it to be longer
so I have more time to catch the others! Em x

Wednesday was no more than adequate in terms of staying in
touch – and quite frankly I was starting to accept that I'd lost
touch. By Thursday, my mood was definitely low. I was trying to
look on the bright side but I wasn't convincing anyone, not least
myself.

Email sent from Pindar, 24 April
I am hoping that someone will remind me why I like yacht racing
when I have finally finished this race. . . . . No, its not really that bad,
the stars are still shining, but now everything is steady, I'm going for
some well needed naps, and maybe it'll all look a little better in a
couple of hours. . . . . . Em x

Any positive thoughts I'd had had gone and hidden in the
same place as the breeze. I was so keen to finish on a high. But
then you don't always get what you want. I think those days
taught me a valuable lesson, though not necessarily one that's
easy to act on. What I'd discovered was that in ocean racing you
need to take risks and push hard every moment of every day but
you also have to hold something back. Because when the going
gets tough – and that could be in hot, flat, windless seas just as
much as in a mountainous, freezing, swell – if you haven't held

something back, some physical and emotional reserve, what's left to keep you together?

There had been times on the journey, not least the mast climb or during storms, when I hadn't held back because I was forced to give everything I had. And I'd survived. But giving *that* much of my body and mind, to within fractions of thinking that I really didn't have anything else to give, was not something I could choose to switch on and off. Basically, I learnt that I dealt with what was thrown at me during periods of crisis. But at other times, it simply wasn't possible to draw upon every reserve. I could push as hard as I could, but it still wasn't enough.

Up ahead, Simone seemed to be facing his own extreme pressures – and then finding the strength to deal with them. He had been up to the top of *Tiscali*'s rig eleven times in two days and had told the race HQ: 'My body is shattered. I spent over 4 hours up the mast at one time but I haven't slept for 24hrs, as I need to push the boat even harder and the weather here is so confusing. I can't sail into very strong winds with this damage so I will avoid the low pressure.'

The saving grace for him was that at least Thierry and I were effectively stranded behind him and we weren't in a position to dent his advantage. Simone was still more than 200 miles ahead of me and despite his mast problems his speed hadn't dropped drastically below mine. So the slog went on.

Email sent from Pindar, 25 April
Another slow day on the fine ship Pindar. It is actually quite hard work to go this slowly, honestly! Every puff of wind you have to be absolutely ready for or it has gone by the time you are ready for it, the autopilot doesn't work too well under 4 kts of boatspeed and not at all under 3 kts unless you trick it into thinking the boat is

going faster than it really is. But then, it's not so responsive and usally ends up 'alarming' at you for some other reason than too little boatspeed . . . .

I have shifted weight (of sails and other heavy bits) to leeward when there is no wind, but over 6kts you really want that back up to windward to counter the heeling. The majority of the time I have beeen handsteering, but I managed to find some more jobs to do today to keep me from locking up at the helm; including climbing to the first spreader to repair a small tear in the reacher.

I am preparing myself mentally for another few days of light wind and although I am still closely following everyone's courses, I am trying to think only how to get out of this dead zone of wind! Going now to grab some sleep as the pilot is happy we are doing 5 kts. Goodnight, Em x

During those long, dull days heading to the finish, I tried hard to think of anything positive to improve my mood. In some ways I would rather have been back in Brazil on an extended stopover. At least we'd had some fun there.

One day, all the skippers had had a race in Optimists, the tiny training dinghies that I grew up racing, against all the local kids who were learning at the sailing centre. I believe that these kids had been taken off the street and had been learning for a while. They were very basic boats and could have done with a little work, but they were perfect for teaching the kids and it was more than amusing for them to race against the skippers of these great 60-foot ocean-going surfboards that we were racing. I was very proud to have been beaten by only one of my competitors, who was maybe only eight years old and sailed very well. I hope he has been given a chance to take his talent further.

Another funny day in Brazil was when we took Andrew

Pindar and Henry Chappell out sailing. We did some fun sailing amongst some testing and as the wind died and the temperature rose, we decided it was time to take a swim. We all had swimwear under our shorts except Henry. We took all our sails down and stopped the boat, threw a safety line out of the back so we had something to hold on to if the boat started drifting away, and we all jumped over. Even with the boat just drifting at one knot we had to swim to keep up with it, or hold on to the rope. Henry watched us all cool down nicely and enjoy our swimming so decided to jump in with us, skinny-dipping. He thought it was a great idea until we all got to climbing out of the water. He hadn't thought about the complications of climbing into the boat and very gingerly stepping over the high safety lines that were designed to keep me on the boat but were doing a good job of keeping him off. We were almost dry and ready to set sail again by the time he had landed spreadeagled on the deck, only just intact!

Such amusing memories did keep my spirits up, but it was a battle.

•

By Saturday, 26 April, I was still some 1,500 miles from Newport but I had the first sign that we were heading back into populated waters.

Email sent from Pindar, 26 April
I saw my first sign of life today; a massive German cruise ship a few miles away. I called up for a radio check and a chat, I got the radio check but the bridge probaby gets so many guests visiting that they seemed to have no interest in a chat with me. I suppose that having hundreds of paying guests onboard they will have had enough of people that they didn't crave some kind of feeback like me, who

could have talked about weather and nothing in particualr for a few minutes! Hey ho, so it was straight back to me and my little world of trimming sails and lookng for more wind on the horizon! Off for a nap now, Em x

Sunday was another beautiful day on the water, marred only by the positions reports and two loud cracks, which sounded like gunshots and made me jump out of my skin. It was Concorde or some other supersonic plane. I'd heard it plenty of times but it still gave me a fright.

Monday was mostly windless again but Tuesday provided me with 20 knots that lasted for hours. That almost had me feeling positive on Wednesday.

Email sent from Pindar, 30 April
The miles over the last couple of days have really gone down, and as I write this, I have about 850nm to go. Still a fair bit more than my competitors, but I am doing everything I can in this light air to keep the boatspeed up. Unfortunately I will have more of the light air to go through than the others, but that won't stop me pushing to the end!

Bernard crossed the finishing line on Thursday, 1 May, claiming a well-earned victory in the leg and in the race overall. By 2 p.m. that day I pretty much knew my fate was sealed. The poll report showed Simone lying closest to Newport with 373 miles to go, followed by Bruce (498 miles), Thierry (549 miles) and me (615 miles). If things stayed as they were, Bernard would finish first overall, Thierry would be second and Simone third.

The wind had risen somewhat but was shifty and changeable. It basically did a 360-degree turn. I started in the morning on the wind and then as the hours went on I was reaching, then running, then needed to gybe, so was running on the other gybe, away from the wind. Then I was reaching again early afternoon and by the evening I was close to the wind, going off course, and needed to tack. So I ended up back in exactly the same sail setting and sailing in the same direction as I was that morning. It was quite bizarre to have such a slow, steady change with very little change in wind speed.

The accumulation of frustrations and the tediously slow progress to the finish had started to blur my perspective. I'd been in regular touch with Team Pindar, receiving all the usual generous, unquestioning support. They were doing all they could to keep my spirits up and get me to the finish. I remember Andrew Pindar saying for the umpteenth time how proud he was and what a wonderful achievement it had been already, and that there wasn't long to go now and to hang in there.

But the disappointment of the final leg and apparent inevitability of losing my podium place at the final hurdle made it hard to feel successful. No doubt, after 30,000 miles or so, I should have been trying to enjoy the last few days, savour the last hours and appreciate what I had done. Yet at that moment I just wanted it all to be over.

The disappointment was huge but the way to keep myself going as fast as possible was that there was always a chance that something might happen in my favour and that the hard push right to the line would never be wasted. Because the quicker I got there and finished the last leg, and the race, the quicker I could have a drink of champagne with my family and friends.

The twist in the tale arrived at the weekend. On Friday, 2 May, I received news of a fast-moving low-pressure system that was storming up the east coast of the States. The forecast for the Saturday was bad. The winds were going to be pretty ferocious. The eye of this system was probably going to pass directly over my intended course. I knew it was going to be intense but I tried to block this out. It wasn't what I needed.

Email sent from Pindar, 2 May
As it is coming up so quick it is likely to be very intense, and worse so because it will be crossing The Gulf Stream at the time too, so wave heights will probably cause some drama too! At the moment it is nice to think of some fast sailing, with waves over the deck, wind in the hair and all that. . . . I am likely to tell you a different story on Saturday night when I will be dreaming of doing 6kts in the blazing sunshine – such is life. For me though, this will be the last 500 miles in this boat, so whatever hits me I intend to enjoy the best of it!
Em x

Simone was dismasted as the storm raged overnight on the Friday into the Saturday. In heavy seas and winds of 50 knots, he heard a bang as *Tiscali* lurched. His mast had snapped just above the top spreaders and his mainsail was flapping wildly. 'I immediately started to secure the mast to see if I could save it,' he said later. 'If I could keep that section of the mast in the boat I knew I would be able to make the finish. In any case I knew I was going to make the finish even if I had to swim towing the boat.'

Luckily for Simone, he was close enough to Newport to limp through the storm and cross the line on the Saturday morning, despite his crippled boat.

Out at sea, the storm was taking one last chance to hammer both *Pindar* and me. It was awful. The seas were very bad because we had the wind against the Gulf Stream. The waves were steep, causing the boat to pitch and slam constantly. I was thrown around the cabin and took one final battering. I did momentarily consider that we might be sunk at the very last hurdle. And then I stopped thinking at all. I just wanted to be out of it. I just wanted it all to stop.

By the Saturday night, Thierry had finished in third place in the leg to claim second overall. The first three skippers across the line had claimed the podium places for the race. Bruce was 35 miles from port. I was 165 miles behind him. The numbers were irrelevant.

> *Email sent from Pinday, Saturday 3 May*
> Still foul weather and foul waves, but I am hoping that by sunrise tomorrow, the wind will have gone aft and died a little and I will be able to move around this crazy boat more easily as it stops jumping off big waves into the holes in between! The radar has given up trying to stay on as each big wave slams the boat it turns itself off. The autopilot has died a couple of times, but it kind of screams at you and gives you a clue to the problem with a fault number flashing on the screen . . . Back to it; my last 160nm. I am already exhausted and I know it will be a long night again, especially without the radar working! . . . Still smiling, just,
> Em x

As dawn arrived on the final day of my voyage, Sunday, 4 May, I couldn't quite believe what I was seeing. I'd had so much wind for a few days, and waves that could have shattered bones, but suddenly the night lifted to reveal flat, calm water and very little wind. What wind was left at daybreak died out during the morning. I was left maybe 10 miles from the finish, not moving at all.

Billy Black and his assistant Marianne came miles out to watch me arrive. Andrew Pindar was onboard too. We drifted close to each other for a while. They were watching me attempt to pull up a spinnaker and try to set it. But there was so little wind that the sail didn't even rustle in the breeze. I took it down again and then small breaths of wind started moving me a little bit. Then the wind shifted and eventually, in the early afternoon, it started building and I was finally able to sail towards the line. I was close now. Very close.

17

The mirror-calm water didn't have a ripple on it as *Pindar* flew over the finish line at 10 knots. I immediately fired off a flare because that's what single-handed sailors do, and then suddenly there were loads of people jumping on to the boat. I started to pick out faces in the supporters' launch nearby. Mum and Dad were there, and my sister Philippa who'd told me a few days earlier via email that she wouldn't be able to make it! Even my great-aunt Biddy, aged eighty-four, had flown across the Atlantic to share my big moment.

I find it hard to describe, even now, what the moment of completion felt like. For eight months and tens of thousands of miles I had been inching towards some imaginary peak. Now I was there. I'd done it. There'd be no more loneliness or safety scares or three-minute meals or three-day storms or windless frustration or sleepless nights or sleepless days or poll positions or struggling or doubts or pain. It was over.

I'd fallen short of the podium place that had been within my grasp for so long. But so what? Three brave, resilient, experienced ocean-racing yachtsmen who had shown skill and courage and doggedness and flair had beaten me. There was no shame in that. I was still the youngest person ever to finish the Around Alone and the first British woman to do so. More than that, I'd sailed around the world alone.

Perhaps I should have felt like I was at the top of that imaginary peak, on top of the world. Perhaps I should have felt simply like surveying the view, like breathing the air, like crying and laughing, awash with joy. But I didn't.

I felt relieved. That was the first sensation, a huge rush of relief right through me. It was over. Thank goodness. And that was my peak. After that I almost felt as though it wasn't a mountain that I'd scaled but a roller-coaster. And the moment at the very top was just that – a moment. I thought, 'Wow' and then we were off again, hurtling forward. I barely had time to catch my breath.

Pindar was swarming with people, including Andrew Pindar and various PR executives and race officials, who had to make their mandatory checks. Later I found out that my mum and dad had been asked not to step aboard at that stage. They'd been told the PR people had priority and the boat mustn't get too crowded. When I heard that I thought it was pretty sad. They'd flown from Scotland to give me a hug at the moment of arrival and then been told they couldn't. I didn't realize this at the time, it only vaguely registered that they were hanging back. I thought maybe they didn't want to get caught in the crush. If I'd known they'd been told not to climb aboard I'd have insisted that they did just that. After all I'd been through there was no such thing as too many people aboard *Pindar* as far as I was concerned. I wouldn't have cared if we'd sunk.

I was so disappointed when I eventually found out, and it seemed completely meaningless. Surely the finish should have been all about hugs and tears of joy and more importantly seeing the support I had received all the way around? The fact that the two most important people I would have wanted on board were told not to be there was devastating. I was glad though to hear later that it was neither Pitch nor Pindar who had told them but some rogue person who probably just wanted a clearer picture of the scene.

Mum and Dad eventually came aboard later when we arrived at the customs pontoon. I got my hugs then. Then we motored the last 100 metres to the arrivals dock. It was packed. The reception was incredible. I disembarked and was passed from one TV camera to another and then on to radio interviewers via mobile phone. And all the time people were congratulating me. I couldn't really take it all in. I said thanks to everyone and sprayed champagne everywhere and from there on in I let the adrenalin take over. It kept me going for quite some time.

The press conference was unreal. 'How does it feel?' I was asked about twenty times in slightly different ways.

'Amazing,' I said. It seemed a better answer than 'Numb, thanks.'

After the press conference I went straight into more interviews and then to dinner with friends and family. It was late by the time I got there but I still hadn't had a chance to shower or change clothes. Hence I found myself giving yet more interviews during the late evening, some of which required going outside and standing around in the thermals which I'd been wearing at sea. I stayed up past 2 a.m., sipping champagne as I waited to do live breakfast-time interviews with stations in the UK.

The PR, the journalists and the repeated questions were all part of my paying back Pindar for all their support. The more I can shout about their support and their company amongst questions about the race, the more the support will continue. It was a very intense period. The PR machine was rolling smoothly and maybe a little too well, and I was overwhelmed by it. I didn't dislike it, in fact I quite enjoyed a lot of it and I would love to do all of it again, but not two months' worth of work in a couple of weeks and not when I was fit for nothing and just wanted more than anything to climb into my warm cosy bed and not wake up for two weeks. I was so exhausted that nothing would have been more tempting than to find the most comfortable bed and stay there. I am sure I missed a lot of what was going on around me as my eyes were half closed. The catch-22 though was that this would be news for only a short time and would then be history. I had to do all the publicity work we could fit in then or never, and I guess it goes with the saying, when it rains it pours. It is hard to maintain a long, steady stream of constant recognition and brand recognition over an extended period of time in this sport because there are very definite points on the racing calendar that are media worthy: the starts and finishes of races. There can't be a constant report of achievements as in a team sport like rugby, for instance, where there are enough events and games on regularly for every member of the public, even those who don't follow the sport closely, to recognize the name or the face. Hence I knew then better than ever that it had all to fit in as quickly as possible and I should be able to drop when it had died down. In fact it took longer to die down than we'd expected and then of course we jumped straight into the next project. We were on a roll and it would have been crazy to try to slow it all down; we couldn't afford the time to do that and so we just kept speeding on. Oh well, I can rest again in December, was my thought at the time.

The following morning, or rather about five hours later, I had an early start for another round of interviews at Belle's café. I had lunch with my parents, whom I'd hardly had a chance to see since arriving, and then an early dinner before heading to Boston airport to catch the red eye overnight flight to London.

As we landed at Heathrow, I was amazed to hear my name called after we'd got off the plane but before we made it to customs. I was fast-tracked through and then stunned to see yet more press and photographers and film crews. My brother Dave was there, and Tracy Edwards. I gave a couple of short interviews and was then whisked away in a BBC Breakfast Show car to central London. I did the rounds at the BBC and various radio stations, then the lunchtime news. Next it was off to Pitch's office, where some more interviews had been arranged, and then a photoshoot in a nearby square. Thank goodness my autopilot was working. I was frazzled. At one stage in the late afternoon I fell asleep in the car between appointments and eventually had to find a bed to sleep in.

The interview round continued the following day and then I flew to Scotland, where I attended a reception at Helensburgh Sailing Club, where I'd learnt to sail. Quite a few local children had been allowed out of school to come and see my 'homecoming' and I was again taken aback by the amount of people who wanted to say 'Well done.' I found it hard to take in and great to be home, if only briefly. Before I knew it I was on a plane back south and then off to America again for a series of events to mark the end of the race officially.

One of the events, in Newport, was a meeting with a class of schoolchildren who'd come up from New Jersey for the day. They were second-graders, taught by a lady called Miss Guzzo and nicknamed 'The Guzzo Gang'. They'd followed my progress throughout the race and held fundraising events all the way through so they could afford to make this big trip to Rhode Island to meet the skippers and see the boats at the end. The kids had each kept a log book throughout the Around Alone as though they'd been racing themselves, and they'd made up dances to re-enact events that happened to us skippers during the race. I was flattered and not a little surprised to see all the effort that gone into the choreography of 'The Emma Dance', which entailed the sewing of imaginary sails and the scaling of imaginary masts.

On 17 May, thirteen days after ending the race – thirteen days in which I'd hardly stopped moving – I attended the official race prize-giving ceremony. As the race committee had not found a title sponsor for the race, the major individual team backers – including Pindar, Tommy Hilfiger and HSBC – took it upon themselves to throw the best prize-giving party they could muster. It was a massive success. Andrew Pindar was rightly lauded for all his work, especially for helping out other skippers, including both Derek and Simone, after their respective dismastings. It was my turn to be proud.

We heard from Derek that night via a radio link-up. He was still at sea, completing the fifth leg. He eventually finished the race at the end of May, having amassed enough points to come third overall in Class II. His elapsed time at sea during the Around Alone amounted to an incredible 246 days. This, more than anything, underlined Derek's tenacity to stick at his task against all the odds. In comparison, my elapsed time had been 132 days at sea while Bernard Stamm completed his circumnavigation in 116 days.

After the link-up with Derek, Simone made a long and amusing speech about his future plans. He said he was considering joining the clergy so that he could make 'special accommodation' for the wives of skippers while their husbands were at sea. 'Father Simone will take care of all their needs,' he said mischievously. It was the last time most of us saw Simone.

The day after the prizegiving I flew with Andrew Pindar from America straight to Nice in France, and then on to Monaco by helicopter to attend the glitzy Laureus Sports Awards, which I'd been invited to attend as a guest. I'd never been to Monaco before and I'd never seen a bigger display of wealth. After a cocktail party on the Monday night, we spent Tuesday out on the water aboard a luxury powerboat watching some match racing in the Laureus Regatta, one of several events linked to the awards. A friend of mine, Andy Green, an America's Cup veteran, won the event. He received a flashy watch for taking part and a Mercedes for actually winning! I felt like I was in a different world. The whole scenario was made all the more surreal because I watched the racing while sipping champagne in the company of Daley Thompson and Seb Coe.

The awards ceremony the next day was a black-tie do and I found myself surrounded by some of the biggest names in sport – Serena Williams, David Coulthard, Ronaldo, Tanni Grey Thompson, Lance Armstrong, Paula Radcliffe and hundreds of others I see on TV on a regular basis. As for the other guests, it felt truly odd to be mingling with Prince Albert of Monaco, Arnold Schwarzenegger and Kylie Minogue! And then when we went to catch a taxi to a nightclub, we ended up sharing with Michael Johnson, one of the greatest runners the world has known. I wasn't so much starstruck as wondering what planet I was on.

At no time did I consider that I was an extraordinary person or that I was in an elite who have achieved an outstanding human feat. Nor did I feel I was especially gifted at my sport. I had wanted to sail around the world in the Around Alone. Only in the hectic month after the race and the months after that did I realize what we had managed to do as a team. My sense of achievement has since grown and so has my desire to get back out there, and sail as part of a winning crew around the world or across more oceans. I have once again had the support from Pindar to fund us and we have built a very strong team around us. Once again it is a team thing and I am lucky to find myself with a strong team around me. I certainly have not lost my desire to compete, in fact it has grown, and I look forward to racing again, but this time with a crew.

•

I flew back to London the day after the awards in Monaco and opened the new Carnaby Street branch of Henri-Lloyd, who are my clothing sponsors. In the early evening I started to fade and went home to bed.

The next day I caught the Eurostar at Waterloo, this time on family business. My brother Andy and his family were moving to Paris and I was a helper for the weekend. On arrival I stuck my head out of the train to look for my sister-in-law Juliette and my nephew Callum. The first thing I caught sight of was a trolley piled high with bags and shopping and a baby's car seat and a pram and then I realized why Juliette had been so keen for me to be there. After a night in their rented apartment in the centre of Paris, we picked up Andy and Juliette's new car – a secondhand Espace – and drove to their new house in the suburbs. We arrived at the same time as a truck with their belongings, and as Juliette spent the day directing the removal men, I entertained eighteen-month-old Callum.

It turned into a Richards family weekend. My sister Philippa and her boyfriend Tom were there, as was my brother Dave with his girlfriend Pippa. Mike Sanderson was there too because we were heading down to Cherbourg the next day to set up the base for the new *Pindar* (the old *Hexagon*, which had been successfully purchased from Graham Dalton). The weekend was really the first chance I'd had to slow down since finishing the race. Or rather, it would have been a chance to slow down if we hadn't been helping Andy and Juliette move into their new home. But it was fun, a weekend of late dinners, French wine and family chat. And then it was back to work.

On Monday Mike and I went to Cherbourg to make arrangements at the shipyard where the new *Pindar* would be repaired and refitted. (It was here that finishing touches were being made to the 140-foot super-maxi, *Mari Cha IV*, which would become the fastest offshore racing monohull ever. In October 2003 she shattered the transatlantic record by making the crossing from America to Britain in six days. During the same voyage, the crew smashed the twenty-four-hour distance record, sailing 525.7 nautical miles in one twenty-four-hour period, which was the first time any monohull had done more than 500 miles in a day. Mike was part of the design team and was racing skipper.)

By Tuesday I was back in London for a dinner with HSBC as a thank you for all the work we'd done on the education programme. On Wednesday we flew to New York as guests of Scott Kennedy, who'd shown so much support during my voyage. I went to his kids' school to see all the work they'd done throughout the year following my progress. They gave me a hero's welcome, which was humbling again. We spent the weekend in New York and then flew back to England on Sunday for a week of schools' visits for HSBC. On Friday I went back to France, where I was staying until the new boat arrived. Although I had a flat in Cowes it was uninhabitable, as it had been for a couple of years. I had an electrician who had promised to 'project manage' the stripping of old paint and wallpaper, the installation of a bathroom and kitchen, and replastering and painting. I'd known it would be a long process but I hadn't known it would take twelve months! It was easier to leave them to it and stay in France.

The summer continued to zoom past. There was so much to do that I really had no time to sit back and think about the race. I was just trying to keep up with all my post-race commitments and every single day seemed to be packed with pre-arranged events. If I wasn't attending some event related to the Around Alone or Pindar business, then I was preparing for the arrival of the new *Pindar* and planning all the work that would be needed to get her into shape. Mike and I had confirmed we were going to enter the Transat Jacques Vabre, which effectively meant I'd stepped from one roller-coaster to the next without stopping in between.

The boat arrived in England, at Tilbury docks aboard a container ship, shortly after we got back from our trip to New York. She was in such a sorry state that we couldn't believe we (Pindar) had paid so much money for her. I'd last seen her looking quite awesome as *Hexagon* leaving Tauranga only four months before. Since then she'd not only lost her mast but suffered damage to a lot of her hull. There were plenty of other things wrong too. We hadn't actually seen the boat since agreeing to buy her but we'd been assured that she just needed some touching up.

Mike and a couple of his *Mari Cha IV* crew went to Tilbury to block the hole in the boat where the keel had been removed. The keel and the boat's cradle were going to be moved to France by truck but getting the boat across the Channel turned into a major mission. We eventually gave up on persuading the transport department to let us travel by road and then take her over on the ferry to Cherbourg, so we ended up towing her to France using the *Hatherleigh*.

Conditions were fine when we set off but by the time we left the Thames estuary the 15-knot forecast had turned to 25 knots of wind on the nose. To make matters worse, the temporary 'plug' in the bottom of the boat was leaking badly and the boat was filling up. We lashed the helm so I could go down below and operate the manual bilge pump. The electronic pump wasn't working. While I was pumping water out, Mike was trying to fix the problem, which necessitated drilling a hole under thigh-deep oily water in the pitch dark.

At one stage Mike asked me if I'd seen a rag anywhere. I found something in the gloom and chucked it to him, joking that it was probably a pair of Graham's discarded underpants. I was mortified when Mike held the 'rag' up in front of his head torch and we discovered that that was precisely what they were. We didn't know whether to laugh or cry. We both knew enough about ocean racing to realize that Graham had probably worn those pants for four weeks without taking them off. Ughh!

Mike managed to fix a tube through the plug in the bottom of the boat and it provided sufficient drainage to keep the water inside at a manageable level. With constant checking it served its purpose of getting us safely to France. When we arrived the yard was very efficient about getting the boat out of the water and into the shed. Work got under way soon afterwards and continued through the summer.

A few days after the delivery I was back in London to take up an invitation by the All England Club to the Royal Box at Wimbledon. It was another bizarre, if thoroughly enjoyable, experience. I sat next to Tracy Edwards and Gary Lineker and behind Jonny Wilkinson, Matthew Pinsent and Steve Redgrave.

We watched matches involving Tim Henman, Andre Agassi and Jennifer Capriati and wanted to take some pictures. Unfortunately I'd forgotten to take a camera so I bought a disposable one. I'd never realized quite how noisy the click on those things can be until I took a photo when everyone else was sitting there in hushed silence. And as for the racket – excuse the pun – when I used the manual wind-on button, that was something else. Still, when I got the film developed I had a fine set of photographs of people's backs and heads.

At the end of the day's tennis, when I was having a final sip of champagne on the balcony overlooking other courts before leaving, I checked my messages on my phone. One of them was urgent, from Mary Ambler, who had been managing the PR for Around Alone. She broke the unbelievable news of Simone's sudden and tragic death. He'd been with his wife at the time, aboard his boat, which was in harbour. He'd died of natural causes. I struggled to take it in. In fact I don't think I did start to take it in properly until months afterwards. It was devastating that his life could end so suddenly after all he'd been through.

Next I headed north to Scarborough, where Pindar's HQ is based. It was my first chance since the race ended to see all the Pindar staff and thank them for their support. I did a couple of evening speeches and attended school speech day. I was there to present prizes and say a few words. I'd never been to such an occasion and had no idea what to expect, but they thanked me with a bunch of flowers and a box of wine so it can't have been all bad. A few days later I was in Glasgow to collect a Young Alumni of the Year award from the university and in between I was back in Cherbourg working on the boat.

Not long afterwards I was back in England for the British Grand Prix as a guest of Sir John Bond. I was treated like a queen. I was flown by helicopter from Battersea to Silverstone and dropped off only a short ride from the paddock, where I met up with Sir Jackie Stewart and the drivers from the Jaguar team. I visited the pits, had a look at some of the technology in the cars and then headed back to the paddock. Jackie Stewart asked me if I'd like to go out on to the grid with him in the five minutes before the start of the race. It was an absolute privilege and I was walking around in some kind of dream state. My mum told me afterwards that she and Dad had been looking out for us in the crowds on the telly. She was convinced she'd seen me standing next to Jackie just before the race. 'Don't be so daft,' my dad had said. 'Emma wouldn't be standing around on the grid just before a Formula 1 race, would she?'

The whole day had been another extraordinary experience. A few months earlier I'd never been to Monaco, Wimbledon or any Grand Prix and now I'd been to all those places and done numerous other incredible things, all because I'd finished fourth in a yacht race. It was quite literally unbelievable. If I didn't stop to think about it, then it was probably only because I'm not sure that I would have been able to digest what was happening.

The morning after the Grand Prix I was at Heathrow again, ready to fly back to America, where I spent a week visiting AlphaGraphics stores in Boston before heading to Long Island. I was there as a guest of Mike Voucas for a sales conference arranged by his company Yellow Book, one of Pindar's major clients. I spoke about my adventures and the next day took Stephanie, Mike's daughter, out sailing. She'd reached a stage where she was more than capable of winning races but always ended up crewing instead of helming when she really wanted to helm. We challenged her friends there to some races and won, with Stephanie at the helm, learning a few more go-fast tips!

Next stop was Boston for another conference and then back to the UK, ready to drop and in need of a little time out. I'd been really enjoying myself and had had so many amazing opportunities to do so but I just hadn't given myself any proper time to rest. There was no time then, either. The following week was Cowes Week, which was hectic, and involved a lot of corporate responsibilities, and then it was back to France to do more work on the boat and then back to Weymouth for a day to present the prizes at the Optimist National Championships. I'd started sailing in an Opti and it gave me great pleasure to do the presentations. I was thanked with a plate, which I've been using ever since.

It was that night after the Opti championships in the middle of August that I finally felt the whole of my year starting to catch up with me. My travel back to France had been arranged for me and I'd been booked on a ferry that was due to arrive in Cherbourg at 2 a.m. That was fine by me. It would be nice to be sleeping in my own bed instead of another hotel room somewhere or a friend's sofa.

But when I arrived at the terminal the ferry had been delayed and I felt a wave of disappointment. I was suddenly sick and tired of all the rushing, all the travel. I just felt exhausted and fed up. The ferry was only delayed for two hours but something had clicked. I got back at 4 a.m. I vowed that I had to stop saying yes to everything I was asked to do. I'd made that vow before, though. And we had less than a month to finish work on the boat before we started our qualifier for the TJV.

18

Some things don't work out the way you expect. Some don't work out the way you hope. Some just don't work.

The Transat Jacques Vabre of 2003 was one of them, and ultimately I was grateful for that. The preparation didn't really go as planned. Where had I heard that before? We didn't quite understand the can of worms we'd opened in buying the boat. This was not Graham Dalton's fault in any sense because we'd agreed to buy the boat in its 'as is, where is' state, so we'd taken the risk. The new *Pindar* was a good boat but each thing we tried to fix or service turned into a new problem or expense. The boat was late getting back into the water. We were late doing our qualifier. We managed, but it wasn't plain sailing.

By the time we officially launched her, in Scarborough on 26 September 2003, a little more than a month before the TJV, I felt ready for some proper rest. The launch was a splendid occasion. The boat looked perfect. We had 500 guests on the dockside and there was a real sense of a new chapter opening for Team Pindar. And I *was* looking forward to the TJV, and to racing with Mike, who I knew would be a formidable ally in a strong field.

But I'd been working almost non-stop for four years and the notion I'd held in my head during the Around Alone that I'd take a couple of months to unwind when it was finished hadn't come to fruition. If anything, I had become busier and busier, carried along by the momentum. The end hadn't been the end. It had just been the start of a different kind of challenge, mostly enjoyable, but draining none the less.

I am not the kind of person who would naturally sit around scratching my chin and trying to work out the meaning of my Around Alone. It was a yacht race, not a Damascus conversion. That's certainly what I thought in those months immediately afterwards. I'd entered it. I'd endured it. I'd enjoyed most of it. I'd completed it. I was getting sick and tired of talking about it. I had nothing new to say about it. Couldn't I just have a few weeks totally away from everything to recover from it, and then move on and leave it behind? Yet the weeks off didn't come, and then it was back to work on the TJV, and before I knew it we were back in France, preparing to set sail on 1 November.

The monohull fleet, including us, was sent off into storm conditions that were deemed too harsh for the multi-hull fleet. Their start was delayed because the race organizers judged that the risks for the multi-hulls were too high. They'd set off when things had calmed down a bit. The logic in sending the 60-foot monohulls out to sea as planned was that they were supposed to be fit to sail around the world in any conditions. They should be able to handle a few days of storms at the start of a 4,000-mile, two-week race.

I'd been a bit fluey and had pretty much lost my voice in the days before the start but we – *Pindar*, Mike and I – were essentially shipshape and up for it anyway. We'd done the best that we could with the boat. We'd got her into the best race condition in the time available. We'd worked hard to make her lighter and faster than our competitors. And as for the weather:

well, it might be a bit bumpy to start with but after four or five days we should be sailing downwind and getting faster in the trade winds.

When we saw the weather forecast we'd half-joked that we had at least some chance of surviving the first few days. Mike actually told one journalist: 'After three days it will be a 50–50 call as to which boats make it through and which don't.'

We didn't last three days. The wind was up to 50 knots on the first night, the Saturday. The seas were huge and horrible and there was a lot of crashing around. The wind instruments failed so we had no idea of the strength of the wind after that and it clearly wasn't an option to climb up the mast and fix the instruments immediately.

Conditions on board took a serious turn for the worse in the early hours of Monday morning. I was down below and had just climbed into the windward bunk. Neither of us had had a wink of sleep since leaving Le Havre because we'd spent the whole time fire-fighting. As soon as one little problem had been fixed, another had arisen. The wind was up and down around the 50-knot mark.

Up on deck, Mike had noticed there was a low battery warning on the instruments so he switched to autopilot while he nipped below to fire up the engine. He mentioned that the battery voltage was high just as the autopilot failed and the boat went straight into a crash tack. I heard a massive surge of water. It was coming from *inside* the boat, somewhere aft.

The cockpit drain hose, a simple bit of pipe that drains water from the cockpit, had detached. Instead of draining water from the cockpit out to the back of the boat it was draining water into the bottom of the boat. It was a dreadful sight. There was a lot of water. This triggered a series of events that scuppered our race.

All the water coming over the decks meant that the aft compartment had filled quickly, swamping electrical equipment, including the autopilots, which was why they had failed.

This was the latest of a string of problems. None of them individually would have stopped us, but together they were adding up to too many. We weren't racing any more.

We had to make a decision about whether to continue. No sailor likes to abandon a race but our hand had been forced. We couldn't continue in that state, although repairs were still a theoretical option. We headed for Brest to assess the damage.

We arrived on the Monday morning, already knowing our decision. We had the option to replace the autopilot, fix the other little problems, replace the solent that had been destroyed and restart. But we knew we would be twenty-four hours behind the boats that had weathered the storm. Several hadn't. We figured that after restarting late we wouldn't be competitive. We wouldn't actually be able to win. And as the purpose of the new boat was to win, we called it a day. I slept for sixteen hours that night.

It was a massive disappointment for our race to end the way it did. It was disappointing not only for Mike and me but for everyone involved, including the guys who'd worked on the boat, the people from Pindar who had been in Le Havre to support us, and those who'd been planning to be at the finish.

We'd been so psyched up to do well. Despite the problems, we knew we had enormous potential in the boat. Then it ended with me just wishing we hadn't had 50 knots on the nose and that we hadn't had so many *almost* insignificant breakages and that we hadn't struggled so hard to get the boat ready without using more manpower earlier in the process. But all these things *had* happened.

Yet after the disappointment and days of self-examination

about what we could and should have done differently came the relief. Huge relief. I realized that this finally meant I'd be able to take some time off and that there was an end in sight to my pressing engagements. We spent two weeks working to put the boat to bed for the winter and fix a few things. And then, at last, there was time to rest, and think.

Shortly after our enforced retirement from the TJV, I heard that I was to receive an MBE for services to British sailing. I was sworn to secrecy until it was announced on New Year's Day. I felt I didn't really deserve it. As is said in our little world: 'You are only as good as your last race.' And we had just retired from the TJV. I was flattered, of course, that my achievement in the Around Alone was so highly recognized and glad that Pindar and I had at least managed to work with HSBC on their education programme during the race.

•

We flew to New Zealand for an extended break in December. In one sense I was still working – writing this book. But in another sense I began, at last, to put myself back together and make some sense of the many things that had happened.

By writing it all down, it started to become real. I wouldn't usually use the word catharsis, if only because I can't spell it without using a dictionary. But I did begin to appreciate, for the first time, that all these weird, wonderful, painful, frightening, nerve-racking, exhilarating, draining, soul-destroying, life-affirming and downright extraordinary things had actually happened to *me*. I started to pick up the thousands of pieces of the crazy, blurred jigsaw of the previous two years and began to reflect on things that had passed me by at the time or that I'd simply been too tired or busy or scared to think about.

The process didn't manifest itself in some tsunami of realization, some overpowering emotional wave, and I have New Zealand to thank for that. It gave me time and space, away from the snowball of pressures and accumulated stress that had been building over the previous four years. It gave me an environment in which to reflect, on my own, uninterrupted by daily questioning and organizing – almost.

While writing, I'd dwell, for example, on just how terrified I had been up that mast in the South Atlantic. And then I looked around me, at the garden or the countryside or a supermarket, and felt that the bad times were in a different world, in the past. I'd think, 'I'd never be able to do that again,' but also know that in the same situation, I would be able to. Because I'd done it.

Or I'd be thinking about that mystery boat off Africa, and feel chilled again at quite how vulnerable I'd felt. But then I'd take a long bath and watch a TV comedy with popcorn or have friends around for dinner and feel the chill ebb away.

Or I'd picture Simone, making some daft speech at a party or grinning aboard *Tiscali*, and I'd feel profoundly sad. This was not just for his passing in itself, but because after the gargantuan struggles of his Around Alone, it somehow seemed so perverse, so utterly unfair, that he should have died precisely at a time when he might have expected safety. But then I'd think about it again and conclude something totally different, like life itself is so fragile, so finite, why not live it to the full?

I've had hundreds of these moments. And they keep on coming. The Around Alone was the toughest thing I have ever done. It tested me to limits I didn't know existed. I saw more and experienced more than I'd ever dreamt possible. And I came through it, alive and healthy. The bad parts no longer feel as bad. It's amazing how quickly you forget how bad a storm is as soon as it's passed. That's human nature, it's self-protection. But it's also amazing how vividly I am able to remember. And I'm glad. There were large parts of being alone that I hated, and I don't want to forget that. (That way, repetition lies.)

As for regrets, of course there are regrets. But in the grand scheme of things they are so trifling that I'd drive myself nuts to fret about them.

So I didn't get a gennaker down quick enough and got myself into a mess. It happened. I learnt from it. I survived.

So I didn't head up the coast of South America but got stuck in the Doldrums and came fourth instead of (maybe) third. It didn't matter. It doesn't matter.

So I didn't insist that I could really, really, really do without just one more round of interviews and one more visit to such and such. And I sometimes fell out with people and they sometimes fell out with me, and I sometimes resented the intrusion of the race into my life, and at times I just wanted to say 'Enough' and walk away. But these things happen, every day in every walk of life. We got through it. We ultimately pulled together. We got to the finish line.

No amount of hindsight would have changed everything. That's the thing about hindsight. It's only applicable after the fact, when it's useless. I prefer instead to think about the future, and doing things right next time.

I want to make a point of going back to Scotland to see my friends, and not solely for weddings and funerals. In March 2004 I went home for the memorial service of my friend Pete, who'd died earlier that month when his light aircraft fell out of the sky. We'd been good mates for a long time. We'd done a lot of sailing together as teenagers. We'd stayed in touch. Most of our close-knit group of friends still saw each other all the time. But when he died I'd only seen him a few times in the previous six years. His dad was really interested in what I'd been doing. He'd read about it. I wished I'd known more about what everyone in Scotland had been doing. I wish I'd known what to say to make it all better. I didn't know what to say.

That's certainly one way I've changed – I've become too busy – and one day I want that to change back again. I certainly want to spend more time with my friends and family. But I've also learnt more about making the most of time: of life itself as well as of every constituent part, be it ten minutes' rest during a busy day in a race situation, or a couple of months in New Zealand.

I'm also starting to feel that maybe the whole routine of being away for long periods of time isn't something I want indefinitely. I like getting home and being surrounded by familiar things (even if, in my new flat, that only means three beanbags and a TV) instead of being in hotels or crew houses or on people's floors.

I like being able to cook what I want for dinner, from a whole range of ingredients, instead of eating quick food aboard boats or choosing from menus.

But then I still love sailing. That was always the point for me, getting aboard my Opti or Mirror and heading off up the Gareloch or around the Sugar Ship. Feeling the elements on my skin and relishing the freedom. Feeling alive and invigorated and as though anything, at any one moment, was possible.

That hasn't changed.

I still have dreams I want to fulfil, races I want to enter and plenty more sailing I want to do.

Because that's something else the last few years have taught me. I want to sail around the world again. Just not around alone.

Epilogue

Dateline: Boston 13 June 2004

You couldn't wish for a more beautiful dawn.

The light from the rising sun melted up through the horizon to paint the sky in a hundred shades of red and orange and yellow.

The sea was calm as it stirred to a new day, all twinkling ripples as far as the eye could see.

Even the wind – eight to ten knots of fresh, rejuvenating breeze – seemed to arrive on cue, as if by special delivery.

And there was *Pindar*, our new *Pindar*, about to finish her first trans-Atlantic race in our colours, gliding towards America in magnificent silhouette.

•

I wasn't on board this time. Mike was the skipper, sailing towards the conclusion of his first solo competition, the Transat between Plymouth and Boston. Instead of being in charge of the boat, I was a member of Team Pindar waiting for an arrival. Instead of coming to the end of a trans-Atlantic crossing hoping to catch sight of our photographer Billy Black's boat, I was aboard Billy's boat, searching the horizon for *Pindar*.

On previous trips, including the end of my own first solo race, at the end of most of the legs and the final finish of the Around Alone, Billy and his assistant, Marianne, had been among the first to see me in. Now I was with them on the other side, watching a sail in the distance become more distinct and then a dot on the deck become a person. It was a great feeling, perhaps even more exciting to be a greeter than a sailor about to be overwhelmed by people and cameras.

After 13 intense, record-breaking days of thrills, spills, tension and neck-and-neck racing, Mike had outstripped all our expectations to finish third among the 60-foot monohulls. At times he'd held the lead and if he hadn't sustained damage to his daggerboards, the result may have been even better.

It was an amazing achievement considering this was Mike's first ever solo ocean race. The quality of the field – 37 skippers from nine countries – was about as high as it gets. The class winner, Mike Golding aboard *Ecover*, is among the very best.

Aboard *Pindar*, Mike was only just pipped into third by Switzerland's Dominique Wavre, aboard *Temenos*, in the final stages.

Mike, Mike and Dominique all smashed Yves Parlier's 1992 record race time by more than a day and a half.

Other seasoned, never-say-die veterans had failed to finish at all. My friend Bernard Stamm, who won the Around Alone, was among them, losing the keel on *Cheminées Poujoulat-Armor Lux*, forcing him to abandon ship, safely thankfully. Rescued by a tanker called Emma . . .

•

I sailed my own first single-handed race in the Transat four years ago, from Plymouth to Newport, Rhode Island. I was lucky enough to win my class, the 50-footers. But as a shore-bound member of Team Pindar in 2004, my view from the other side has been, if anything, doubly inspiring.

It has allowed me to appreciate even more how much of a team effort solo racing can be. I knew that already from my Around Alone, which would never have been possible without so much support from so many people. But by following Mike's progress, hour-by-hour, mile-by-mile, I have come to realise quite how fervently everyone at Team Pindar believes in us, the sailors. Also, by admiring Mike's performance, from a distance, I have a greater appreciation of how my own races, especially the Around Alone, might have been seen.

I can see that we, Team Pindar, and me, as its 'frontman', didn't do too badly after all in the Around Alone, even though during the later legs it felt to me like a chore that would never end. I'd also felt I'd let everyone down by losing the podium position I had held for so long. Time has added perspective. Living and breathing with Mike through his Transat, albeit from thousands of miles away, has added perspective. We, Team Pindar, can do amazing things together.

Life is imperfect. Everything we do is imperfect, and the time factor is a part of that, there's never enough, whether it's the pursuit of a round-the-world yacht race or an attempt to write a book that tells the story of that race. But then what would be the point of knowing nothing can be better, that there are no more dreams left to fulfil?

I hope I'll always do my best, and give my all, to chase those dreams. And on days that dawn like this one, it sometimes feels like I could get there.

Glossary

aft – back of the boat

ballast – weight

ballast tank – a tank that holds water as ballast

block – pulley

boom – a spar that sticks out from the mast or deck to hold the foot of the mainsail in place

bow – front of the boat

to broach – to tip the boat over

dinghy – small boat

Doldrums – a region of the ocean near the equator, characterized by calms, light winds or squalls

forestay – a stay extending from the head of the mast to the bow of the boat

420 – a type of two-man dinghy; a squad of sailors in the 420-class dinghy

furler – a bit of gear that furls the sail around itself while still up the mast

gennaker – a big asymmetrical sail that flies out of the front of the boat

gimbal – or 'leveller', swings so it stays horizontal even when the boat heels

to gybe – to turn away from the wind

halyard – a rope used for raising or lowering the sails

to heel over – to lean over (of the boat)

hitches – knots

hull (multi- etc.) – the shell of the boat that sits in the water, a multi-hull has more than one hull

jammer – a cleat that jams a rope

jib – foresail

keel – the weighted fin that sticks out of the bottom of the boat to keep it upright

Laser dinghy – type of small one-man boat

leech – the aft edge of a sail

luff – the forward edge of a sail

mainsheet – rope that controls the mainsail

Mirror dinghy – type of small two-man boat

Optimist – type of small one-man boat for youths

pontoon – small dock in a marina

port – left

to reach – to sail with the wind from the side (on the beam of the boat)

to reef – to reduce the size of the sail

rig – mast

rudder – a foil or flat structure that twists to steer the boat

sextant – instrument used for celestial navigation

sheet – rope used to control the sail

skiff – a dinghy that planes on the surface of the water, not pushing through it

solent – a jib

spinnaker – big floating sail that you fly off the front of the boat

starboard – right

to tack itself (boat) – to turn through the eye of the wind

tiller – is attached to the rudder stock and rudder to steer the boat

trade winds – a wind that comes as a consequence of global circulation patterns

Tropic of Capricorn – one of the five major circles of latitude that mark the earth; the parallel of latitude that runs approx 23.5° south of the equator

tugboat – a boat that pulls another boat

twin elliptical hulls – two hulls shaped like ellipses

yacht – tends to mean a boat with a lead keel on it though in some countries a yacht is any boat that sails, including dinghies